Making Up with Mom

Making Up with Mom

WHY MOTHERS AND DAUGHTERS DISAGREE ABOUT KIDS, CAREERS, AND CASSEROLES (AND WHAT TO DO ABOUT IT)

Julie Halpert and Deborah Carr, Ph.D.

THOMAS DUNNE BOOKS

ST. MARTIN'S PRESS ⚹ NEW YORK

THOMAS DUNNE BOOKS.
An imprint of St. Martin's Press.

www.thomasdunnebooks.com
www.stmartins.com

Book design by Gretchen Achilles

Library of Congress Cataloging-in-Publication Data

Halpert, Julie.
    Making up with mom : why mothers and daughters disagree about kids, careers, and casseroles (and what to do about it) / Julie Halpert and Deborah Carr.—1st ed.
        p.   cm.
    ISBN-13: 978-0-312-36881-4
    ISBN-10: 0-312-36881-X
    1. Parent and adult child.   2. Mothers and daughters.   3. Interpersonal communication.   I. Title.
    Includes bibliographical references and index.

HQ755.86 .H35   2008
646.7'8—dc22

                                                        2008006623

First Edition: April 2008

10 9 8 7 6 5 4 3 2 1

To my parents, Joanna and Alvin Edelson, who blessed me with an idyllic, stress-free childhood; to the love of my life, my husband, Scott, my best supporter during good times and bad, who makes everything possible; and to my precious children, Alyson, Garrett, and Madeline, who continually remind me how wonderful it is to be a mother.

—J.H.

To my mother, Naomi Bojar Carr, who has always marched to the beat of her own drum, and lovingly encouraged her daughters and sons to do the same.

—D.C.

Contents

PROLOGUE

Julie's Story

Let's flash back to eight years ago, when my children were 2, 5, and 8. It's a chaotic morning in our house, and my mother, who lives an hour away, is here to witness the usual craziness. I dash downstairs where my husband, always one step ahead of me in the mornings, is in the kitchen making our kids a breakfast of instant oatmeal and Eggo waffles. The kids get ready to shovel down their food, but the older two both want the same Hercules bowl. "I want it!" says the oldest. "No, you got it yesterday. It's *my* turn!" says her younger brother. Each grabs the bowl in a tug of war that eventually causes the mighty Hercules to fall and break. Orange juice is spilled in the fray. Our kitchen is being remodeled, and my toddler, now covered head to toe with oatmeal, sits in her high chair, unfazed by the ongoing construction, while a workman drills into a cupboard directly underneath her. In the midst of the commotion, the phone rings and the sitter calls: "Sorry!" she screams through her phone, "I'm just running a bit late!" "How late?" I start to ask—but she's already hung up. While I worry about this latest catastrophe, my husband says good-bye and slips quietly out the door to work.

As I hustle my older daughter off to school, my son decides it's time for a full-out tantrum. He's hitting his little sister, whom I can hear screaming from the other room: "Mooom!" I look around and survey the wreckage of my home. Beds aren't made. Pajamas and dirty underwear are strewn by the television. Dishes clutter the table and sink. It will stay that way, since I'm heading to my home office where I work as a freelance journalist.

I could handle all of this, but to make things more difficult, I'm bombarded with advice from my mother, who has been calmly observing the chaos from the sidelines. "You need to be more *firm* with your children and have them clean up their breakfast," she advises. We go head to head as she continues her well-intentioned barrage of questions. "Why do you always *entertain* your children? If you let them amuse themselves, you'll have more time to keep your kitchen organized." That leads to the final proclamation: "You should get your floors refinished. They look completely worn."

I also notice my mother is giving me *that* look. If you're a mother and you have a mother, you probably know the look. It's the doubting glance that makes you question your parenting skills and your competence as an adult. It's the look that says, "In my day, we didn't rush off to work when our kids were little. Instead, we kept a clean house, raised respectful, well-dressed children, and cooked them hearty breakfasts of pancakes, eggs, and toast."

As I watch my mother scrub my kitchen sink and finish washing my windows—a job she began last night, when she bristled at the buildup of dust—I marvel at how different my life as a mother is from hers when I was growing up. Like my husband and me, my parents had three children, and my mother worked as a teacher. But the household where I grew up seemed very different to me. For one, I cannot recall the kind of chaos I see in my house.

This feeling that I'm not measuring up to my mother's expectations has nagged at me repeatedly throughout my adulthood. My mother has second-guessed several of my major life decisions, saying things like "Why don't you become a lawyer instead of a journalist?" and "How could you pay so much money for an eighty-year-old house? It needs a lot of work." And then there are the smaller issues that pop up on a regular basis, such as "How can you possibly entertain without putting doilies on your dessert trays?" "Wide-pleated shades would look better than the dilapidated ones you have hanging on your windows." And "How can you let your teenage daughter overpluck her eyebrows?"

I'm absolutely certain, based on countless conversations I've had with other women my age, that my irritation with my mother isn't unique. I knew there had to be thousands of other women like my mother and me: women who loved each other and wanted to support each other, but instead ended up sniping over matters big and small. I started thinking: could there be a better way? Just as I appreciate having my mother as an ally rather than a critic, I'm certain she would prefer that I wasn't so resentful of her suggestions. She's just trying to help.

But right now, that doesn't seem possible.

When Julie Met Deborah

One morning, when I was mulling over my relationship with my mother, I came across a *New York Times* article that grabbed my attention. The headline for Lisa Belkin's "Life's Work" column that day read: "Anxious? Sleepless? In a Survey, Your Mom, Again, Tells You Why."[1] The article featured the findings of a new academic study on mother-daughter relationships, conducted by sociologist Deborah Carr. What I found fascinating was that Deborah was interested in the flip side of mother-daughter relationships: How do women in their sixties and seventies today feel about the fact that their daughters—beneficiaries of the feminist movement—have infinitely more options than they had as young women decades earlier? Are they jealous of their daughters' high-powered work lives? Are they envious of the fact that their daughters' husbands do more household chores than their spouses did thirty years ago? Do their daughters' career accomplishments trigger any regrets for those women who took a more traditional, family-oriented path when they were younger?

Deborah's study revealed a surprising finding that I intuitively knew was true. Mothers of a generation ago aren't jealous of their daughters' boundless choices and opportunities; rather, they feel sorry for and worry incessantly about them. Daughters who are trying to "do it all"—run corporations, raise baby geniuses, and maintain loving marriages—are exhausted. When their well-intentioned mothers offer advice or share stories about how things were "so much easier" back in the good old days of the 1950s and 1960s, their daughters flippantly snap, "You just don't understand."

I quickly contacted Deborah and we talked excitedly about our ideas. We both knew mothers and daughters have been getting on each other's nerves for as long as there have been mothers and daughters. What's new today is that the two generations of women have often had vastly different upbringings and opportunities. As a result, many hold radically different views toward two of life's most important domains: family and work. Whether we have children, how we raise them, the ways we spend our money, our career choices, how we define a healthy marriage—these are just a few of the issues where today's mothers and daughters often find they're not "getting" each other. These disagreements can create a significant strain on mother-daughter relationships even when those connections are, or have been, healthy and strong.

We found that mothers often can't relate when their daughters feel compelled to be both supermoms and super-careerwomen, and they're worried their daughters are going to crack under the pressure. They also fear for their grandchildren, who they feel are being spoiled with expensive toys and lax discipline. Daughters often curtly dismiss their mothers' advice as obsolete or irrelevant, wrongly thinking their mothers don't know what it's like to work and raise a child in a hyper-competitive, materialist world. Deborah and I agreed that the time was ripe for a book that explored these issues of divisiveness—and provided practical advice for resolving them. That's how *Making Up with Mom* was born.

Since deciding to write this book, we've spoken with dozens of women from all walks of life. At playgrounds and Pilates classes, in grocery stores and on airplanes, during mother-toddler groups and singles cocktail parties, women stopped what they were doing and eagerly shared their stories with us. We've interviewed nearly a hundred mothers and daughters from throughout the United States. Almost all the women we interviewed said they had a close and loving relationship with their mother, but their relationship became tenser after they started making important life choices—about work, marriage, babies, and finances—that diverged from the decisions their mothers had made decades earlier. They were heartened to discover they weren't alone and were hungry for practical guidance on improving their relationships. They were eager to devour stories of other strained mother-daughter relationships.

We also talked to more than a dozen therapists, physicians, psychologists, sociologists, and other professionals, who offered expert advice for closing this generational divide. Quotes from this team of experts are drawn from our personal interviews with Elizabeth Berger, Ellen Berman, Margaret Buttenheim, Renée A. Cohen, Roni Cohen-Sandler, Julia Davies, Bella DePaulo, Susan English, Pamela High, Barbara Howard, Donna Mayerson, Tom Merrill, John Northman, Carl Pickhardt, Bobbie Sandoz-Merrill, Diane Sanford, Pamela Smock, Janis Spindel, Tom Sullivan, and Howard Weinblatt. These interviews took place between May 2006 and April 2007.

We hope this book will help mothers and daughters gain the support they crave during these complicated times.

Making Up with Mom

CHAPTER 1

Mothers and Daughters: Why We Get Under Each Other's Skin

A mother is one to whom you hurry when you are troubled.

—EMILY DICKINSON

A daughter is the happy memories of the past, the joyful moments of the present, and the hope and promise of the future.

Young women today have vastly more options than their mothers and grandmothers did decades ago. "Should I become a doctor, a writer, or a stay-at-home mom?" "Should I get married or live with my boyfriend?" "Do I want children?" Women in their twenties, thirties, and forties today are wrestling with deeply personal, life-altering decisions about work and family. Life choices are inevitably accompanied by self-doubt, regret, and nagging questions about the path not taken, so young women need all the affirmation and support they can get. But the very people whose support they crave most—their mothers—often can't get on board with their choices. This frustrates mothers and leaves daughters questioning themselves. It also creates a sometimes cataclysmic rift between the two generations, even for women who have always had a close and loving relationship.

A mother's simple question, like "How can you trust a nanny to watch your children all day?" can bring her poised, accomplished CEO daughter to tears or provoke a nasty response more suitable to a surly teenager than a leader of industry. Why can't mothers and daughters today see eye-to-eye when it comes to important choices about love, work, children, money, and personal fulfillment? Why does a mother's approval still matter so much, even to the most confident and self-possessed daughter? And when daughters choose paths different from their mothers', why is it so painful for the older generation?

Why Mother-Daughter Relationships Are So Important

The mother-daughter bond is the closest and most emotionally intense of all relationships. But as daughters grow older, the natural evolution of becoming an independent woman creates a forceful current against that unifying bond. Mothers start out as the primary caregivers and role models for their daughters. Many secretly hope and expect their daughters will turn out just like them. Yet as daughters mature, they must become physically, psychologically, and financially independent. In their attempts to carve out their own unique identities, daughters often choose paths that are intentionally different from their mothers'.

Psychologists have argued that the mother-daughter relationship reaches its lowest, most contentious point during the teen years, when daughters fight their hardest to be "individuals." That's the age when daughters dye their hair purple, write morose poetry, stay out all night, or strive to be a star athlete—so they can prove they're *not* their mother's daughters. But those rebellious years quickly fade. Many psychologists believe that the mother-daughter relationship reaches a glorious turning point when the daughter becomes a mother herself. The younger generation of women can relate to their mothers' experiences, and their relationships recover from the tempestuous drama of the adolescent years.

Yet the underlying assumption here is that daughters will be the *same kind* of wives and parents as their mothers had been. Quite often, that's not the case. With young women reinventing marriage, pregnancy, career, and parenthood, we found in our interviews that mother-daughter relationships can take a turn for the worse once a daughter becomes a wife, mother, and worker. Daughters who enjoyed warm, easygoing relationships with their mothers begin to butt heads once the daughter starts raising her kids or running her household *her way*. The reason? By doing things her own way, a daughter may be unintentionally conveying the message that her method is *better* than her mother's. At the same time, mothers want badly to remain close with their daughters. Many feel the need to "fix" things when they don't like the direction their daughters are headed. So, they may resort to unsolicited advice, which their daughters invariably interpret as criticism or disapproval.[1]

That perceived criticism is painful because a mother's endorsement and affirmation means the world to her daughter, even if she's a confident woman with a long list of professional accomplishments. As women have more choices today, they inevitably experience at least some self-doubt or regret. The term "cognitive dissonance" applies frequently to young women when, after choosing between two options, they feel a nagging sense of discontent and need to ask themselves, "Did I do the right thing?" This discomfort will only be exacerbated when their mothers question their decisions.[2] Often, the only way to resolve these conflicting feelings is to stubbornly stick to the original choice—even if they recognize that the decision wasn't necessarily in their best interest. As we'll show in our interviews, when mothers question their already insecure daughters' choices about love, marriage, and work, the relationship can take a turn for the worse.

The Ups and Downs of Mother-Daughter Relationships

Adult daughters and their aging mothers can frustrate each other because they have a hard time acknowledging that the other has changed over the years. A grown woman may still view her mother as the inflexible disciplinarian who wouldn't let her attend a midnight movie "because I said so." And a mother may have a hard time accepting that her daughter, the girl who once didn't know how to make toast, is now a chef at a four-star restaurant. It's even harder for the mother to accept that, as she becomes older and her health declines, her daughter may be cooking meals for her—rather than vice versa. Mothers are accustomed to teaching and protecting their daughters and may not easily accept that their daughters have grown into smart, competent women who no longer need their mothers' help.

Many of the daughters we spoke with said they had concealed a major life event—illness, an abortion, marital woes—from their mother because they feared she would become upset and overly emotional, or that she would pass harsh judgment. Yet as their mothers age, those intense emotional responses they had as young mothers fade. Psychologists say that as adults mature into their sixties and older, their "emotional reactivity" declines. That means that they are less emotional when joys and crises come their way. A mother who would have flown off the handle at her daughter's misbehavior thirty years ago may simply roll with the punches today. That's because older women have experienced enough ups and downs in life to have perspective, and are now better at taking things in stride. But their daughters don't always realize this, so they shield their mothers from the truth. And that creates a climate of pain and distrust.[3]

Daughters today also fail to recognize that their mothers are entering a new phase of life, as well—focusing on their own personal accomplishments, such as going back to school or developing a new hobby, after devoting earlier years to their family. Some of the mothers we interviewed had led traditional, family-centered lives in their twenties and thirties, but once their children left the nest, they went back to work, got college degrees, and in some cases, divorced their husbands. As these older women carved out new lives for themselves, they also were better able to relate to their daughters' struggles than they had been decades earlier.

Taking the Pulse of Your Relationship

Psychologists have developed dozens of theories to characterize mother-daughter relationships, yet we realize that no two relationships are exactly alike. For starters, we invite readers to take the quiz that follows; it may provide some insights into what's good and bad about your mother-daughter relationship. We hope this quiz will help you identify strengths and weak spots in your own relationship.

QUESTION 1

DAUGHTERS: Your mother invites you and your family over for a home-cooked dinner. You:

   a. tell her you have tickets to see *American Idol Live* with your family that night, even though you don't.

   b. agree, but bring a box of macaroni and cheese for your kids, since they don't like her cooking.

   c. take a deep breath and grudgingly agree.

   d. happily say yes, knowing you'll be treated to a wonderful meal and lively conversation.

MOTHERS: You've invited your daughter and her family for dinner and have spent the afternoon preparing your daughter's favorite dish. As you are about to serve, your daughter heats up a bowl of Kraft macaroni and cheese for her kids. You:

   a. tell her to take it away immediately and insist your grandkids eat what you prepared.

   b. decide to go to your favorite restaurant next time, where everyone can order what they want.

   c. let your daughter serve the macaroni, but then silently seethe all night because she's hurt your feelings.

   d. gently ask your daughter why she felt the need to bring the macaroni and ask if your grandchildren might try some of the specialty dish as well.

QUESTION 2

DAUGHTERS: Your mother has rented a condo in Florida for the month and has invited you and your family to visit for a week. Your children burst into your mother's living room, kick off their boots, and start chasing each other. Your mother tells them to put their boots in the closet and keep their voices down, so as not to disturb the neighbors. You:

   a. tell your mother that you and your family will never vacation with her again.

   b. quietly tell the kids that it's fine if they want to run around for a little while.

   c. tell your children that they must obey Grandma's rules when they're at her house and to go outside if they're planning on running around.

   d. explain to your mother that your children have been sitting on a plane for four hours and ask if she can allow them to let off some steam.

MOTHERS: You've invited your daughter and her family to stay with you at your winter condo in Florida for a week. As soon as your grandkids walk in the door, they kick off their boots and start running around and yelling. Your daughter laughs it off and does nothing to discipline them. You:

   a. tell your daughter you'll never invite her family to your vacation spot again.

   b. tell your grandchildren they need to put away their boots and keep their voices down.

   c. say nothing, even if their unruly behavior bothers you. Disciplining your grandchildren is your daughter's job.

   d. take your daughter aside and ask if the two of you might come up with some ground rules to keep the kids in line when they visit.

QUESTION 3

DAUGHTERS: You've just gone shopping and treated yourself to a new spaghetti-strap tank top and snug-fitting cropped pants. When your mother sees you, she raises her eyebrow and says, "Oh, is *that* what you girls are wearing today?" You:

    a. tell your mother that the last time she could squeeze into slim-cut pants was during the Eisenhower administration.

    b. tell your mother that your husband likes your new outfit and his opinion matters more than hers.

    c. quietly take her advice—even though you and she have very different styles—and ask her to go shopping with you for a new outfit.

    d. let her know that you appreciate her input, but would prefer to make your own choices about what you wear.

MOTHERS: Your daughter has just bought a new spaghetti-strap tank top and snug-fitting cropped pants. You think the outfit is too revealing and doesn't flatter her curvaceous figure. You:

    a. tell her she is an adult and shouldn't be shopping in the teen department.

    b. ask if the pants come in a larger size, and whether she has a long sweater to go over the tank top.

    c. say nothing, since what she wears is her decision, even if you don't think it's flattering.

    d. ask if it's okay to give advice on her outfit, and then gently tell her that other styles would be more becoming on her lovely figure.

QUESTION 4

DAUGHTERS: Your mom comes from out of town to visit for the week. As soon as she walks in your house, she sees a mass of wrinkled towels falling out of your tiny linen closet. Immediately, she starts to reorganize. You:

    a. tell her to sit down and stop messing with your stuff.

    b. let her go at it, but then run to your husband and complain about how annoying she is.

c. do nothing, since you don't want to hurt her feelings.

d. agree to let her help, provided you can do it together and show her where you like things to go.

MOTHERS: You are visiting your daughter for the week. As you walk into the house, you see dishes in the sink and towels spilling out of the linen closet. You:

a. tell your daughter that her house is a mess and she should hire a cleaning woman if she doesn't have the time to straighten up.

b. immediately start cleaning.

c. ignore the mess, since it's your daughter's house and you have no place commenting on how she runs it.

d. tell her that you realize how overwhelmed she is, and ask her if she would like you to help clean her house or offer to pay for a cleaning service.

QUESTION 5

DAUGHTERS: When your mom offers to babysit, you:

a. tell her you and your husband don't need a sitter. You spend all your leisure time with your children.

b. agree, but give her a list of rules she must follow, including appropriate foods to eat and a bedtime ritual.

c. agree, even though you have a regular, paid babysitter you prefer to use.

d. happily accept. A free night out and the children get to see their beloved grandma—what could be better!

MOTHERS: When your daughter asks you to babysit, you:

a. say no. You're very busy and don't have the time.

b. reluctantly agree, but tell her it needs to be at your house. You have a better stocked refrigerator and your home is tidier.

    c. agree, even though it means giving up your monthly bridge game.

    d. happily agree, delighted by the chance to spend time with your grand-children.

QUESTION 6

DAUGHTERS: You've been dating the man of your dreams for four months, and have finally brought him to your mom's house for dinner. Your mother grills him on why he's a vegetarian, making him squirm and run for the door as soon as dinner is over. You:

    a. apologize to your beau, yell at your mother for her insulting behavior, and leave before dessert is served.

    b. make light of her behavior, telling your boyfriend not to take her too se-riously.

    c. say nothing, so as not to create any additional tension.

    d. take your mother aside and tell her that you'd rather she not interrogate your boyfriend about his dietary preferences.

MOTHERS: Your daughter calls to tell you she's met the man of her dreams and wants to bring him for dinner. Within the first half-hour he tells you that he's a staunch vegetarian, that "meat is murder," and that he couldn't possibly eat your pot roast. At dinner, he interrupts your daughter and rolls his eyes when she shares her political views. You:

    a. let him know firmly that you want him out of your daughter's life.

    b. slip your daughter the phone number of your cardiologist's unmarried son.

    c. say nothing, and hope your daughter comes to realize what a jerk he is.

    d. speak to your daughter privately, gently expressing your concerns about his insensitive behavior.

QUESTION 7

DAUGHTERS: You just celebrated your fifth wedding anniversary and have no children. At a lunch with your mother, she expresses concern that you're waiting too long and tells you that you should have a child soon. You:

    a. tell her that you'll start your family when you're good and ready, and that it's none of her business.

    b. mention that you don't want to struggle the way she and your father did, so you're waiting until you're financially secure before you have a child.

    c. try to change the subject.

    d. acknowledge her concerns, but firmly tell her that this is a personal decision between you and your husband.

MOTHERS: Your 35-year-old daughter has been married for five years but has no children. You're worried she'll have a hard time getting pregnant if she doesn't start trying soon. You:

    a. tell her that she better make getting pregnant a priority—pronto. You're the only one of your friends who doesn't have a grandchild yet.

    b. recount a story about a lonely, childless cousin of yours, and ask her, "Who will take care of you when you're older?"

    c. say nothing, since it's her life and her decision.

    d. let her know your concerns about fertility difficulties as women age and ask if it's okay to share your feelings on the subject.

QUESTION 8

DAUGHTERS: You've been named partner at your law firm. You're thrilled and can't wait to share the news with your mother. Her immediate response is, "You're home with the kids so little as it is. Do you really think it's a good idea to accept that promotion?" You:

    a. tell her she couldn't possibly understand what's best for you career-wise, since she's never had a real job.

    b. block out what she says, and let your mind wander to the thought of your new corner office.

c. quietly agree that the promotion will take you away from your family more.

d. let her know you understand her concern and suggest brainstorming together on the best way for your family to adapt to your changing work situation.

MOTHERS: Your daughter calls you, ecstatic with her good news. She's been named a partner at her law firm. You're worried about the long hours involved, since she already sees her kids so seldom and often seems tired and irritable. You:

a. tell her not to accept it; it's a selfish move that will hurt her children.

b. congratulate her and let her know you would have enjoyed a career like hers, but *someone* had to stay home and take care of the kids.

c. tell her you're proud of her and keep your concerns mum, even though you're worried about how your grandchildren will adjust to her long work hours.

d. applaud her good news and tell her how proud you are of her accomplishment. Then offer to help her adapt to her new work schedule.

QUESTION 9

DAUGHTERS: Congratulations! You've won a weeklong Caribbean cruise for two. The catch? You must take your mother as your guest. You:

a. say, "No thanks." Even tropical breezes and margaritas on the lido deck couldn't get you to spend a week captive with your mother.

b. agree to go, but tell your mother to hang out with the seniors at the shuffleboard deck, while you sun yourself by the pool.

c. agree to go, even though you don't want to. How bad can it be?

d. jump at the chance! What a nice way to spend uninterrupted time with your mother, in wonderful surroundings.

MOTHERS: Congratulations! You've won a weeklong Caribbean cruise for two. The catch? You must take your daughter as your guest. You:

a. say, "No thanks." Even tropical breezes and margaritas on the lido deck couldn't get you to spend a week captive with your daughter.

b. agree to go, but tell your daughter to hang out with the other young people by the pool, while you enjoy cards with your peers.

c. agree to go, even though you don't want to. How bad can it be?

d. jump at the chance! What a nice way to spend uninterrupted time with your daughter, in wonderful surroundings.

WHAT KIND OF MOTHER-DAUGHTER RELATIONSHIP DO YOU HAVE?

DAUGHTERS:

If you answered mostly a's . . . You're the Dueling Daughter. You'd rather have a root canal than spend the afternoon with your mother. You two bicker often, and you tend to snap at her, interpreting her advice as criticism. Your challenge is to develop patience and not judge every word out of your mother's mouth; she may just surprise you with valuable insights, if only you'll let her.

If you answered mostly b's . . . You're the Dismissive Daughter. You rarely insult or fight with your mother, but your actions are often hurtful. You'll do what you think is right, often with little regard for how she feels. Your challenge is to think about the consequences of your actions and ask yourself how you would feel if your children quietly did the opposite of what you advised.

If you answered mostly c's . . . You're the In-Denial Daughter. Even though your mother's questions and advice annoy you occasionally, you fear conflict, so you hold your tongue when you're upset. If you continue to sweep things under the rug rather than openly confront your mother about how you feel, you'll have a relationship marked by frustration and dishonesty. Your challenge is to develop the courage to share your thoughts with your mother.

If you answered mostly d's . . . Congratulations, you're the Divine Daughter. This is as good as it gets. You're the accepting, loving daughter who views her mother more as a friend than an authority figure. You appreciate your mother for who she is. When you disagree with her suggestions, you tactfully share your feelings and keep the lines of communication open. Your goal is to share the secrets of your success with other women in your life.

MOTHERS:

If you answered mostly a's . . . You're the Maligning Mom. You often feel like you've given birth to an alien and can't understand why your daughter behaves as she does. Rather than just accepting her the way she is, you feel the need to barrage her with advice. Although your intentions may be good, your words end up hurting your daughter and making her snap back. Your challenge is to develop patience and not condemn everything your daughter does or says. She may just surprise you with her good judgment and competence, if only you'll let her.

If you answered mostly b's . . . You're the Meddling Mom. You seldom insult or pick fights with your daughter, but your actions speak louder than words. By dismissing your daughter's feelings or opinions and doing what you think is right, you send the message that she's not a competent adult. Even though you want what's best for her and often choose your words carefully, your actions may be hurtful. Your challenge is to think about the consequences of your actions, and ask yourself how you would feel if your own mother quietly did things that undermined your authority and credibility.

If you answered mostly c's . . . You're the Mum Mom, afraid anything you say will be interpreted as judgmental or critical by your daughter. You feel it's not your place to tell your daughter what you think. You're afraid to share your concerns, so you often seethe silently. Your challenge is to develop the courage to be open and honest with your daughter, yet do so in a way that won't offend her.

If you answered mostly d's . . . Congratulations, you're the Model Mom. You share your concerns in an empathetic way that's helpful, not judgmental or critical. You openly appreciate your daughter's good traits, and treat her more as a friend than as the child you've raised. Your challenge is to help your friends and sisters achieve the kind of relationship you have with your daughter.

Delving into the Lives of Mothers and Daughters

Making Up with Mom: Why Mothers and Daughters Disagree About Kids, Careers, and Casseroles (and What to Do About It) is neither an academic study nor a typical self-help guide, with checklists and magic formulas for the perfect relationship. The heart and soul of our book rests with the stories of mothers and daughters. We spoke with approximately one hundred women from ages 25 to 79, from all parts of the United States. We interviewed homemakers, engineers, nursing home attendants, professors, doctors, lawyers, and others. Our interview subjects were ethnically diverse: blacks, whites, Asians, and Latinas. We also interviewed lesbians, childless women, mothers of large families, recent immigrants, and women whose ancestors arrived in the United States shortly after the Mayflower docked. We've supplemented our evocative interview data with statistics and expert advice offered by a team of therapists, pediatricians, sociologists, psychologists, gerontologists, financial advisers, and even a professional matchmaker. These experts helped put the stories into context and offer constructive tips to help mothers and daughters work through their conflicts.

We found our interview subjects primarily through word-of-mouth. We first relied on what sociologists call "snowball sampling." That means we queried our friends, colleagues, and acquaintances and asked them whether they and their mothers disagreed about at least one of their fundamental life choices—a romantic partner, job, child-rearing strategy, and so on. We also asked them to forward our e-mail query to their friends, colleagues, acquaintances, and family members. We contacted roughly half of our subjects this way. We also located subjects through Internet postings and ads placed on Web sites, like iVillage, HipMama, and local newsletters, such as the Berkeley (California) Parents Network. We posted our query on Web sites targeting specific communities of women, including childless women, stepdaughters, lesbians, women of color, stay-at-home moms, and career women. We were delighted to receive dozens of responses from women who were eager to share their stories. Even before we spoke directly to these women, we received detailed, thoughtful, animated e-mail messages conveying their tales of joy and frustration with their mother-daughter relationship.

In a few cases, we recruited the older generation of women first, through venues such as grandparenting Web sites. More typically, we enlisted the daughters first. Then, we faced a much more daunting task: getting their mothers to talk to us. In a handful of cases, the daughters described their mothers as ogres and we were a bit hesitant about contacting them. We worried their mothers would be reluctant to talk to us, fearful they would be held up as examples of "Mommy Dearest" types. Our fears were quickly put to rest. Most were eager to speak with us, as were their daughters. Of course, some women declined: they didn't want to dredge up painful memories and share their difficult experiences with the public.

We conducted the majority of our interviews over the telephone and spoke separately to the mothers and daughters. In about a dozen cases, however, we met with them in person, often at the same time. In those cases, we were surprised and impressed by the level of honesty and openness we saw. It wasn't uncommon for mothers and daughters to shed tears as they relived difficult moments of their past. Most of our interviews lasted from forty-five minutes to two hours. Prior to the interviews, we mailed both mothers and daughters a brief questionnaire asking about their background, to highlight the best and worst aspects of their relationship. In our interviews, we seldom made it through the full set of questions we had prepared. Most mothers and daughters had one or two sore spots that they wanted to discuss, so we let them talk about the issues they found most important.

We expected that many women would use the interview as a forum for griping about their mother's or daughter's annoying quirks and habits. But that didn't happen. Certainly, mothers and daughters aired their frustrations with one another, but they often shared compassionate and wise insights as to why they thought the other behaved as she did. We heard many words of praise and appreciation. Most women we interviewed said at one point or another, "We have a good relationship, despite everything," or "Of all the things I've done in my life, I'm proudest of my daughter," or "I wouldn't be who I am without my mother."

Nearly every woman we interviewed one-on-one also asked us the same question: "Are you going to tell my mother/daughter what I said about her?" Our answer was a resounding no, although we reminded the mothers and daughters that they would probably discover what the other said once the book was published. Our job as authors and researchers was to listen, probe, and accurately describe what the mothers and daughters told us. We did not want to interfere in their relationships or play the role of mediator of long-standing squabbles. We hope our interviews with the mothers and daughters opened communication channels on issues that have been long simmering.

Even more importantly, it is not our job as authors to play the blame game. We don't take a position on who is right in each conflict. Rather, we let the mothers and daughters speak for themselves, and consulted our team of therapists and experts to weigh in with their thoughts and advice.

The poignant, occasionally humorous, and often touching stories of real mothers and daughters make up the core of our book. In order to protect the anonymity of our interviewees, we changed their names, and in some cases, minor details of their biographies: for instance, the city where they currently live. Every other detail has been accurately recounted to the best of our abilities. We believe these stories make for fascinating reading and that mothers and daughters everywhere will be able to relate to these tales of tension, torment, and triumph. We hope that the publication of this book gives the mothers and daughters we interviewed an opportunity to fully hear each other's perspectives in an objective manner, and in doing so, begin to heal their wounds. We also hope this book will invite other mothers and daughters to speak their minds and share their concerns with each other as they work to resolve their own personal generational divide.

CHAPTER 2

From *Good Housekeeping* to *Working Woman:* Why Are Mothers and Daughters So Different Today?

A woman's place is in the home.

A woman's place is in House . . . the House of Representatives.

—BELLA ABZUG (1970)

From appearances alone, Lisa Jones is obviously her mother's daughter. She shares her mother Anita Hecht's willowy frame and calm demeanor. Both women have the right jewelry to complement every outfit, perfectly styled hair, and inquisitive green eyes. But that's where the similarities end. The life choices they've made couldn't be more different. Anita married at age 25 in 1960 and spent the next twenty years running her home and caring for her husband and her five spirited children. Lisa, a program director for a nonprofit organization in Michigan, has worked full-time since her two children were infants. While Anita whipped up home-cooked meals and dreamed up elaborate games for her five children, 44-year-old Lisa serves meals that "can be prepared in less than ten minutes" and she relies on day care, private-school teachers, and camp counselors to provide fun and games for her sons.

Suzanne Balin hasn't given much thought to how she might someday cook meals for her future children. At age 38, Suzanne works seventy hours a week as a health-care consultant in Boston and lives alone with her two cats. Although she'd like to be married with children someday, she hasn't yet found her "other half." She's also not sure that she's willing to trade her lifestyle—giving lectures throughout the country, the impromptu weekend jaunts to the beach, the lingering meals at ethnic restaurants, and season tickets to the ballet—for the life of a wife and mother. In other words, she's not sure she's cut out to live her mother Norma Balin's life.

When Norma was in her thirties, nearly forty years ago, her life was a mirror image of Anita Hecht's. Her days revolved around caring for her five children and husband. Although Norma is a talented singer and former first-grade teacher who nearly finished a master's degree in education before marrying, she put those interests aside when she gave birth to her first child in 1965. With the energy and smarts of a Fortune 500 CEO, Norma spent each day cooking favorite meals for her children, taking them on walks to story hour at the library, helping with class projects, and making sure that the children were reasonably clean and quiet when their father, Harry, came home from a long day of repairing televisions. As Norma recalled, "Harry worked hard all day. He deserved to have a little peace and quiet at home."

Just ten years after Norma and Anita married and had children, however, the world was changing. In the late 1960s and early 1970s, the feminist movement was in full swing and women just a decade younger than Norma and Anita were redefining the ways American women think about work and family. Among the women blazing new trails were Marla Beech and Pamela Chalmers, both age 59, who earned graduate degrees in fields like public administration and continued to work even when their babies were just a few months old. Marla and Pamela loved their work and wanted to prove that women were just as capable as men in the workplace. Today, their daughters don't feel they need to fight as hard as their mothers did, and are much more laid-back in how they think about their careers. While Marla is an executive at an engineering firm, her daughter, Cassie, has chosen to work in day care. And while Pamela has worked around the clock as a corporate recruiter, her daughter, Monica, is a freelance campaign manager who is happy to take off a few months between jobs. Monica and Cassie don't worry about proving themselves at work; they know they'll do just fine, and assume that they'll be respected just as much as their male colleagues.

As our vignettes reveal, women's lives have been transformed over the past five decades. Women in the 1950s and early 1960s married at around age 20, had their first baby within a year or two of their wedding day, and then had two or three more children within the next three to five years. Most worked prior to marrying—as schoolteachers, nurses, stenographers, or saleswomen—yet quit their jobs a few months into their first pregnancy and stayed home with their children until they were grown. Many had always wanted to be full-time mothers, while others quietly and without protest cast aside their earlier career dreams to play the supporting role of homemaker to their husband's starring role of breadwinner.

Young women today, in contrast, are determined to "have it all": the husband, the children, and the globe-trotting career. Beneficiaries of the 1960s women's movement, most married women in their twenties, thirties, and forties today are blending rewarding careers with marriage, children, and housework, while their single friends are devoting their nonworking hours to dating, volunteering, social outings with friends, and, in some cases, childrearing. Women today dwell in a universe very different from the one their mothers inhabited as young women a few decades ago. Yet like their mothers, these young women are making sacrifices. Time spent at work means time *not* spent with one's children, one's husband, or the promising blind date who may someday become one's husband. Even more troubling, the expectations for what women *should* do today are rising. Women are expected to be career dynamos while raising happy, healthy children with Nobel Prize winner potential, looking fit and gorgeous for their husbands, and running marathons on the weekends. They're trying to "do it all," yet feel like they are doing none of it well. Given these pressures, emotional support and affirmation from their mothers is more important than ever.[1]

Given the fundamental differences in the sacrifices made by these two generations of women, can they ever really understand one another? How can traditional family–focused mothers of the 1950s and

1960s support their career-oriented daughters, who often rely on fast food and babysitters while they're at work? How can these daughters develop an appreciation of their mothers' insights, intelligence, creativity, and inner strength when the older generation of women received neither hefty paychecks nor public accolades for their very private accomplishments?

Mothers and daughters today are living at a unique moment in history. In this chapter, we will take a whirlwind journey from the 1950s to the present, weaving together historical facts, statistical figures, cultural images, and vignettes from women's real lives to show how social, cultural and economic forces have created such divergent life paths for two generations of women. We will talk about three sweeping changes that have had a powerful impact on women's lives over the past five decades:

- The rise of the working mom

- The increasing acceptability of singlehood, divorce, and cohabitation

- New job opportunities for women

Moms at Work

The most profound change in the American family in the twentieth century has been the influx of mothers into the paid workforce, especially mothers of infants and young children. Women have always worked, whether on the family farm in the nineteenth century, in the textile mills in the early twentieth century, or in secretarial pools and department stores in the mid-twentieth century. And poor women, immigrants, and African Americans have juggled paid work and parenting for much of the past century. What's changed is that the majority of American mothers today are managing work and family roles *simultaneously* rather than *sequentially*.

The typical working woman in the 1950s and early 1960s was either a single "career gal" in her twenties or an "empty nester," a woman whose grown children had left home. Paid work came either before or after raising children. It wasn't until the 1970s that married women with young children began to enter the labor force in droves. Two-thirds of women with preschool children now work for pay; just one in ten did so in 1950. Even mothers of infants are working in record numbers; roughly half of women with babies under one year old are back in the workforce within months of giving birth.

As mothers have swarmed into the workforce, popular notions of the typical American family have been transformed. The traditional *Father Knows Best* family, with a stay-at-home wife, a breadwinner husband, and three or four children has become a relic of the past. Rather, in the majority of American families today both husbands and wives are working. As our interviews show, working women and their husbands are juggling challenges that are foreign to their parents.

Families also are shrinking in size. In the 1950s and 1960s, when most women stayed home with their little ones, a large brood was perfectly desirable and acceptable. Today, women who are committed to their careers find that one or two kids is the ideal family size. Couples today can easily choose how many kids to have and when to have them because they have access to effective birth control. But it's not just reproductive technology that's changed. Women's personal goals are also different.

Most women today want children, just as their mothers did. But many are also dedicated to their careers. They realize that the more children they have, the less time they can devote to climbing the corporate ladder. Single women often want to date and play the field in their twenties and thirties and don't want to settle down until they've found the right person. Others seek the freedom to travel, chase their dreams, and try out a few careers before settling on the one that's right for them. Yet each of these pursuits may prevent women from having large families even if they wanted them. Women who put off having children until their careers and relationships are secure may find that their emotional and biological readiness for children are out of sync. A couple who tries to start a family when the wife is in her late thirties may be able to have only one or two children even if they had originally hoped to have three or four.

Annie Sobota, a 37-year-old gerontologist in Ann Arbor, Michigan, discovered that the hard way. Annie and her husband, Eric, had difficulty conceiving a child and had their first daughter, Emily, after several rounds of invasive, distressing, and costly fertility treatments. When Emily turned two, Annie and Eric set up an appointment for another round of fertility treatments. "Miraculously," says Annie, they didn't need the treatments the second time, since Annie was able to conceive naturally. Annie realizes the rarity of her good fortune. Our interviews with career-focused daughters and their mothers revealed the joys but also the heartache women face when choosing when to have children and the ways that these decisions are tightly tied to their work choices. As we'll see in Chapter 4, women today have much greater control when it comes to child-rearing choices—yet their mothers often worry that these choices may carry difficult consequences.

Going It Alone: Alternatives to Marriage and Parenthood

If the dual-earner couple is the most important change in family life in the twentieth century, following close behind is the expanding list of alternatives to the traditional role of wife and mother. Many late baby boom and Generation X women are single well into their thirties and forties. Some still dream about meeting and marrying Mr. Right, while others accept that they may never walk down the aisle. Married couples are choosing to be or are reluctantly finding themselves childless. Unmarried women are having children on their own and married women who later divorce are often raising their children alone. Women today are abandoning, or are being forced to abandon, the merged role of wife and mother, the very role around which their own mothers often organized their lives and identities.

The Single Life
Young women today don't take a long and happy marriage for granted the way their mothers often did. But even women who have given up their girlhood dream of a white wedding are encouraged by

an important statistic generated by the U.S. Census Bureau: well over 90 percent of all American women will eventually marry, just as their mothers did. But that day will come much later than it did for Mom.

"Delayed marriage," as demographers call it, has transformed the ways that husbands and wives relate to each other and their work. In the 1950s and 1960s, young adults often moved straight from their parents' home (or college dorm or military barracks) to their newly-wed apartment. Young men often went from relying on their mother's cooking and cleaning to their wife's domestic skills. Today, in contrast, young adults live on their own, with roommates, or with a romantic partner for several years before they marry. As a result, new husbands are more skilled with a vacuum cleaner than their fathers were, and brides are better equipped than their mothers to balance their checkbook and fix the toilet.

Married couples today are more likely than their parents to share household tasks and child care because both spouses have experience with both "male" and "female" tasks from their days of living single. Delayed marriage also means that newlyweds have more years of work experience under their belts than their parents did. Many single women spend their twenties and thirties climbing the corporate ladder or attending graduate school, and they are unwilling to give up this important part of life when they marry and have children. The women we feature in Chapter 3 have chosen to sidestep or delay marriage, or to cohabit with their boyfriends rather than marry. These choices were unthinkable just four decades ago, and women in their sixties and seventies often can't support their daughters' decisions. This often leads to tremendous distress for both generations of women.

When Marriage Ends . . .

In the 1950s and 1960s, divorce was infrequent. Most Americans believed that feuding couples should "stay together for the sake of the children." A divorced woman was often shamed, and the D word was whispered behind closed doors, far away from the earshot of children. By the 1970s, however, an estimated one-third to one-half of all marriages ended in divorce, and that pattern continues to hold true today.

The rise in divorce rates isn't due solely to changing attitudes about what's best for the kids. Women today have the financial resources and job skills that enable them to leave a failing marriage. Four decades ago, a stay-at-home mother with three children and no marketable job skills often felt that she couldn't afford to go it alone. Today, young women can provide for themselves and their children if their marriages end. That doesn't mean that divorced mothers have it easy today. The challenges of paying bills, going to work, shuttling the kids to and from their dad's home, and keeping a clean house are far more difficult for these women. For many such women, their mothers are their biggest supporters and confidantes. Yet others say their mothers view their divorce as a sign of a character flaw or unrealistically high standards for what a marriage should be.

Child-Free Women

In the 1950s and 1960s, most Americans believed that a woman's main purpose in life was to have children. Women and their husbands who did not want children were often considered selfish, while those who couldn't have children were pitied. Most married couples today do have children, just as they did fifty years ago, but growing numbers do not: today, roughly one in five women in their early forties is childless compared to just one in ten in the mid-1970s.[2] Many of these women are childless due to infertility, or they plan to bear or adopt a child in the future.

Experts believe that a growing number of women today really don't want children. They're well aware of the toll that children may take on their earnings and career prospects. Those who opt not to have children often find that their choice creates a wedge between them and their mothers, who are eager to become grandmothers. In Chapter 4, we hear from daughters whose childbearing choices don't always conform to their mothers' visions.

Education and Careers: Unlimited Possibilities

Just as young women today have myriad paths they can follow in their personal lives, they also have many more choices for their education and careers than their mothers had. Women today are receiving bachelor's degrees and graduate degrees at unprecedented levels and are entering professions that barely registered in their mothers' dreams. The ways that women think and feel about their work have also changed dramatically.

Several decades ago, women took jobs that were expected of them, while women today are carefully choosing careers that mesh with their skills and interests. Shirley Stein, a 67-year old former schoolteacher from Farmington Hills, Michigan, recalls, "I wanted to be a journalist, but my mother said, 'Be a teacher.' For a woman in my generation, to have professional success meant becoming a teacher." Florence Lehman, age 64, who lives in Baraboo, Wisconsin, sees the issue of choice as one of the key differences between her life and that of her daughter. Florence worked at the telephone company as a clerk when her children were in school, while her 30-year-old daughter landed a career as a children's book illustrator. Florence is impressed that her daughter gets paid to draw all day. "She's doing what she really likes to do. I don't know that at the telephone company I was doing what I really liked to do." Women of her generation "were pushed, or told what to do," she says.

Working women today may even be more emotionally attached to their work than their husbands and male colleagues—making it more difficult for them to give up their careers for family, as their mothers did. Young women growing up in the 1970s and 1980s were raised to believe that they could succeed at any job they set their mind to, but many still received the subtle message that if one spouse had to stay home with their children, it would be them, not their husbands. As a result, these young women felt free to choose jobs based on their passions and talents, rather than the simple desire to make money. Because they and their parents believed that the woman's income would be secondary to her husband's, they could opt for personally rewarding career paths like writing, biomedical research, or teaching philosophy.

Yet once these young women entered the workforce, many found themselves more devoted to their careers than they had anticipated. They didn't want to leave their jobs once they had kids. Others feared that if they took time off, they would never regain their footing at work. This is something their mothers often don't understand. Women who were schoolteachers or department store saleswomen in the 1960s and 1970s could take a few years off work without fear of falling behind on their climb up the career ladder. Today's working women, in contrast, worry that even a brief leave will take a toll on their careers. Women scientists, doctors, lawyers, computer programmers, editors, and professors who take time off to raise their children fear that they'll lose the skills, knowledge, and connections that are so critical to their future success.

Their worry is well founded. Dozens of studies show that women who take time off from work or cut back to part-time hours take a hit in earnings and never catch up with their peers who stay in the workforce.[3] "Face time," being seen at work, is a factor that many employers consider when deciding whether an employee has the commitment and work ethic necessary to get that big promotion. Even female bosses haven't broken out of this outdated mind-set. Shelly Lazarus, CEO of advertising agency Ogilvy & Mather, angered working mothers by forbidding part-time or flex-time employees to become partners. "Just because you're a woman with a child, you can't be allowed a lower standard of performance," she said. As our interviews in Chapter 5 reveal, women today are trying to be stars at work and supermoms at home and their efforts to do both are leaving them exhausted, frustrated, and the target of their mothers' worry and concern.

The "Good Mother" Ideal

It's hard for women today to fathom how different their mothers' lives were when they were growing up. Women growing up in the 1940s through the early 1960s were told that they should be happy to put their own ambitions aside so that they could support their husbands and children. A good woman was defined as a devoted mother and homemaker. A working wife was often viewed as an uncaring or uncommitted mother and a shameful indication of her husband's financial failure.

Even goal-oriented young women studying at the nation's most prestigious colleges weren't spared such messages. In 1955, the graduating seniors at Smith College listened as progressive liberal Adlai Stevenson told them they should confine their intellectual skills to the home front: "As wives and mothers . . . you can do [homework] in the living room with a baby in your lap, or in the kitchen with a can opener in your hands. If you're really clever, maybe you can even practice your [home economics] on that unsuspecting husband while he's watching television."[4]

How have expectations for women's lives changed so radically in just a few decades? Legislative changes have had a tremendous impact on women's opportunities. Throughout much of the twentieth century, gender-based discrimination was legal in the workplace. Married and pregnant women were regularly barred or fired from teaching and office jobs. Employers believed that married women would be preoccupied with their husbands and would only leave their jobs when they became pregnant. Smart, able women who wanted to juggle work and family weren't given a chance.

As Seen on TV

Cultural images, too, have shaped how women view their choices. A generation ago, movies, television shows, and "expert advice" books sent women a loud and clear message: "good women" stay at home with their children and "bad women" chase their own personal goals. Working mothers were considered such an oddity that in the cardinal edition of Dr. Spock's *Baby and Child Care,* the challenges facing working mothers were touched on briefly in a section entitled "Special Problems." Children of working mothers were lumped together with disabled children and children who had been born prematurely. Television images idealized the lives of married women. *Leave It to Beaver*'s June Cleaver wore pleated skirts and pearls as she vacuumed her living room and prepared meals for her husband and two sons. Working women, divorced women, and self-assured single women (other than the occasional spunky widow) were virtually absent from the television and movie screens of the 1950s and early 1960s.

By contrast, women who were born in the 1950s through the late

1970s were inundated with the message that they could be or do any-thing they wanted. In 1972, the record album *Free to Be . . . You and Me* became a favorite of young children. Girls were told that "mom-mies" could be "ranchers or poetry makers, or doctors or teachers, or cleaners or bakers," while "daddies" were "busy with children," but also were "writers or grocery sellers or painters or welders." In the 1980s and early 1990s, young women watched their married peers land prestigious careers and negotiate complex work arrangements with their spouses. They saw public relations executive Jamie Buch-man support her sporadically employed filmmaker husband, Paul, on *Mad About You*. At the same time, *Growing Pains*'s Maggie Seaver, mother of three, worked as a newspaper reporter and television an-chor while her psychiatrist husband worked out of his home office. In the series finale, the Seaver family relocated from New York to Wash-ington, D.C., so that Maggie could take a position as a prominent sen-ator's press secretary.

Young women also learned that it was possible for an unmarried woman to support herself financially, yet still be sexy and engaging to potential suitors. In the early 1970s, *The Mary Tyler Moore Show*'s Mary Richards, a television news producer, was financially indepen-dent, attractive, and hardly subject to spells of loneliness or social re-jection. A few years later, *One Day at a Time* divorcée Ann Romano supported herself and her two teenage daughters while proudly pro-claiming herself a "liberated woman, master of her fate." Three de-cades later, the four single women in *Sex and the City* lived a carefree life any married woman would envy, finding success as a newspaper columnist, a lawyer, an art gallery manager, and the owner of a public relations firm. Although few women would choose a career or spouse because their favorite TV character did, cultural images show women what's possible. For today's young women, the possibilities are light-years away from those that were available to their mothers.

The Political Is Personal

Social scientists and cultural commentators like to describe the stay-at-home mothers of the 1950s and 1960s as oppressed victims of sexism whose choices were confined by cultural and normative pressures. The women we spoke with would never describe their lives in such self-pitying terms. Not one had seen a "women need not apply" sign hanging on a shop door. Few were told outright that "a woman's place is in the home," and even fewer made it their personal mission to follow the make-believe model set forth by television characters June Cleaver or Harriet Nelson. The obstacles were much subtler and beneath the surface: the disapproving father, the boyfriend who assumed that his girlfriend would follow him anywhere regardless of her own educational plans, the neighbor who shook her head disapprovingly when a young mother headed to work in the morning. Shirley Stein recounted the "disdain" she felt when she returned to teaching while her children were young, in order to supplement her husband's modest income. "My mother-in-law was disappointed in me," she recalls. "She didn't want me to go back to work."

When mothers of earlier decades reflect on why they chose the path of homemaker, many say that they simply couldn't have imagined it any another way. Although some had entertained the idea of a career, most simply followed the paths of their mothers and grandmothers before them. Irene Swenson, age 64, from Des Moines, Iowa, recalls her career plans when she was growing up in rural Wisconsin in the 1950s: "I didn't make any great plans for my career because at that time it was basically, you graduate from high school, get married, and have a family. That was the focus at the time. That's the way it was."

Some women mentioned their parents' refusal to support their education or career plans, although these stories were quite rare. Betty Knaup, 65, of Phoenix, Arizona, was one of the few to recount such an obstacle: "When I wanted to go to college, my father threw the recruiter out of the house. He thought girls shouldn't go to college." Other women were stifled by a much more subtle pressure: to be a devoted and attractive girlfriend. Lois Culver, 64, of Waunakee, Wisconsin, was afraid her ambition would hurt her relationship with her boyfriend. "I wanted to be a librarian, but I was afraid that I would lose my boyfriend if I went away to school. We had a good beauty school in town, so I went there instead."

Most young women today find it unthinkable that ambition

would make them unappealing to men. Smart, educated, assertive women with their own corner office and Ivy League M.B.A. have become the new trophy wives. According to a recent poll by dating Web site Match.com, 48 percent of both men and women reported that they were dating and preferred to date partners who earn the same income they do, while 20 percent of men said that they were dating women who earned more than them. Many young men today are relieved to no longer be the sole earner, a burden many watched their frustrated fathers shoulder.

The Economy and Women's Choices

When women talk about their career choices, most focus on the emotional rewards and downsides. They say that staying home with children brings them joy or that an intellectually challenging career brings them a sense of accomplishment. But women's choices also reflect economic realities. Many women stayed at home with their children in the 1950s, 1960s, and 1970s because their families could afford to live on one income; others went to work because they had to. Although many women today work because they love their jobs, it's also the case that their families couldn't swing the monthly mortgage payments on their husband's income alone. To fully grasp the very different life paths of two generations of women requires a glimpse into the importance of economics.

It's the Economy, Mom

Many young women today look back at their own childhood in amazement. How was it possible for their parents to feed and clothe the family, take summer vacations, and send four or five kids to college on a single income, almost always their father's? For most of the women we spoke with, that single income came from the hard labor of a television repairman, high school teacher, or foreman at the General Motors plant. Economists tell us that it *was* possible to maintain a desirable standard of living on one income at that time. Although dual-earner couples today are often made to feel like lavish spendthrifts who fritter away their second income on frivolous luxuries, the truth is that making ends meet simply is harder for many of today's working parents. The costs of life's necessities—housing (and property taxes), medical care, college tuition—have risen at a rapid clip, and men's and women's earnings aren't keeping up with these expenses. It isn't as easy to provide food, shelter, and schooling for kids today on one income as it was forty years ago.

Keeping Up with the Joneses (and the Gates and the Trumps?)

Most of the young working women we spoke with say that they work because they enjoy their jobs or because they can't raise their children on their husband's income alone. But a handful work to maintain the lifestyle to which they've become accustomed. Their standard of living requires two incomes to provide many of life's luxuries. Several of the young women we spoke with said they knew that their mothers condemned their spending and work habits, but they feel entitled to spend their hard-earned salaries as they wish. The fancy gym membership, the private school education, the Nintendo Wii for their son's thirteenth birthday, the yearly vacations to Aspen: these are the reasons why some women and their husbands are working so hard today. At least that's the opinion of Jean Raines, a 74-year-old woman in Livonia, Michigan, who worked as a nurse. Raines is in awe of the Christmas gifts that her "spoiled" grandchildren receive each year. "They have such an abundance of gifts at such an early age. They have the latest gizmo, the latest outfit." Dr. Juliet Schor, a sociology professor at Boston College and author of *The Overspent American,* agrees that at least part of the reason why couples are working so hard today is that they want more. This pattern, Schor observes, casts families today into the "cycle of work and spend."[5]

Over the past twenty-five years, the "culture of spending" has intensified, according to Schor. Home sizes have increased and small eco-friendly cars have given way to bigger, gas-guzzling SUVs even as gas prices have skyrocketed. Americans now regard celebrities as their benchmark for what they should want. It's not just adults who have gotten swept up into consumer culture. Marketing firms have discovered that children and teenagers today are their meal ticket. Children, egged on by television commercials and media images, have always nagged their parents for the latest novelty: the coonskin cap or hula hoop in the 1950s, Cabbage Patch dolls in the 1980s, Furbies, Beanie Babies, and Pokemon cards in the 1990s, and iPod nanos today. What's changed is the sheer number of these media images and the price of the items that kids are demanding. According to the American Academy of Pediatrics, the average American child sees twenty thousand ads per year, or roughly fifty-five ads per day. It's not surprising, then, that parents are parting with more money each year to buy those products hawked in ads during Saturday morning cartoons.

Some economists believe that parents today have a much harder time saying "No, we can't afford it" than their own parents did. Why? Because children and adults today have warped expectations for what they "need." In order to raise the happiest, healthiest, smartest, most well-behaved children with the most promising prospects for the future, parents often feel the need to provide the best teachers, computers, hobbies, summer camps, and homes for those children.

When the women we spoke with described their economic need to work, their criteria for "need" were quite varied. In some cases, it meant money for mortgage payments and college savings. In other cases, it meant enough money to support their children's Paris Hilton wannabe lifestyle. Regardless of how women define need, the outcome is the same: working families, even middle-class families with two working parents, feel that they're scrambling to get by. Even the highly educated aren't spared from financial anxiety; an estimated one-third of families where the main breadwinner is a college graduate report that they have no savings. As we'll see in Chapter 7, these spending patterns are simply incomprehensible to their mothers, who managed to save for the future despite their families' much lower incomes.

Getting Personal: How Work and Family Affect Women's Inner Lives

We've described how two generations of women have carved out work and family lives that comply with or defy the expectations held up for them. But how do these different choices affect women's inner lives and personal relationships? And how do these choices affect the very ways mothers and daughters relate to one another?

Life at Home

A generation ago, the boundaries separating men's work and women's work were clearly drawn and seen as impenetrable. Although wives were frustrated when their husbands neglected to put their socks in the laundry basket or pick up milk on the way home from work, most women believed that household chores were *their job.* Maybe they were exhausted from keeping house and caring for the kids, but they felt their husbands were just as tired from their long day at the office or on the assembly line. Husbands and wives were each holding up their end of the marital bargain, and complaining about it wasn't productive. As Anita Hecht, a Michigan homemaker, recalls without a trace of resentment, "in my day, all the domestic responsibilities belonged to me."

For today's young women and their husbands, the boundaries between his and her work are continually blurring and shifting. Few husbands today can claim the title of sole breadwinner, as their fathers did. Wives' earnings are no longer considered secondary. Nearly one in four working women outearns their employed husbands today, according to a Bureau of Labor Statistics report.[6] Money is a powerful influence on how husbands and wives relate to one another. Stay-at-home mothers of a generation ago often felt trapped and powerless because they were fully dependent on their husband's earnings, while their daughters are equals with, and in some cases a threat to, their husbands.

One common way working women today cope with the overwhelming demands of employment and parenthood is by cutting back on housework. Many studies show that the number of hours women spend on housework has dropped steadily over the past three decades. Men are doing more around the house than their fathers did, but not enough to balance out the cutbacks their wives are making. While mothers in the 1950s and 1960s expected that they'd do more housework than their husbands and would keep quiet about the imbalance, their career-minded daughters have no problem vocalizing their dissatisfaction with the "second shift" of housework that they face at the end of their workday.

According to a recent survey, 80 percent of working mothers say that they handle far more of the household chores than their spouses. In order to make up for this housekeeping shortfall, couples are relying on fast food, ready-made meals, housekeepers, and laundry services. Couples who can't afford such luxuries have to lower their standards regarding what constitutes a clean house, often to the chagrin of their white glove–testing mothers. Although working couples may have to give short shrift to the cleanliness of their kitchen floors and window sills, they're not giving short shrift to their children. Recent studies show that mothers spend roughly the same amount of time with each of their children today as they did twenty or thirty years ago.[7] How is this possible? If working women today are at home less often than their mothers were, how can they report the same number of hours caring for their children?

First, mothers today have fewer children than their mothers did. Tucking one child into bed simply takes less time than tucking in five. Second, when researchers delve behind these statistics, they find that although mothers today are around their children less often than mothers in the past, they devote those scarce hours expressly to child-focused activities. In past decades, mothers were home with their children all day, but many of those hours were spent on housework, rather than directly relating to their kids. Mothers often let their children entertain one another while they prepared dinner and folded laundry.

If working mothers and fathers are managing to keep their homes reasonably tidy and are spending as much time playing with their children as past generations, then what gives? Time and energy are in limited supply, so young women must be sacrificing *something*. That "something" is their own physical and emotional health. In her book *The Second Shift,* sociologist Arlie Hochschild observed that working mothers talk about sleep "the way a hungry person talks about food."[8]

It's not surprising that the daughters we spoke with frequently reported exhaustion and their worried mothers responded by expressing their concern and offering advice. Carrie Smith, a pediatric cardiologist, struggles to balance round-the-clock shifts at the hospital with intensive parenting of her two daughters. She admits that she's trying to live up to the ideals set by both her professional father and homemaker mother, but that may be just too much for one person. Carrie feels she has no choice but to cut back on her sleep, much to her mother's concern.

The Third Shift: Guilt

For many working mothers today, managing the second shift of housework and child care isn't nearly as difficult as managing the third shift, which is, according to researcher Michele Bolton, the time at the end of the day when women are finished with work and have put their children to bed.[9] This is the time when they mull over their day—the time when working mothers "second guess their motives, doubt their choices and question their tradeoffs at the end of the day."

At the core of the third shift is feeling guilty about time away from the kids. Working parents often lament that they don't spend as much time with their children as they would like. They also worry that they're putting their children's lives in the hands of strangers. Working parents today often live far away from their own parents, brothers, and sisters, and simply can't rely on family to care for their children. While mothers of the 1950s and 1960s often lived in the same city—and in some cases, the same city block—as their mothers, sisters, and aunts, today's working women have often moved hundreds of miles from their hometowns to pursue their careers. With so many women at work today, very few friends or neighbors are available to provide child care. Rather, children spend much more time in after-school programs and group care and far less time playing outside with friends than they did in the 1960s and 1970s. It's a rare neighborhood today where the sidewalks are filled with children playing frozen tag after school; more than two-thirds of all children ages 5 to 12 with a working mother spend their after-school hours with someone other than a parent.

For working women and especially working women who use paid child care, guilt is almost inescapable. A recent Gallup Poll showed that most Americans believe one parent—the mother—should be home with their child during the day. These data are brought to life in a telling passage in the 2002 novel *I Don't Know How She Does It*, by Allison Pearson.[10] The novel's heroine, Kate Reddy, is the manager of a hedge fund and mother of two small children. Kate offers the following observation about her office's politics: "If a man has pictures of his kids on his desk, it enhances his humanity; if a woman has them, it decreases hers. Why? Because he's not supposed to be home with the children. She is."

Many working mothers feel guilty for relying on day-care centers, private child-care workers, or nannies to help raise their children. Nearly all the daughters we spoke to talked about compensating for their absence in some ways. Kara Bellini, a stockbroker, is more likely than her mother was to buy her daughter the latest pair of designer jeans or a much-desired but overpriced toy. For many working women, the indulgences are small in the scheme of things, yet their mothers see these concessions as a misguided way to soothe parental guilt.

It's not just neglected children that women feel guilty about. As they focus their precious nonworking hours on their children, working mothers say they inevitably neglect their husbands. Many women we spoke with confided that the romance was gone from their marriage, as other demands like kids' schedules took precedence. They talked honestly about how their dual workday made them so exhausted that they often felt they weren't being good wives, just as they felt they weren't being good mothers. Becca Halligan, 37, a program evaluation specialist in Madison, Wisconsin, says she and her husband, the parents of two daughters, are so worn out from work that they barely talk anymore. At Becca's mother's urging, the two booked a cruise—their first vacation alone together in seven years. The experience was wonderful and reminded them of the importance of couple time. Women like Becca share their struggles in Chapter 9 and talk about how their efforts to work and raise children are leaving them emotionally and physically depleted.

In the eyes of career-oriented women today, though, these struggles—indulging a child's costly birthday wish, the sleep deprivation, the rumination and self-doubt, the dust bunnies under the bed, scarce time with their husbands—are a relatively modest price to pay for the opportunity to work at a job they truly enjoy. For most working women, employment brings a sense of accomplishment and purpose that they can't imagine finding anywhere else.

Many women also believe that a lack of professional fulfillment haunted their mothers when they were growing up. Several told us that they have consciously fashioned their work lives, with all the accompanying stress and strain, so that they would never relive their mothers' misery. Just as mothers worry about their daughters being "exhausted" and "stressed," the daughters fear that if they give up their hectic work lives they will feel the same sadness and lack of personal fulfillment that their mothers experienced.

Is This All?

The daughters' memories of their mothers' unhappiness mesh surprisingly tightly with the reports of academics and feminist activists. Many homemakers were unhappy, anxious, and socially isolated. That unhappiness—"the problem with no name"—is the main observation of Betty Friedan's *Feminine Mystique,* a book that many credit with unleashing the women's movement of the 1960s. Friedan wrote about the malaise that housewives felt as they tended to the needs of their husbands and children, yet neglected their own desires and dreams.

Psychologists say that the mother-daughter tie is the closest of any parent-child bond. But it is also the one most frequently marked by ambivalence and strain. A concerned mother's attempt to offer a helping hand may be interpreted as critical or intrusive. A busy daughter's desire to do it all without asking for her mother's help or advice may be interpreted as shutting her out or ignoring her. We hope that by providing a historical and cultural lens for understanding mothers' and daughters' choices, and by offering glimpses into their daily joys and disappointments, we can help to foster more understanding, empathy, and supportive relationships across the generations.

CHAPTER 3

Courtship, Cohabitation, and China Patterns: Choices About Love and Marriage

It's just as easy to marry a rich man as a poor man.

You're not getting any younger. Do you want to end up an old maid?

This relationship with Lisa. Are you sure it isn't just a phase?

As long as there have been mothers and daughters, there have been mothers dreaming of their daughter's wedding day. The perfect white taffeta dress, the perfect ceremony, and most importantly, the perfect groom—a handsome, hardworking man who would be their daughter's ticket to a blissful and financially secure future. Mrs. Bennett, the mother of five daughters in Jane Austen's *Pride and Prejudice,* could hardly contain her excitement over a potential son-in-law: "a single man of large fortune. . . . What a fine thing for our girls!" Almost two hundred years later, Bridget Jones's mother schemed to marry off her 30-something chain-smoking, martini-swilling journalist daughter to a stuffy human rights lawyer. But matrimonially minded mothers are now finding their daughters may not appreciate their efforts to bring a son-in-law into the family.

Young women are more likely than ever to stay single into their thirties and forties, to live with a boyfriend rather than marry him, or enter a loving long-term relationship with another woman. Those women who are marrying may be saying no to high-earning doctors and lawyers, and yes to stay-at-home dads, graphic artists, and ski bums turned Web page designers. What's changed is that women don't *have* to marry: with education, investments, and income to spare, many are partnering for love alone rather than financial security, and for shared passions rather than a shared cultural or religious background. Some women who find that marriage isn't all it's cracked up to be are divorcing and starting new lives on their own—often to the chagrin and sadness of their mothers.

We've talked to young women with a variety of romantic histories: financially secure women who live in nonmarital bliss with their long-term boyfriends, single young urbanites who prefer playing the field to playing house, unhappy single women who don't need to be reminded they haven't had a date in a six months, divorcees who have left their seemingly "perfect" husbands, and lesbians who marry their longtime loves and have children. What many of these women share is the nagging feeling that their mothers just don't get why they're doing what they're doing. As young women today take risks in their personal lives, they crave support from their mothers, rather than judgment. And mothers need to get on board with their daughters' choices. In 2007, the U.S. Census Bureau revealed that, for the first time, a majority—51 percent—of American women are now unmarried.[1] As we'll see in the stories of Jenny and Marilyn Schultz, Kara and Val Birmingham, and others, it's a tough—but not impossible—task to get Mom's blessing, even if there's no mother-of-the-bride dress in her future.

"I'm Not Ready to Get Married": Is Singlehood a Refusal to Grow Up?

If the women of *Sex and the City* were looking to add a politically active, socially conscious friend to their quartet, Diana Gladwell would be their pick. A law school graduate living in New York City, Diana, age 27, is fervently committed to fighting for the rights of women and children, protecting the environment from global warming, and warding off four more years of Republican leadership. That doesn't mean she's immune to the temptation of pricy designer shoes or an occasional meal at a four-star restaurant. Like many of her friends, Diana, a slim brunette with close-cropped hair and an edgy fashion sense, enjoys dating, traveling to off-the-beaten-path vacation spots, and spending her money freely—even if she's strapped by law school debt and sky-high Manhattan rents. She's not looking to get married any time soon and is perfectly happy to date men with whom she doesn't see a long-term future. Diana worked hard to get through college and law school and she isn't ready to settle into a life of suburban, domestic complacency.

Diana's mother, Nanette Westfall, age 46, is trying to embrace her daughter's live-for-the-moment philosophy, but she's having a tough time. When Nanette was in her twenties, she was a divorced Air Force officer, raising 6-year-old Diana on her own. Nanette grew up in a small town in Florida and joined the U.S. Air Force immediately after graduating from high school. "No one really guided me to go to college," recalls Nanette. "I couldn't see wasting the money because I didn't know what I wanted to do." Her father worked three jobs to make ends meet and her mother took in ironing from neighbors. She thought the military would be a wise career move: "I got to travel, plus growing up in the South, it was a good thing to do."

She joined the Air Force at age 17 and became romantically involved with a fellow enlistee. At 19, she got pregnant with Diana. "It wasn't a planned pregnancy," she tells us. Nanette married Diana's father, but the marriage lasted only five years, ending when her husband walked out on her and their young daughter. She reenlisted in the Air Force "because I needed the income. It was the easiest way to earn money and put a roof over our heads." She first had a job as a medical technician in obstetrics and quickly worked her way up to intelligence. Nanette's financial and personal struggles were resolved when she remarried at age 27. Her second husband, an Air Force fighter pilot, provided a stable and loving home for Nanette and Diana. Still, Nanette learned the hard way how to take care of herself and her daughter. She wishes her daughter would absorb some of her life management skills.

Nanette can't muster much sympathy when Diana complains about her financial situation—the heavy debt from law school, the exorbitant rent for a tiny New York apartment, the cost of trying to maintain a diet rich in organic foods. When Nanette was her daughter's age, she had the more daunting responsibility of holding down a job and raising a child, while Diana struggles to cover rent for one. "I tell her, 'I couldn't pay ten dollars for an organic cantaloupe like you do. I had a family to feed,'" says Nanette.

Nanette also can't understand why Diana won't marry one of her perfectly nice boyfriends. Nanette is particularly saddened that Diana didn't marry her former boyfriend Jim, whom she dated throughout college. Nanette and her husband always admired Jim. "He was a nice, clean-cut kid who worked hard to put himself through school. He didn't always agree with Diana, but he was always very supportive of her," says Nanette. Nanette says the relationship ended when Diana decided to move to California after graduation, though she later returned to New York City for law school. She says her daughter gave Jim an ultimatum: follow her out west or date someone else.

Diana sees the breakup differently. She says she and Jim were growing in opposite directions and had different emotional responses to the world—especially after Diana fell into a depressive funk after 9/11. "My parents really wanted me to marry him," she says. She recalls her mother making "really hurtful" snide comments after the breakup. "I was only twenty-one then and unhappy in the relationship. I thought I was making a really smart decision, but she kept saying, 'I'm afraid you'll never let your guard down and get close to someone and get married.'"

What Diana saw as a deliberate and mature decision, her mother saw as partly pathology and partly a desire to avoid becoming an adult. Nanette fears that her first marriage to an abusive alcoholic—Diana's biological father—is preventing Diana from marrying. "She has such high expectations for everyone," she says. "I made this poor decision, and now she has to suffer as a result." Nanette thinks her daughter can't trust men because her father abandoned them.

She also believes her daughter acts and thinks like an adolescent, and that she lives for the moment. Although Diana recently graduated law school, she decided not to practice law. Instead, she hopes to work for a nonprofit organization that fights for the rights of battered women. Diana wants to lead a life consistent with her personal values and political views, even if it means less income than she'd have as a corporate lawyer. Nanette, however, thinks her daughter's refusal to practice law is another indication of immaturity, and that she needs to get a "real job" to pay her bills. "Sometimes, I just want to say to her, 'Grow up.' In the real world where I live, people work nine to five. That isn't her world," Nanette says. Nanette's life has been about her husband and children, and she wishes her daughter would follow her model, get married, and have children. "Then she'd understand what it's like to be a responsible adult."

The strain in their relationship reflects the fact that Diana and Nanette hold different opinions about what makes for a meaningful adult life. Nanette believes that being an adult means holding down a steady job, marrying, and having children, while Diana says it means making choices that work for her, even if they're choices that others might deem irrational or selfish.

Social scientists say that people in their twenties and thirties today are reinventing the term "adulthood." According to Dr. Frank Furstenberg, a sociology professor at University of Pennsylvania, "Many [young women] have not fully become adults yet—traditionally defined as finishing school, landing a job with benefits, marrying, and parenting—because they are not ready."[2] But, Dr. Furstenberg's research shows that parents like Nanette should cast aside the notion that their daughters are irresponsible or immature. Rather than equating adulthood with marriage and full-time employment, Nanette should recognize that "this is a time of unparalleled freedom from family responsibilities and [provides] an opportunity for self-exploration and development." Dr. Furstenberg's research suggests two strategies that women like Nanette and Diana can use to overcome obstacles in their relationship.

ADVICE FOR MOTHERS

Accept that definitions of adulthood have changed. Nanette equates adulthood with being a married parent with a full-time job. Most Americans feel the same way. National surveys show that 96 percent of Americans say "financial independence" and "full-time work" are the defining accomplishments of adult life, while 94 percent think a young person isn't officially an adult until he or she "is able to support a family." Yet data from the U.S. Census Bureau show that only a fraction of Diana's peers are actually behaving like adults by age 30—that is, they have finished school, left their parents' home, gotten married, had a child, and achieved financial independence. In the year 2000, just 46 percent of women and 31 percent of men had reached all five milestones. Forty years ago, 77 percent of women and 65 percent of men had done so.[3]

The delayed transition to traditionally defined adulthood isn't due to irresponsibility, but rather to changes in the economy. Real estate costs have skyrocketed. Debt from college loans can be staggering. Master's degrees are required for many jobs, so young women are staying in school well into their twenties and older. Young people whose parents divorced don't want to jump hastily into marriage and prefer to date many people before settling down. Furstenberg says "the timetable of the 1950s is no longer applicable. It is high time to . . . address the realities of the longer and more demanding transition to adulthood."[4] Rather than judging her daughter and comparing Diana's struggles with her own, Nanette should recognize that Diana is doing the best she can and she's adjusting to the realities of a new economy.

ADVICE FOR DAUGHTERS

Explain that nontraditional choices are often thoughtful choices. Diana is not content to marry her college boyfriend simply because they dated for three years. Nor is she willing to become a lawyer because she went to law school. She's proud of the fact that she's taking time to think about what she wants in a career. Unfortunately, her mother did not have the same luxury. Nanette didn't have the opportunity to go to college. She married because she became pregnant. She reenlisted in the Air Force because she needed money. It's natural that Nanette would resent not having the choices her daughter has. It's also understandable that she's disappointed by her daughter's "rejection" of seemingly perfect options—like her college boyfriend, Jim, or a high-paying job in a law firm.

Mother and daughter will continue to butt heads until Nanette recognizes that her daughter has choices she lacked—and with choice comes acceptance of both the path taken and the path not taken. Dr. John Northman, a family psychologist based in Amherst, New York, says that mothers need to recognize they have done their job successfully if they've raised their daughters to make autonomous choices, regardless of whether they agree with them. "What one aims to do as a parent is raise a child from age zero to twenty, teaching them a variety of skills and perspectives, so that at age twenty or so they can go out into the world and function as a successful adult," he says. As an autonomous adult, the child might make choices the parent disagrees with. "I think it's an error to equate 'love' with congruence of life choices," Dr. Northman advises. What Diana can do is openly and honestly talk to her mother about why she's made the decisions she's made—without being defensive or haughty. She should also let her mother know that she is grateful for her options and recognizes that they are due, at least in part, to the sacrifices her mother has made.

Single and Loving It: Daughters' Decisions About Marriage

Although Diana Gladwell relished her single life, her mother, Nanette, couldn't shake off the uneasy feeling her unmarried daughter was scarred because her father abandoned her as a child. Nanette is not alone in her worries. Several of the mothers we spoke with suspected that the difficulties they had in their own marriages—whether boredom, entrapment, or abuse—created emotional obstacles for their daughters. Women of a generation ago often didn't have the financial means to leave a troubled marriage. Even those with a job and money of their own found that the stigma of divorce was powerful enough to keep them in unsatisfying marriages. Mothers like Genevieve Canvasser, whose daughter Johanna Jones married for the first time at age 46, view their daughters' late marriages, or permanent singlehood, as a sign of deep-seated commitment issues. Genevieve had spent more than twenty years worrying that her single daughter would end up alone, unable to shake the emotional pain of growing up with an abusive father.

Mothers like Genevieve and Nanette fear their "emotionally scarred" daughters are turning their backs on marriage altogether or delaying marriage until after they've resolved their personal demons. But their daughters gave us very different explanations for their singlehood. Women like Johanna Jones, beneficiaries of the 1960s feminist movement, say they're spending their twenties and thirties pursuing careers and hobbies, and figuring out who they really are. Women today don't want to become someone's "other half" until they feel they are psychologically and financially whole on their own.

We met with Genevieve, 76, and her daughters, Johanna Jones, 50, and Jesse Slater, 53, when they were visiting Jesse's Michigan home over a July fourth weekend. What began as a pleasant family reunion turned into a tense afternoon of dredging up painful memories from the girls' childhood. Jesse remembered that their father was a "cold, mean, and irrational" man who was abusive to them and their mother. With a hint of bitterness, she recalled that one night when she was 6, her parents returned home from a movie and found her jumping on her bed, causing a spring to pop out of the mattress. Her father "was furious" and told her that the bed was expensive and she would have to quit her dance lessons to pay for it. She stopped dancing then and never returned to it. Jesse said her father grew up in a home with physical violence, and he emotionally abused Jesse and her siblings when he became a parent.

During our conversation, Jesse and Johanna asked their mother why she tolerated cruel treatment from her husband. Genevieve replied that her husband told her, "If you didn't go to college, you don't have a brain," so Genevieve, who wasn't college-educated, was in no position to challenge him. "I felt my husband knew everything and I didn't know anything," she said. Her husband eventually left her in 1964, after carrying on a two-year affair with a woman he met while doing research in England. Johanna was 7 years old at the time, and she and her three siblings took over household chores while their mother went back to work as a nurse. Eventually, in 1975, Genevieve remarried; her current husband, according to Jesse and Johanna, is also emotionally unstable.

Years of growing up with an abusive biological father and an erratic stepfather have taken a toll. Jesse was fortunate; she fell in love and got married at 34. Johanna, by contrast, had no intention of falling for anyone, fearful of following in her mother's footsteps: "My mother let my dad walk all over her and she blamed herself for things that weren't her fault. I didn't want to be like her." Johanna took great efforts to avoid her mother's fate. She has embraced life as a free spirit and looks every bit the part. A massage therapist, Johanna now has long gray hair, pulled back in a loose ponytail. She wears small wire-rimmed spectacles and favors floor-length peasant dresses. After establishing a successful spa practice in California in her early twenties, she decided her round-the-clock work schedule was too stressful and moved to a rural part of Hawaii.

A self-described loner, Johanna was at peace in her remote Hawaiian jungle home, but her mother was worried. Once when Johanna was visiting her mother, Genevieve asked her if she was a lesbian and told her if she was, she should feel free to bring her girlfriend home. "She sent me a *Modern Bride* magazine and wanted me to marry a doctor and get a real job," Johanna recalled. Genevieve defended her actions: "I worried about Johanna" being all alone in the wilderness, without a companion. On a visit to her daughter's home, Genevieve recalls, "there was nothing there." She saw her daughter herding goats and learning about Hawaiian healing systems and asked her, "What are you doing with your life?" But Johanna insists she was happy at the time and had no interest in settling into a traditional marriage. "I'm very selfish, individualistic, and not tolerant of other's habits," she admits.

Although Johanna was comfortable with her offbeat lifestyle, she did worry that her mother "didn't really get me" and that "I was disappointing her in some way" by not marrying. Johanna told her mother she wouldn't marry someone unless they got along well and she loved him. Ultimately, Johanna married at 46 and has moved from the jungle to the more "civilized" area of Maui. She and her husband have a refreshing "daily harmony" she never experienced before. He's even agreed to do things Johanna's way, giving up television and junk food. "He doesn't agitate my emotional volatility," she says. In her own way,

Johanna has found her perfect match, but the long search for meaning and love created a tense mother-daughter relationship in the process.

What should mothers like Genevieve do when their daughters seem to turn their backs on marriage?

ADVICE FOR MOTHERS

Compare your definition of "single" with your daughter's. For Genevieve, her daughter's singlehood represented loneliness and social isolation—quite literally, as she saw her daughter living alone in a secluded jungle. For Johanna, though, singlehood was a path to personal freedom and exploration. Johanna didn't feel lonely; rather, she felt unencumbered and free to pursue her interests in holistic health. The belief that singlehood is synonymous with sadness and misery is a common view in American society, says psychologist Bella DePaulo: "Even the most accomplished single people are called upon to defend their lives in a way that married people are not."[5]

If Johanna felt that singlehood was the best path for her (at least when she was in her twenties and thirties), then her mother needed to support her choice, says Dr. Diane Sanford, a family therapist specializing in women's health and relationships, and president of Women's Healthcare Partnership in St. Louis, Missouri. Dr. Sanford says "we shouldn't interfere with our children and try to pin our hopes and dreams on them. Sending *Modern Bride* to your daughter is just obnoxious." Matchmaker Janis Spindel, author of *Get Serious About Getting Married,* agrees. "A daughter doesn't need to be reminded she's single. The more a mother nags, the less likely that marriage is going to happen."[6]

What can daughters like Johanna do to assuage their mother's worries?

ADVICE FOR DAUGHTERS

Make a relationship contract. Although Johanna claims she was happy on her own, the therapists we spoke with cautioned that she may have been using her career and her alternative lifestyle as a way to hide from real intimacy. By trying to have a romantic life that's very different from her mother's abusive marriages, she's designing a life based on what she *doesn't* want rather than what she *does* want. Before entering a successful relationship, women need to articulate what they truly want, according to Dr. Tom Merrill, a forensic psychologist based in Honolulu, Hawaii, and Phoenix, Arizona, who specializes in relationships. He and his wife, Bobbie Sandoz-Merrill, a social worker, are coauthors of *Settle for More*.[7]

Dr. Merrill suggests that women like Johanna sit down and make a list of what they want in a relationship—like honesty, open communication, love, and acceptance. Women who are already in a relationship could ask their partner to make their own list and see if both sets of goals match. "I don't see how two people can count on a relationship working unless they really know they want the same things," says Dr. Merrill. When you take the time to explore what you want, you're more likely to find someone who fits your needs, instead of choosing someone based on a reaction to your parents' flawed relationship.

"We Don't Need a Piece of Paper": Living Together Without Marrying

Jenny Schultz, 33, and her longtime boyfriend, Greg Harris, 40, look like they just stepped out of a J.Crew catalog. Blond and athletic, they recently relocated to Utah from Michigan and are thrilled they can hit the ski slopes on a moment's notice. The couple relocated for Jenny's new job as a college professor, and after seven years of dating, they've just bought a hundred-year-old bungalow together. They enjoy spending weekends renovating their house, and are so busy with treks to Home Depot and Jenny's demanding work schedule and pursuit of tenure that getting married is "pretty low on our list of priorities right now," according to Jenny.

This laid-back attitude toward marriage does not go over well with Jenny's mother, Marilyn Schultz, 57. Marilyn, a self-described homemaker, can't understand why her daughter won't marry. She fears

Greg is dragging his heels and isn't really committed to Jenny. Marilyn is not shy about sharing her worries with her daughter.

Marilyn says Greg is "not *really* a son-in-law" and won't include him in family photos or e-mails. "My mother still doesn't fully accept him because we're not married," laments Jenny. She feels hurt that her mother won't acknowledge the seriousness of her relationship with Greg. Although Marilyn would never go so far as to refer to Jenny's arrangement as "shacking up" or "living in sin," she frequently sends little slights Jenny's way.

For example, every year at Christmas, her mother leaves out bright red holiday stockings for her two children and her daughter-in-law, but Greg doesn't get one. "She'll make these little jabs like 'He's not part of the family yet. Why should he get a stocking?' " Jenny is quick to point out that Greg has spent the last five Christmases with the Schultz family. When Jenny's childhood dog died, Marilyn sent an e-mail message to everyone in their family, including her son and daughter-in-law but not Greg, "even though Greg and I have been together longer than my brother and his wife." On another occasion, when Jenny's grandfather died, she and Greg immediately flew out to be with her family in Ohio. Marilyn acted surprised that Greg had accompanied Jenny. "He doesn't need to be here," she said. Jenny replied, "He doesn't *need* to be here. I want him to be here." She often asks herself if her mother would "act differently if we were legally married."

In Jenny's mind, there's no difference between her relationship with Greg and her brother's relationship with his wife. Jenny says that in many ways, she and Greg "are more committed to each other than most married people are." They've written their wills and are the beneficiaries of each other's estate. Still, her mother does not embrace Greg in the same way she embraces her daughter-in-law. Marilyn believes that she needs to protect her daughter from a man who won't commit. On a recent family vacation to South Carolina, Marilyn and Greg took a bike ride together. The outing turned out to be stressful for both. Marilyn confronted Greg and asked him, "Why won't you marry Jenny? You should be honored to be a part of our family."

Marilyn thinks their lack of legal commitment to each other must reflect some weakness in their relationship. She also questions Jenny's emotional commitment to Greg: "You're not gushy and excited when you talk about him," she often says to Jenny. Jenny acknowledges this. "I'm not a mushy person. I don't talk about how happy I am with Greg. So she reads into that, that I'm not committed." Jenny explains that she and Greg aren't opposed to marriage; they just haven't gotten around to it yet. She wanted to finish her Ph.D. and start her new job as a professor before heading to the altar. She also wants to avoid having a "big Catholic wedding," which she knows her mother would insist on.

It's not surprising that Marilyn can't accept her daughter's timetable for marrying. Marilyn married shortly after graduating high school in 1969, and had two children soon thereafter. Although the sexual revolution was starting to unfold on college campuses at that time, Marilyn's small town in Ohio was still living as if it were the 1950s. After graduating high school, Marilyn began work as a dental assistant. One of her first patients was a young Vietnam veteran, Matthew Schultz, who had come in to have his wisdom teeth removed. They married shortly after their first date and Marilyn spent the next eighteen years raising her daughter, Jenny, and son, Kyle, while running a small arts and crafts business out of her basement, and continuing part-time work as a dental assistant. Still, she considers being a wife and mother her two most important accomplishments.

That fast track from first date to marriage is becoming a relic of the past. Dating now leads to cohabitation, which may or may not lead to marriage. The number of unmarried couples living together increased tenfold from 1960 to 2000, according to the U.S. Census Bureau. About 10 million people are now living with a partner of the opposite sex; that's about 8 percent of all couples households in the United States. Most unmarried couples who live together are Jenny's peers—men and women ages 25 to 34. What's more, roughly half of all people marrying today have lived with their partner before marrying.[8]

Living with a partner is really a trial run for marriage, according to Dr. Pamela Smock, a sociology professor at the University of Michigan and an expert on cohabitation. Dr. Smock says young women today "are trying cohabitation because they believe this will help them choose the right marriage partner and avoid a divorce."[9] Studies of couples who live together show that within five years of living together, about half of couples marry, 40 percent split up, and the rest continue to live together. These statistics should give some comfort to Marilyn; the odds are in favor of Jenny and Greg eventually marrying. But if they don't, it's probably for the best, according to Smock. Living together before marriage "makes sense to young people if they're serious about each other at all," and if they want to be sure they're marrying for the right reasons.

Still, what can Marilyn do to relieve her anxiety about Jenny's living situation?

ADVICE FOR MOTHERS

Recognize that a wedding is not a marriage. Dr. Northman encourages Marilyn to think about the differences between a wedding and a marriage. "A *wedding* is a life cycle event, whereas a *marriage* is something that starts when you begin dating and that changes and grows over a lifetime. Jenny should have the wrong kind of wedding and a right marriage, rather than vice versa." Marilyn could try to understand what Jenny loves about Greg, and should accept that the two are more focused on their relationship with one another than they are with the ritual of a wedding. He also says Marilyn should ask herself: "Why are you holding on so tenaciously?" If she truly has concerns about Jenny and Greg's relationship, then she should gingerly raise these issues and allow her daughter to talk honestly and openly, without fear that her mother will forever have a tainted impression of Greg.

"It's Just as Easy to Marry a Rich Man as a Poor Man": When Mothers Disapprove of Daughters' Husbands

The one comment we heard more than any other in our interviews with mothers was that they want what's best for their daughters. And "what's best" often meant marrying a financially stable man so their daughters would not have to worry about their economic security. Mothers from all backgrounds—from former socialites to impoverished single mothers—generally agreed that "it's just as easy to marry a rich man as a poor man." This is a surprisingly common view, even in the twenty-first century, when women have advanced degrees and career prospects that are often better than their husbands'. As matchmaker Janis Spindel says, "Why shouldn't women have it all?" There are enough issues to deal with when you're getting married. You shouldn't start a marriage with financial struggles, which can add more stress to the mix, Spindel warns. Mothers are telling their daughters the same thing.

Eleanor Kowalski, age 56, fled Poland in 1982 because of her husband Sam's anticommunist activities. She complains that her daughter Megan Harper's husband "is not much for her." She wishes her son-in-law were more ambitious so that Megan wouldn't have to work part-time as a social worker while raising her young son. "He doesn't have any drive to make money, to accomplish something," says Eleanor. Megan, age 29, counters that her husband, Craig, a computer programmer, is "kindhearted, loving, and caring." The two communicate well, work through their disputes, and are committed to staying together. Megan says her mother judges men based on their earnings, not on their character. "It wouldn't have mattered who I married," she said. "The only thing that matters is his profession, not his personality." She says her husband doesn't strive to be in a position of power, that he's "laid-back," and happily lets Megan "take the lead," which is why the two get along so well. Megan is hurt by her mother's disapproval, but knows her mother's concern is the product of her difficult past. Eleanor felt trapped in a marriage to an abusive man for twenty-five years and she struggled to support herself and her children after she finally gained the courage to leave him. Eleanor wants Megan and her son to have the financial and emotional stability she craved as a young mother.

Socialite Sally Handleman, 71, was crushed when her daughter, Jill Handleman, 42, stopped dating the son of a prominent political figure. Jill recalls that her mother was "incredibly upset" when she broke up with her boyfriend, whom Jill describes as a "depressed alcoholic." Ultimately, Jill married a "lovely man," a video producer who is a perfect match for her. His family has "no name" in the community, but he is "kind, honest and funny," she says. "My mom really loved it when we dated people of social standing," agrees Lindsay, Jill's younger sister. She encouraged them to make social status a priority in choosing a mate, but neither daughter followed her advice. Sally, by contrast, had married for money and status and was miserable during her frosty marriage. She found her passion in a seven-year-long extramarital affair with Gerald Jones, the architect who redesigned the family home. The affair ended up destroying her marriage and her relationship with her daughters, who can't fathom that their mother's obsession with wealth and social status would overshadow her desire for a truly loving relationship. When cleaning her mother's house recently, Jill found a note Sally had written during the time of the affair. It was a list of pros and cons, comparing her husband, Ronald, and her lover. Jill said the note described Gerald as "more loving, but Dad had more money and more prestige." Interestingly, Sally told us, "I never even thought of marrying Gerald." When her husband eventually left her, Sally was saddened because "it dramatically changed my social life."

Terri Romero, a 44-year-old marketing executive, knows her mother, Louise Goldfarb, was more than a tad disappointed that Terri married a "penniless Puerto Rican–Italian graphic artist from the Bronx." Louise, a Manhattanite, had her heart set on Terri marrying her former boyfriend Joel, a Jewish medical student. Terri says Joel was the "ideal husband" in her mother's eyes, "though not the ideal for me," because he was verbally abusive and had a secret cocaine habit. Her mother adored Joel, whom she saw as a polite future physician who "had it all on paper." But, Terri says, "he was cruel to me and didn't love me." Louise admits that when Terri and Joel broke up, she said to her daughter, "Are you stupid? He's a doll. He's so sweet." Terri replied, "Ma, you don't know what happened." "In my heart, I kept thinking, 'What could be wrong?'" says Louise.

Women like Terri, Jill, and Megan view love and marriage in quite different terms than their mothers. That's not to say their mothers didn't love their husbands (although Sally admits she married for money and not love). Rather, the expectations for whom women "should" marry have changed drastically in recent decades. In the 1950s and early 1960s, the average American woman married in her late teens and early twenties, so most would meet their future husbands in their neighborhoods and high schools. Typically, young women and their beaus came from the same social class, ethnicity, and religious background. Today, women often meet their husbands in college or graduate school, often hundreds of miles from home, or in their first jobs or through friends and social activities. It's not surprising then, that men and women today are more likely to marry those from different ethnic, socioeconomic, or religious backgrounds.[10]

The traits women look for in a spouse have also changed in recent decades. According to Dr. David Popenoe, professor of sociology at Rutgers University and director of the National Marriage Project, young women and men today want a "soul mate," not a financial supporter. The National Marriage Project surveyed thousands of 20-something Americans and found that an astounding 94 percent of single men and women agree that "when you marry you want your spouse to be your soul mate, first and foremost," and 82 percent agreed "it is unwise for a woman to rely on marriage for financial security." Less than half believe "it is important to find a spouse who shares their own religion."[11]

Many women today no longer expect that they will live on their husbands' incomes alone. In roughly one-third of marriages today, wives earn more than their husbands. Generation X men are more likely than their fathers to cut back on their work hours and share housework and child care with their wives. Married couples today operate as peers or equals, according to University of Washington sociologist Dr. Pepper Schwartz, so women feel less pressure to marry a man for financial stability. More than 80 percent of women surveyed in the National Marriage Project agree "it is more important to have a husband who can communicate about his deepest feelings than a husband who makes a good living."[12]

Although Terri, Jill, and Megan may be in sync with the women of their generation, this still doesn't erase the tension in their relationships with their mothers. How can they make their mothers understand their romantic choices? And how can the daughters come to appreciate their mothers' valuable perspectives on love and marriage?

ADVICE FOR MOTHERS

Share your concerns with your daughter in a gentle way. Donna Mayerson, a psychologist and parenting coach with Hummingbird Coaching Services in Cincinnati, Ohio, suggests that mothers feel free to express their concerns, but they should do so in a kind rather than a judgmental or scolding manner. For example, Eleanor tends to express her anxiety in the form of disapproval. Instead, she could be direct with Megan about her worries and what she wants for her daughter. Phrasing her worries as complaints about Megan's husband will only cause Megan to become defensive.

ADVICE FOR DAUGHTERS

Be open with your mother about why you've chosen whom you've chosen. The daughters we spoke with admitted they sometimes weren't forthright with their mothers when it came to discussing issues like love, intimacy, and relationships, and this secrecy dated back to their teen years. For instance, Terri hasn't felt comfortable sharing personal issues with her mother ever since Louise read her diary when she was 14. As Terri recalled, "There was some pretty wild stuff in there." At the time, Louise told her, "Don't worry. I only read the good parts." If Terri could have trusted her, she would have felt safe telling her mother her "perfect" ex-boyfriend, the medical student, had a long history of drug abuse. Daughters were often reluctant to discuss their romantic relationships with their mothers when they were young for fear of being judged, misunderstood, or even reprimanded for having a sexual relationship when they were unmarried. But as adult women, they should have confidence that their mothers are more open now than they were twenty years earlier, and might be more understanding of their daughters' romantic choices.

Partners for Life: Relationship Choices of Lesbian Daughters

Most mothers would be overjoyed to see their daughter happily settled down with the love of her life, in a nice home and with an adorable child. But when the daughter's beloved is another woman, it may take her mother some time to warm up. That was the case with Kara Birmingham, 37, and her mother, Val, 61. Kara, a computer software engineer, lives with her longtime partner, Renee, 43, and their 4-year-old daughter, Annabelle, in Indianapolis. Although Val is a devoted grandmother to Annabelle and she has politely (if not warmly) embraced Renee as a daughter-in-law, both Kara and Val are still recovering from the difficult years leading up to this point. Kara knows deep down that her mother hasn't truly accepted that she's a lesbian and thinks this is merely a "stage" that will pass. "She thinks issues that happened in my life have 'made' me a temporary lesbian, rather than accepting who I really am," Kara explains.

Kara can understand why her mother feels that way. She believes it reflects her mother's conventional religious upbringing and the fact that Kara didn't come out as a lesbian until she was in her late twenties. "When I was growing up, we were the stereotypical American family living in a small midwestern town," Kara recalls. Her mother stayed at home with Kara and her brother, and she raised them while their father worked. They went to church every Sunday. "I guess you could say we were raised with basic right-wing values, where you grow up with a mother and father in the home." She calls her upbringing sheltered. "I wasn't exposed to anything political, and I was really naïve."

Kara and Val agree they've always had a good relationship. Kara says, "She made me feel I could do anything I strived to do. But part of that was assuming I would marry and have a family." Kara did get married at age 20, after dropping out of college in her sophomore year. Her marriage was miserable: "He was bad news. I stayed in the relationship for eight years out of habit." Kara always felt ill at ease in her marriage, just as she felt a bit out of place growing up in her small Indiana town—though she didn't figure out *why* until her midtwenties. "I remember exactly when I discovered I was gay. I was lying in bed and it hit me like a ton of bricks." She had never known anyone who was gay and it had never crossed her mind before. But then everything was falling into place. "I never felt like I fit in anywhere, even as small child. Some people sense there's something different about them, even when they're that young. I just couldn't figure it out."

When Kara realized she was a lesbian, she went out and bought herself a computer with Internet access so that she could research gay and lesbian issues. She knew that she couldn't educate herself by relying on resources in rural Indiana. "If I had tried to find a lesbian resource center, I would have been laughed out of town."

The Internet turned out to be a lifeline, and her partner, Renee, was one of the first people she met in an Internet chat room. They became friends and communicated by e-mail for more than six months. They were both still married and struggling with the same issues. "We stayed in contact, and then we realized there was something more there." They eventually met in person and Kara moved to be with Renee a couple of years later.

The path from Kara's unhappy marriage to her loving relationship with Renee wasn't a smooth one. But Kara believes the struggles she encountered turned out to be a blessing for her. They brought her daughter, Annabelle, into her life. Kara recalls that shortly after she left her husband, she needed to figure out whether she was "truly gay." She went out with a male friend one night, got drunk, and slept with him. "I thought I should give men one more try so that I could figure out whether I was really gay or whether it was just my ex-husband who was wrong for me." That one-night stand got her pregnant. Though that was a low point, she says there's a reason Annabelle was given to her. Giving birth to Annabelle, she says, "is the best thing I've ever done."

Shortly after Annabelle was born, Kara braced herself to tell her mother she was a lesbian. Although Kara and Renee were living together by that point, they referred to one another as "friends" and "roommates." By both Kara and Val's accounts, Kara's coming out was the most difficult period in their relationship. Kara recalled the painful afternoon when she took her mother out to lunch and told her at the restaurant that she was a lesbian: "She was furious and we fought for a couple of weeks." Kara says she was honest and told her mother everything. "She thought that I had been traumatized by men and that I needed therapy." Her mother said she would never come by to see her and Renee, only her granddaughter, Annabelle. A few hours after the screaming match at the restaurant, Val phoned her daughter and said she couldn't believe what she had just done.

Kara knows her mother loves her, yet she also knows that Val does not understand or accept her choices. She also realizes that because of her mother's fundamentalist Christian and conservative Republican political views, she can't fully accept Kara's relationship with Renee. Val tells us the same: "I still don't believe Kara is truly a lesbian. I think it's more experimentation," and an example of "another mistake in her life." She adds that Kara's never had a good relationship with any man, including her father.

Given their fundamentally different views, Kara and Val are not as close as they once were. Val explains: "As far as discussing a lot of gay issues, we just don't talk about them." Val says her daughter is smart enough to know she disagrees with the way that she does things. "I'll accept the way she's living right now, but I don't have to agree with it. We're just on different sides, and we can't argue about it."

Dr. Margaret Buttenheim, a psychologist and member of the clinical faculty at the University of Michigan Center for the Child and the Family, emphasizes that most lesbians have relationships with their mothers that are just as good as those of heterosexual women. Although it may take time for mothers to come around and accept their daughters' choices, most do. She offers two suggestions to help women like Val and Kara move forward.

ADVICE FOR MOTHERS AND DAUGHTERS

Think twice about the "we agree to disagree" approach. For many lesbian daughters, the seemingly simplest plan of action is to temporarily put aside their sexual orientation and their relationship and not discuss it with their mother. There are serious costs to this, warns Dr. Buttenheim. "If they don't talk about such an important part of the daughter's life, her mother won't know who she is anymore." In the long run, the person who will be hurt most is the mother. The mother is going to need her daughter, and, as she gets older, will be more dependent on her daughter than vice versa. This "agree to disagree" strategy, says Dr. Buttenheim, "basically says that we agree to give up on emotional intimacy, and we'll do nothing about it because we think things are hopeless." The better approach is to talk directly about what's happening.

Put family first, ideology second. Dr. Buttenheim observes that "it's hard to make peace when one of the two has a rigid ideology." She suggests the daughter state very bluntly to her mother that they will be losing emotional intimacy if the daughter can't be open about her choices because she is fearful of being judged. She urges Val to think about which values she cherishes most. Politically or religiously conservative mothers should seriously consider whether their ideological stance is more important to them than their relationship with their daughter. Buttenheim notes, "Most religions preach that 'God is love,' so there's something ironic about judging one kind of love as good and another as bad."

When Love Fades: The Stigma of a Daughter's Divorce

Shannon Tyler, a 33-year-old insurance executive in Arizona, is the first to admit she's been unlucky in love. Her first two marriages ended in divorce, but she's convinced "the third time's the charm." Her mother, Margaret Reese, a 55-year-old Iowa native, isn't so sure—and she won't let Shannon forget her first two marital missteps. Margaret thinks her daughter is selfish and that she didn't work hard enough to keep her first two marriages together. Shannon can't conceal her anger when her mother refers to her husband Derrick as "number three" and tells him "his days are numbered." Margaret's skepticism about her daughter's third marriage is compounded by the fact that Shannon met her husband through the Internet. Shannon counters that she had very good reasons for divorcing her first two husbands, and she finally has learned what she wants in a relationship. She wishes her mother could have faith in her decision.

Shannon says she's a different person now than when she first married at age 20. "In my first marriage, I tried to cook, work full-time, and do everything. I thought I had to be just like my mother and I finally realized that I didn't have to be." In Shannon's eyes, her first marriage didn't work because she and her husband had fallen out of love and were growing in different directions. That explanation didn't satisfy her mother. "She thought I was on drugs, an alcoholic, or gay—that was why my marriage fell apart. She had to have a reason and a rationale. She couldn't accept that it just didn't work." Shannon says that she's now older and wiser, and her marriage to Derrick is solid and secure.

Shannon recounted that she and Derrick met through the Web site eHarmony and the courtship progressed slowly and tentatively over e-mail. "When we finally met in person, we realized we're cut out of the same cloth." The two don't eat fish and have the same kind of goals and aspirations. They enjoy travel. They're dedicated to their careers but don't work themselves to death. Still, Margaret couldn't fathom meeting one's husband—a third husband, at that—in cyberspace. When she met Derrick, she said, "Well, he *seems* normal. . . ." Shannon snapped back: "What did you think? That he's going to be a weirdo nutcase?"

Margaret feels someone has to be the voice of reason and says she's being honest with her daughter. She thinks that Shannon has ridiculously high standards when it comes to love. "I think she married these guys and then they didn't live up to her standards, so she left them. Marriage isn't always fun, but you make the best of it and tough it out." Margaret reluctantly admits she is her daughter's worst critic, and she has a hard time acknowledging that there are two sides to every divorce. "Even when my kids were young and they got into fights at school," she recalls, "I never thought it was the other person's fault because I wanted my kids to toughen up." She wanted them to know you can't blame others for your problems and you have to take responsibility.

This tough-love approach has created a rift between Shannon and Margaret. Many daughters told us their mother was their biggest ally when the daughter went through a difficult divorce. For mothers and daughters like Shannon and Margaret, however, seemingly small, long-standing tensions can develop into full-blown feuds when the daughter decides to end a marriage.

Vivian Kleinschmidt, now 77, can relate to Margaret's melancholy. When she first heard the news of her daughter Mary's divorce, it "was like somebody took my heart out of my body and held it in my hand and squeezed it." Sixteen years later, her feelings of sadness are still palpable. Mary believes her mother dwells too much on the divorce and can't understand why her mother can't let go of her pain.

Stacy Fines, 44, also got little support from her mother when she divorced. When Stacy first introduced her fiancé, Nathan, to her mother, Jean Kaplan, age 68, she couldn't have been happier. "He seemed like a nice young man," Jean said. A doctor with a Harvard education, Nathan fulfilled her mother's dream. "Harvard is the place to be from," she said. At 27, Stacy and Nathan married and within two years they started their family, having four children over a span of eight years.

Two years ago, Stacy decided to divorce. The news didn't surprise her mother, who felt Stacy was an uncaring wife who took her loving husband for granted. "I knew that was coming," Jean says. She thinks her daughter showed no interest in her husband's life. He would often travel for business, and when she'd ask Stacy where he was, she would respond that she didn't know. "To me that was so horrible, not to know where he was going," she says. Jean says she and her husband check in with each other at the end of every day. "We talk about everything. We have a wonderful relationship." She hoped that her marriage would provide a positive model for Stacy and was disappointed that her marriage failed. Jean says Stacy never opened up to her about the possibility of divorce or the reasons behind it, so she never had the opportunity to lend a sympathetic ear to her daughter. "She doesn't need anybody," Jean says, sarcastically. Stacy's husband confided his unhappiness to Jean, and she said she supported him. She didn't urge Stacy to stay with him. Instead, after Stacy told her she was getting divorced, "I said, 'Fine.'"

Stacy is hurt that her mother views the divorce as a failing on her part. She says her mother's biggest concern was having to tell her friends that her daughter was getting divorced. "It was not about my happiness," Stacy says. Instead, she believes her mother was worried about how others would react. No one in Stacy's small family has ever divorced, so her mother considers the failed marriage as a blot on the family name. She says her mother's failure to support her during this "huge life-changing event," made an already strained relationship even worse.

Jean Kaplan and Margaret Reese view their daughters' divorces as a sign of a character flaw, rather than as a rational response to a marriage that wasn't working. When Jean and Margaret were newlyweds five decades ago, divorce was rare and divorced persons were often scorned. Since the 1960s and 1970s, though, divorce rates have climbed steadily, reaching a peak in 1980, when roughly 40 percent of marriages ended in divorce. Currently, that figure is about one-third.[13]

While a handful of social critics may attribute the rise in divorce rates to "selfishness," most social scientists explain the pattern as a consequence of women's rising economic independence. Women in earlier generations often didn't have the financial means to support themselves, and many stayed in troubled marriages because they feared for their children's economic well-being. Today, women are able to support themselves and their children outside of marriage. Further, the stigma of divorce has declined, and very few experts would say it's right for unhappy couples to stay together for the "sake of the kids." Women like Stacy and Shannon recognized that their marriages weren't working, and they decided to leave rather than suffer. Why couldn't their mothers understand?

Dr. Ellen Berman, a clinical professor of psychiatry at the University of Pennsylvania School of Medicine and the author of a textbook on marital and family therapy, says there's "something going on" with Stacy and Jean—especially because most mothers can and do support their daughters through a divorce. "Jean really does not like her daughter." She wonders if Jean, as an only child, was made to feel like she was the center of the universe, and thought that her daughter would treat her the same way. She may have had a vision that Stacy would think her mother was wonderful and they would be best friends whose lives were tightly intertwined. The problem is that Jean could never see Stacy as an independent person who was different from her. As a result, Jean was very hurt when her daughter's life choices diverged from her own.

Each of our mother-daughter pairs had its own idiosyncratic concerns, but there were also some tensions shared by all. Our team of therapists drew up a list of tips mothers and daughters can follow when mom doesn't agree with her daughter's romantic choices.

ADVICE FOR MOTHERS

Reveal your concerns, but only if asked. It's okay, if asked, to point out aspects of your daughter's relationship that she may not be thinking about logically or with a clear perspective. It's something the mother may better understand because she's had more life experience and can provide her daughter with the benefit of her hard-earned wisdom.

Don't expect your daughter to pursue your unlived life. Mothers don't want daughters to repeat their mistakes. In Johanna Jones's case, the way her mother, Genevieve, coped with her own tumultuous marriages was to glorify marriage. She wants her daughters to have marriages far better than hers. But she must accept the fact that her daughter Johanna doesn't necessarily want that. "To keep blindly trying to get them to live the life we had or didn't have or wanted to have is not our role," says Dr. Sanford.

Trust your daughter to do the right thing. If mothers have raised their daughters well, they should have faith their daughters will ultimately make the right decisions, according to Dr. Mayerson. For example, Jenny Schultz may not be marrying her boyfriend, but she has followed in her mother's footsteps by having a loving relationship, and by making practical decisions—such as naming her boyfriend the beneficiary of her estate and vice versa. Although Margaret Reese sneers at the fact that her daughter, Shannon Tyler, met her third husband on the Internet, she should trust that Shannon has learned from her first two failed marriages and now knows what she wants in a relationship. Eleanor Kowalski should trust that she has given her daughter, Megan, the tools to become self-reliant and strong. Megan has chosen a mate who provides her with emotional support, love, and open communication. Dr. Mayerson says Eleanor should rest assured that Megan has the personal qualities and survival skills needed to manage whatever life throws her way.

Support your child when times get tough. Dr. Merrill says mothers should support their children in what they do—even if they've made a mistake. When your children are having trouble, that's when they need you the most, he says. It's a shame that Stacy Fines couldn't count on her mother's support during her difficult divorce, says Merrill. A daughter's crisis may last only a few months or years, yet the mother-daughter bond persists for life.

ADVICE FOR DAUGHTERS

Don't rebel just for the sake of rebelling. Making choices about dating, love, and marriage by trying to avoid a mother's mistake "won't necessarily get you a good relationship," says Dr. Merrill. He discourages daughters from behaving reactively and says that could result in relationships that may be as unsatisfying as their parents' were. Instead, daughters should choose a partner and a relationship on the basis of the positive traits they have, rather than the flaws that they lack.

Tell your mother, gently, to lay off. Whether your mother is urging you to get married, stay married, or marry someone other than the one you love, Dr. Merrill suggests taking your mother aside at a calm moment, ideally when things are going well. A daughter can begin by thanking her mother for being so concerned. She can tell her she appreciates her good wishes and desires for a life that works. But then she can say, "I understand you don't agree, but we don't need to have a lot of conversation about it." As we mentioned in the advice to mothers, it's okay for a mother to express her concerns in a gentle way. But ultimately, if her daughter doesn't want to listen, the mother needs to respect that.

Tell your mother how her comments make you feel. Even the most assertive and confident woman has been raised to play nice and to keep the peace. But sometimes timidity can make mother-daughter strains simmer and eventually boil over. Dr. Sanford says that young women need to understand their mothers have their best interests at heart. It's clear that Jenny Schultz's mom, Marilyn, fears that her nonmarriage to Greg is a sign that her relationship is in trouble. And Eleanor Kowalski and Louise Goldfarb want their daughters, Megan and Terri, to marry financially secure men so their daughters and grandchildren will not struggle financially, as they did. Genevieve Canvasser was saddened by what she saw as her single daughter's loneliness. Sandford suggests daughters say something like: "I understand you want these things for me. However, these may not be the things that I want for myself right now. What I really need from you is understanding, support, and encouragement for the choices that I'm making."

Explore your *own* motivations. Daughters tend to dig in their heels and tell their mothers they're choosing certain life paths because they "want to." But Dr. Merrill urges daughters to honestly assess their motivations for why they're doing what they're doing. Sometimes a mother's interrogation may hurt precisely because the daughter knows that Mom is right; mothers often know their daughters better than their daughters know themselves. For instance, Johanna Jones says that she enjoyed her single life and pursuing her interests in New Age religion and alternative medicine. Part of her persona was dressing the part of a woman who didn't care about her appearances. Dr. Merrill wonders whether Johanna was keeping herself "safe" from men by dressing plainly and not making herself attractive, "so she's not much at risk for people banging down her door." He also questions why she chose the socially isolated life in remote Hawaii. "There's no reason that because you don't want to be married, you have to make yourself unattractive and be a hermit."

Try to understand *your mother's* motivations. Just as daughters need to delve into their own motivations for why they're doing what they're doing, they should also try to figure out what's driving their mother's behavior. For example, Eleanor Kowalski is critical of her son-in-law, Craig, because she fears that Megan will repeat Eleanor's past and end up as devastated as Eleanor was. She doesn't trust that Craig is different from her ex-husband, and she's waiting for her daughter's nightmare to unfold. She fears the worst and is trying hard to protect her daughter,

Dr. Mayerson says. Daughters may be able to better accept their mothers' views if they better understand where she's coming from.

ADVICE FOR MOTHERS AND DAUGHTERS

Recognize that mothers' relationships have implications for daughters' choices. If you grow up in a home where there is an abusive relationship, you're going to question whether it's possible to have a loving, caring relationship, says Dr. Sanford. Diana Gladwell's abusive father abandoned her and her mother when she was just 6, leading her mother Nanette Westfall to conclude that her daughter is afraid of committing to a long-term relationship. Jill Handleman saw how her mother Sally married for money rather than love and destroyed her family when she had an affair with her architect. Jill admits that she dated a string of passionate but "totally deadbeat inappropriate bad-boys" when in her twenties, to avoid her mother's fate. She ultimately realized she didn't need to go that far just for the sake of rebellion. Both mothers and daughters should recognize that early experiences don't just fade into a distant memory, and that it takes time and soul-searching—if not professional help—for a woman to overcome the pain of her own and her mother's past.

Set limits on what you discuss and for how long. Sometimes a conversation can go on for too long or veer off into dangerous territory. Dr. Berman suggests mothers and daughters ask themselves whether a problem really has to be "talked out," and if so, for how long. Daughters may want to set limits on the discussion. For instance, when Marilyn Schultz cajoles her cohabiting daughter, Jenny, to marry, Jenny could say, "Mom, this is your problem. I don't want to talk about it. I love you. I'm fine. The subject is closed." Similarly, mothers and daughters may find that a particular issue typically starts festering after a prolonged amount of time together. If so, mothers and daughters can set limits on time spent together. If you stay over an hour and that's when you end up having a tussle, and if it makes sense to do so, leave before things get heated, suggests Sandoz-Merrill.

CHAPTER 4

Having a Baby: Whether, When, How, with Whom, and How Many?

It takes love, not money, to raise a child.

There's no greater joy than being a mother. How could you give that up?

Don't you think that Emma would like a little brother or sister?

Shannon Tyler, a 33-year-old insurance executive, knew it probably wasn't a good idea to buy her mother a T-shirt emblazoned with the words "Ask me about my grand-dog." For 55-year-old Margaret Reese, her daughter's decision to be child-free is no laughing matter. Shannon and her husband, Derrick, have no interest in raising kids and prefer to spend their time traveling, working, golfing, and playing with their two Labradors. For Margaret, though, "a grand-dog isn't good enough." Margaret is desperate to become a grandmother, yet Shannon is 100 percent certain that motherhood is not for her. "I've never really liked kids. I babysat when I was younger and the kids hated me," she explains.

While Shannon has chosen not to have children, 44-year-old Tammy Mahoney, an education professor, knew she and her husband, Tom, would have just two children. Tammy loved growing up in a commotion-filled household with her six brothers and sisters, but a large family isn't compatible with her demanding career as a college professor: "I wanted to have more of my own life than my mother had." Tammy's mother, Betty Mahoney, is a devout Catholic who had seven children, and she tried hard to hide from her children how exhausted she was raising her large brood.

For Shannon, Tammy, and dozens of other young women we interviewed, childbearing is a choice they see as largely within their control.[1] Women born in the period after the 1960s can't remember life before the birth control pill and access to legal abortion. In 1960, the pill was approved by the Food and Drug Administration, and couples quickly abandoned less effective methods, like the IUD or the rhythm method. By 1964, just four years after the pill became widely available, one in four couples relied on it. As couples began to believe it was safe—or even good for them—to proactively control their childbearing, the pill became extremely popular. By the 1980s, more than 80 percent of American women used effective contraceptives, and today, Catholic women are just as likely as other women to use birth control.

While women of a generation ago, like Betty Mahoney, often didn't plan their pregnancies, their daughters are plotting out childbearing with the same careful thought and research that they devoted to their college applications. They're seriously deliberating whether, when, how many, and with whom they'll have their children. And their decisions are shaped by an endless list of considerations, including their career prospects, their spouse's preferences, work schedules, maternity leave policies, the costs of having two children in college at the same time, and even knowledge of their genetic histories.

This rational, scientific approach to motherhood often befuddles their mothers. Women like Betty Mahoney and Margaret Reese frequently told us: "We didn't *think* about everything so much." For them, having babies was a natural step after marrying. All the mothers we interviewed ultimately supported their daughters' childbearing choices, but the road to acceptance was bumpy at best: they worried that an only grandchild would be a lonely grandchild, a childless daughter would have no one to take care of her in old age, or a single mother would be too exhausted and undesirable to ever find a husband. A mother's probing questions are especially troubling to their daughters because the daughters often find themselves second-guessing their choices or sadly find that their best-laid plans can go awry when a marriage ends or infertility issues arise.

A Working Mother's Choice: Rejecting the Boisterous Big Family

The notion of "control"—deciding precisely when, whether, and how many children to have—was foreign to many women a generation ago, especially observant Catholics. Betty Mahoney, now 79, was one of those women. At 19, she married a man who was in the Navy. Within a year she had her first child, and six more followed over the next fourteen years. As an only child, Betty wanted a large family so her children would have friends and a built-in support system. Betty tried to live by the rules of the Catholic Church and didn't use birth control "because I loved God and I loved my husband." None of her pregnancies were planned.

Betty's youngest child, Tammy Mahoney, now 44, says that as one of seven children she always had ready-made playmates. Tammy is perky and energetic, with short dark hair, large expressive eyes, and a wide smile. She eagerly shared with us many warm memories of her childhood antics with her brothers and sisters. After baths on Sunday night, the kids put on their pajamas and huddled around the television to watch *The Ed Sullivan Show*. Tammy shared a bedroom with her sister and two brothers, and the four of them would stay up long after lights-out. With a grin, she recalls nighttime games of "quicksand," where she and her older siblings would mischievously hop from bed to bed, trying not to touch the floor. "We'd jump from the dresser to the twin beds and from the bunk beds to the twin beds. We couldn't understand how our parents knew we were still awake!" Tammy remembers her childhood as a wonderful time with her brothers and sisters, yet she also saw that her mother was often overwhelmed and angry—no doubt a response to the pressures of caring for such a large family.

Before she married, Tammy had dreamed of having five children, her plans buoyed by her happy memories of growing up in a large family. She knew she wanted another baby after she had her first. But ultimately, she stopped after two girls. She had several reasons. First, she had her children when she was 34 and 36, so she was concerned that her age would put her and her baby at risk for health problems. Also, as a full-time education professor, trying to focus on two children while working in an intense job proved to be a huge challenge. "I couldn't imagine how I'd fit any more [children] into my life. I wanted to fully enjoy my time with both girls," she said. Another important factor, says Tammy, was that "I wanted to have more of my own life than I sense my mother had." Tammy feared she would end up resenting her children if they consumed all of her time, as a large family would. Once she had her own children, she was in awe of her mother. "I have a lot more respect for her and her choices and difficulties," she said.

Tammy's husband, Brian, always wanted a small family, so he was relieved when she settled for two. "He had the big V [vasectomy] once I was sure," she said. Tammy said her mother never questioned her about stopping at two children, though she often told her that siblings are important because you always have each other as the years go by. As an only child, Betty was alone when her parents died and that was very hard for her, Tammy said. She wanted to ensure that her own children could share the burdens of health issues and emergencies, as well as the good times. Tammy says that having so many siblings has been wonderful. Betty points out that her two granddaughters will have only each other to lean on as Tammy and her husband face the inevitable challenges that old age brings. But that's a sacrifice Tammy is willing to make, so she can balance her family life with her work demands.

Avoiding Parenthood: Child-Free by Choice

Some women, like Tammy Mahoney, are opting for smaller families than the ones they grew up in, yet others know that parenthood isn't for them. The path to a child-free life, like the path to parenthood, is quite varied. Some don't like children, while others fear their troubled pasts would make them unfit parents. Others don't want to pass down their DNA to a new generation, especially if they're at genetic risk for a serious health concern. Each and every child-free woman we spoke with had given much thought to her decision and wanted respect for their decision *not* to parent. But they also knew their choice would be difficult for their mothers, who were eager to become grandmothers and wanted to see their own daughters experience the joys of parenthood.

Shannon Tyler, the 33-year-old insurance executive whom we met earlier in the chapter, made her decision after years of soul-searching. Shannon is saddened her mother can't accept that she is making a thoughtful and deliberate choice. "I've chosen a career, and I've chosen not to have children. I don't have any desire to have kids, and there are enough children in the world that didn't ask to be born." She admits she never really liked children, but when she was younger she presumed that all women became mothers. "I've tried it on and can't see it in my life." Though she doesn't want the responsibility of her own kids, she adores her friends' children (in small doses), and looks forward to being an aunt, once her younger brother and his wife start having kids.

Her mother, Margaret Reese, has tried hard to change Shannon's mind. "She told me that I was a selfish child for not providing her with grandchildren," Shannon recalls. "She said that I would be lonely when I was old because no one would take care of me" and asked who would mow the lawn if she owned a large home.

Margaret says she has finally accepted Shannon's decision. Still, she can't conceal her bitterness and ambivalence when she talks about her daughter's choice: "I guess she shouldn't have kids. She doesn't have a maternal bone in her body." Despite Shannon's lack of interest in mothering, Margaret still hopes that she'll have children. Margaret recalls her earlier days of trying to persuade her daughter: "I would tell her all the time, 'I would be a wonderful grandma and you need to have kids.'" But her daughter's common refrain was "Yeah, yeah, yeah." Margaret realizes that being a grandmother to Shannon's children probably isn't in the cards for her. "I tell her I understand, but I'm still really sad about it," Margaret says. She blames the decision on Shannon's career. "She's obsessed with that." She has found solace in the fact that her son recently married and he and his wife are planning to have children.

While Shannon viewed motherhood as incompatible with the plans she and her husband made for the future, other women told us a difficult childhood left them emotionally unprepared for parenthood. The fear of passing along a troublesome hereditary condition also was a serious consideration. That was the case with Rena Caldwell, age 44. When Rena was in college, she learned a disturbing family secret for the first time. Her younger sister discovered that when their mother, Sarah, was 18, Sarah's mother (the girls' grandmother) was diagnosed with schizophrenia and she endured intrusive treatments, including electric shock therapy. Later that same year, while Sarah was at school, her mother committed suicide. Sarah never told the girls about this until they found out on their own. But for Rena, the sad discovery answered many of her questions about her mother's parenting. It all began to make sense.

According to Rena, her mother never felt she had a "normal" upbringing and vowed to provide her children with the stable environment she lacked. Within four years of her mother's death, Sarah married. By the time she was 26, she had given birth to three girls and hoped to provide her daughters a safe and secure environment.

Sarah's mother's suicide "was the root of all her issues. It colored everything in her life," Rena explained. She thinks her mother spent her life trying to create the "perfect family" and the "perfect home" that she never had growing up. Rena said she always tried to appear positive and optimistic, even if she didn't genuinely feel that way. She stifled her anger and her true feelings for fear that she would drive others away. Sarah looked the part of the "perfect" young woman and modeled when she was young. Rena describes her as stunningly beautiful: tall, slender, with olive skin, jet black hair, and dark eyes. She dressed impeccably in the latest fashions and furnished her historic colonial home with the most elegant architectural touches.

Whenever there were problems in the family, Sarah tried to deny they existed, Rena said. She couldn't cope when Rena, an insecure child, became severely anorexic as a teen. Sarah pulled her out of therapy as soon as Rena indicated that her mother might be the source of her problems. Rena often wanted to say to her mother, "I'm sorry your mom killed herself. It's not my fault." At the same time that Rena was suffering from anorexia, she tells us her father was diagnosed with clinical depression.

Rena is far happier as an adult, as her cheerful laugh indicates. She now lives in Los Angeles with her boyfriend of six years, a photographer, and she travels the world as a publicist for the motion picture industry. They live a five-hour plane ride from her parents, whom she rarely sees. Rena's difficult childhood sealed her choice not to have children. "I had such a miserable childhood. My parents didn't mean to inflict this on their kids, but they did. Imagine what I could do to a child unintentionally?" she wondered.

Rena says her anxiety-filled childhood was the primary reason she's decided not to have a child, but the specter of a genetic condition also played a role. "It is likely I have some of the genetic stuff that contributes to bipolar disorder, schizophrenia, obsessive-compulsive disorder, and anorexia. So that was a consideration in not having kids," she says. "But the real fear was that I didn't know who I was and hadn't worked out my childhood issues." That, coupled with her genetic predisposition, meant kids "probably weren't a great idea."

Rena's youngest sister also has no children. Rena knows how much her mother wanted grandchildren, so she's grateful that her middle sister, Molly, took the pressure off. According to Rena, Molly has always tried to be the good daughter. She married "the nice Jewish boy" and they have two sons, so Rena enjoys the role of doting aunt. Sarah and her husband recently moved from Michigan to Texas to live in the same town as their grandchildren and also to be geographically closer to Rena and her youngest sister, who lives in the Southwest. (Rena's mother and sisters declined to speak with us.)

A generation ago, women usually assumed that they would have children, even if they didn't necessarily want or plan them. Today, however, many women think long and hard about their decision and do a lot of soul-searching before deciding whether they're capable of being good parents. Often the verdict is no. According to data from the National Survey of Family Growth, more than 40 percent of female college graduates between the ages of 22 and 44 were childless in 2002. About one-third of childless women ages 35 to 44 say that it's "temporary"—meaning that they still plan to have their first baby in the coming years. Just 26 percent say it's "involuntary," and more than 40 percent say they're child-free by choice.[2]

Women like Sarah, however, never really considered the possibility of *not* having children. She had her three daughters in rapid succession, in part to fill a deep emotional void, as her daughter Rena pointed out. But with a stronger sense of self-awareness and a greater understanding of the role of genetics, Rena felt that having children would be too risky. She doesn't want to take the chance of being a deficient mother, or of bearing a child who could be predisposed to a lifetime of sadness—even if that means giving up motherhood and disappointing her own mother.

Parenting coach Dr. Mayerson sheds some light on this situation. Her advice can apply to other mothers and daughters where a mother's troubled past affected her daughter's childbearing decisions.

ADVICE FOR MOTHERS

Recognize that the truth can set you free. When a parent tries to deny or conceal the truth, and creates a façade to mask pain and disappointment, it can be difficult for the child to break free of the façade. It can feel like a betrayal. Discovering the truth about Sarah's past created an opportunity for her daughters to better understand their own childhood experiences. This revelation may have enabled them to break free and make their choices with their eyes wide open. For instance, Rena dealt with this new knowledge by choosing not to take the risk of passing on psychopathology to children.

ADVICE FOR DAUGHTERS

Step back and see life through your mother's eyes. In a relationship like Rena and Sarah's, it's important to empathize with the mother, who has experienced such pain. The daughter should try to understand why her mother behaved as she did and why she feels the way she does. Dr. Mayerson says this story "is painful and hopeful at the same time." Despite the trauma, it speaks to the resilience of the human spirit. Sarah missed out on being mothered herself, but she resolved to "right the wrong" and do things differently for her own daughters. She did this by compartmentalizing or sealing off the painful part of her life. She glossed over or denied anything that didn't fit in with the portrait of domestic tranquility that she so badly wanted to create, including her husband's depression and her daughter's eating disorder.

Dr. Mayerson gives kudos to the decisions Rena made, both in the way she's lived her life and in her decision not to have kids. None of the daughters were privy to the information about their grandmother's suicide until late adolescence. Each of them dealt with the information in a thoughtful way. They all chose lives that reflected the reality of risk factors while assessing what would meet their individual needs.

ADVICE FOR MOTHERS AND DAUGHTERS

Seek out support. When a daughter decides not to have a child, she should recognize that her mother may need to grieve the loss of a grandchild she has long hoped for. It's important for mothers to find ways of experiencing and expressing their feelings of loss and disappointment. It may even be necessary to find support from friends and other family members in coping with these feelings.

Parenting Solo:
Raising Children as a Single Mom by Choice

Women today are more likely than ever before to bypass the altar en route to motherhood. Single women who want children have options that their mothers couldn't have dreamed of, ranging from adoption to shopping for their child's father at the local sperm bank. Some divorced women may decide to expand their family as a solo parent instead of pinning their hopes on a second marriage. Women who choose to have children on their own are finding that the social stigma of single parenthood has faded. Some women who want to become single mothers have adopted daughters from China, which until recently had liberal policies toward unmarried parents. Adopting a child is emancipating for single women, who feel they shouldn't have to sacrifice motherhood just because they don't have a husband. Yet we found that their own mothers are often concerned about the toll that single parenting can take.

Faye Hayman, 69, thinks her daughter is entering motherhood with blinders on, and that she doesn't realize everything that's involved in being a single mother. Even though her daughter, Janine Marks, assures her mother she'll be fine, Faye can't stop worrying.

When we met Janine Marks, a 44-year-old divorced public school teacher, she was running late for an appointment, which isn't surprising given her perpetually hectic schedule. As she opens the door to her mother's sprawling suburban ranch, you can hear the laughter of her three gleeful Chinese-born daughters, who rush in to greet their grandmother, Faye. Janine lives a short fifteen-minute drive from her mother. As Janine sends her girls off to watch a video in another room and settles onto her mother's couch, you can see the striking physical resemblance between mother and daughter. Both are petite and have the same dark eyes. While Faye is soft-spoken, serious, and contemplative, Janine is always smiling, even when discussing painful subjects, and her boisterous laugh is often used to diffuse the tension with her mother. During our conversation, Janine's youngest child, Eva, age 2½, pops in intermittently to give her mom hugs and kisses. Faye looks a bit exasperated. She says this child is particularly needy and attached at the hip to Janine, making her job as mother even harder.

When Janine was married, she and her (now ex-) husband tried unsuccessfully to conceive a child, enduring several grueling rounds of fertility treatments. Those attempts failed, so they decided to adopt a daughter from China. The news of the impending Chinese adoption was hard for Faye to digest. "It was a new concept," she said. There weren't that many Asian children with white parents at the time, said Faye, who is white and Jewish. She had "a million questions. 'Why do you want to do this?' . . . She was more fearful than anything," Janine recalled. "I think fearful is a good word," Faye agreed: she feared AIDS and other diseases that she thought the child could have. But ultimately, Janine convinced her it would work out and she came to accept the impending adoption.

Even so, when Faye caught her first glimpse of her new 9-month-old granddaughter, Amy, her worries resurfaced. Amy weighed only twelve pounds and she couldn't hold her head up, sit up, or roll over, even though she was long past the age when those milestones should be met. She needed to be hospitalized for pneumonia during a layover in Los Angeles on the flight home from China. "It was a worrisome time," Faye recalled. The baby had no muscle tone. She "was like Gumby," she was so limp.

Shortly after Amy turned 2 and was thriving physically, Janine and her husband divorced because they disagreed about parenting styles. Janine said he was too indulgent with their daughter and didn't set boundaries. "It was easier to do it without him," Janine concluded.

A few years after she divorced, when Amy was 5½, Janine, then 40, wanted a sister for her child and decided to adopt another Chinese girl. "I thought she was nuts," Faye recalls. Instead of sharing the parenting with a spouse (her husband has joint custody of Amy), Janine would now be taking on all those responsibilities solo and have no time to herself. Faye was concerned that the stress of single parenthood would exacerbate Janine's health problems: she has Crohn's disease, a serious gastrointestinal disorder. Faye didn't hesitate to let her daughter know her concerns.

"I didn't listen to her," said Janine, laughing while she was sitting on the couch next to her mother. For fourteen months, while Janine was going through the adoption proceedings, the topic was off limits for discussion with her mother. "If we didn't mention it [she thought], the child would go away," Janine said. The two agreed to disagree. Janine adopted her second daughter, Lana, when she was 13 months. Fortunately, she turned out to be a healthy child with an easy disposition.

As Faye started warming up to the idea of Janine parenting two girls on her own, Janine decided she wanted a third child. When Amy was 8 and Lana was 3, she took the plunge again. "I had to be insane," Janine admitted. But she said she didn't feel "finished" with her two. Her oldest was with her ex-husband every other weekend, leaving just Lana with her—and she seemed lonely. "I figured, what's one more?" Janine asked.

Faye didn't like her daughter's cavalier attitude, and she felt Janine shouldn't take on such a huge commitment. "I was very upset," she said. The reasons were the same as before: having to shoulder the responsibilities of raising not one, not two, but three children on a single income, and the physical and emotional strain that would bring. Faye was also concerned because Janine would be adopting a 2-year-old and she had heard "horror stories" about a child's ability to bond with an adoptive parent at that age. "Why is she doing this to herself?" she wondered. Faye was also worried that a prospective husband might be scared off by the fact that Janine already had three children of her own. She joked that Janine should "go back to China and find a Chinese man."

As usual, Faye's worries fell on deaf ears. Janine recently adopted her third child, Eva. Fortunately, there have been no problems with the littlest one forming an attachment with Janine, as evidenced by the many kisses and hugs that Eva gives her mother. But Faye remains concerned that Janine's life is too stressful.

Janine insists that she doesn't feel stressed and points out that as a teacher, she has her summers off. "I enjoy being with my kids," she says. She wishes money weren't so tight, and admits she can't afford to send her children to fancy camps, but, she says, "it's worth the struggle." Even when her marriage was rocky, Janine knew she wanted more children. Having them "keeps me young. I enjoy watching them grow up" and seeing their three distinct personalities emerge. Faye adores her granddaughters and has become resigned to Janine's hectic life. Still, she says, "I worry that she's tired all the time," but "I try not to worry about things I have no control over." Janine wishes her mother would stop fretting and just accept her offbeat lifestyle, since her mother's concerns are a constant source of friction between the two.

Janine is one of a rapidly growing number of women who has decided to be a parent on her own. As more women today earn their own money and recognize the difficulty of finding a suitable mate, they're choosing to parent without a partner. The number of Americans choosing international adoptions has skyrocketed in recent years.[3] In 1990, the U.S. State Department granted about 7,500 visas to foreign babies being adopted by American parents. By 2006, the number topped 20,000, with nearly one-third of the visas going to Chinese orphans. China has been a particularly popular source of babies for single women, because China has had a liberal adoption policy and its babies are usually healthy and well-cared for. Although China changed its policy in 2007, barring single women from adopting its babies, women like Janine will still continue to flock to countries like Guatemala or Vietnam to fulfill their dreams of parenthood.

Other single women are turning to domestic adoptions. An estimated one-third of all children in foster care are adopted by single people. And more women are giving birth on their own; one-third of all babies born to American women today are born to single women. Even though Janine—and millions of women like her—doesn't have a husband or a house with a white picket fence, she's not willing to give up her dreams for a large family. Her choices are a source of endless anxiety for her mother. What can mothers and daughters like Faye and Janine do?

ADVICE FOR MOTHERS

Let your daughter live the life that's right for her. Dr. Diane Sanford says her impression is that Janine really enjoys being a mother and she's quite comfortable devoting her life to her children. "This is the whole choice thing. Everybody gets to decide what's most important to them," she says. Faye needs to ask herself: "Are the things that were fulfilling to me necessarily going to fulfill my daughter?" The role of the mother is to listen to how the daughter is experiencing it, not say what she thinks is right for her daughter. What makes Janine happy may be entirely different than what brought pleasure to Faye as a young mother raising her children. Faye needs to realize that her daughter is a different person, with different hopes and dreams. The most important thing she, and mothers in general, can do is to ask how they can best support their daughters and allow them to pursue their own interests and dreams.

ADVICE FOR DAUGHTERS

Realize your mother wants the best for you. Daughters should realize that their mother's advice and interrogations come out of good intentions. "They really want their children to be happy," Dr. Sanford says.

But they often have a tough time recognizing that what worked for them may not work for the daughters.

When an Exciting Career Beckons: Postponing Parenthood

For many women—especially highly educated, career-focused women—the notion of having babies shortly after marrying seems as quaint as a poodle skirt and saddle shoes. Women like Katie Menkin, Terri Romero, and Tessa Hatfield waited until they were in their thirties to have their children. Even though Katie and Tessa married in their twenties, they wanted to hold out until their careers were established and they and their husbands were financially secure before having children. Katie's mother, Peggy O'Hara, says somewhat sarcastically that Katie and her husband, Carl, wouldn't have children until their home was decorated with the "perfect cherrywood furniture."

For women who married young and started their families right away, the idea of delaying childbearing until one is "ready" seems a preposterous notion. Is one ever really ready to have a child? ask women like Peggy O'Hara, now age 69. When she was a young newlywed in the 1960s, having children shortly after marrying and staying home to raise them was the norm. Peggy married in 1960 and a year later, when she was 23, she had her first child, Katie. Her second, Jeff, was born just eleven months after Katie, and two more followed over the next seven years. Peggy, a religious Catholic, didn't use birth control and didn't plan her children. Although her husband was just starting his career and money was often tight, finances were not a major consideration in deciding when to have a child. Peggy taught high school biology before her children were born, but happily gave that up to stay at home, viewing her college degree as "a fallback." Peggy was completely in step with her peers; everywhere she looked around her apartment complex, "there were clones of myself with little children. It was a very warm atmosphere," she remembers.

Her daughter, Katie Menkin, followed a very different path. Though she married at 27, she waited until she was 34 to have a child. "We were trying to wait for the right time," she said. She and her husband wanted to feel settled, with a house and secure jobs, before they tackled parenthood. By the time she had her first child, Max, Katie had worked for ten years in a variety of government jobs. She now works in the budget office of the New York State government. Her job seniority granted her the freedom to take a six-month parental leave from work when her first child was born, without the fear of losing her high-ranking position. Katie's daughter was born two years after her son and she plans to stop there.

Though Katie feels the decision to postpone parenthood was right for her, her mother doesn't agree. Peggy said there was less pressure in her day for families to focus on material goods, like home ownership or furnishings. And young parents seldom considered finances when deciding whether to have a child. Peggy also worries about her daughter's age. Being an older mother isn't necessarily a problem now, she says, but when her grandchildren are teenagers, "Katie will be fifty. I'm happy that at fifty I didn't have teenagers," she said. At that age, a mother may not have the energy to stay up until three in the morning waiting for her daughter to come home from a date. Peggy also worries that she will be so old by that time that she won't be as active a grandparent as she would like to be.

Katie says that she's content with her choice. She also thinks her mother was spared the burden of figuring out how to factor a career into her childbearing plans. That concept is entirely foreign to Peggy. "She always wanted to be a mom, and I had an established career," Katie explained. Katie is pleased that she and her husband don't need to struggle financially while bringing up their children, which she says added a layer of stress to her parents' lives.

Katie's childbearing worked out perfectly according to her plan. But some women who delay childbearing face difficulty conceiving, while others find that they need to scale back their plans for a large family. Terri Romero, 44, found out the hard way that the chances of conceiving decline steadily for women in their late thirties. Terri, a marketing executive in New York, spent her twenties and early thirties traveling throughout the United States as a reporter for United Press International. She loved her work and enjoyed the challenge of chasing exciting news stories. She didn't get married until 35, and had difficulty getting pregnant. After a traumatic late-stage miscarriage, she had fraternal twin daughters through in-vitro fertilization when she was 37 years old.

As difficult as her ordeal was, Terri faced the added pressure of her mother's not-so-secret desire to be a young grandmother. Her mother, Louise Goldfarb, had dropped subtle hints through the years that she wanted grandchildren: "After I told her I was engaged, she bought me a maternity dress."

Louise, like many of her peers, started having her children very young. She moved to New York City from Detroit shortly after she graduated from college. Her dream was to make it as a stage actress. Instead, she recalls, "I met this young comic who promised to show me the bright lights of Broadway. He was a fantastic salesman, charming and funny." She married him in 1955, within a year of meeting him. They had five children over the next twelve years, although they ultimately divorced after nearly thirty years of marriage. Louise reluctantly admits that she placed tremendous pressure on Terri to get married and have children. "I would have loved for her to get married earlier so I could be a younger grandmother. Maybe that's a selfish thing. My mother was only forty-four when her first grandchild was born." Louise, by contrast, was 65 when Terri had her twin daughters.

Like Terri, Tessa Hatfield, age 47, was in her late thirties when she had her first child. Tessa, who works in the defense industry in Washington, D.C., gave birth to her son, Nate, when she was 38. She was twenty-one years older than her own mother was when she had Tessa. "If I had known how much fun motherhood was, I would have started earlier and had a bucket of kids," Tessa said. Three years after giving birth, she knew her biological clock was ticking and she needed to act fast if she wanted a second child. But that meant more time off work and the possible sacrifice of a big promotion. Since she earned more than her husband at the time (they're now divorced), it's a sacrifice she couldn't afford to make, even though it meant no siblings for her son. One child is still better than none, she says. Tessa was one of four, and says she and her siblings were the focal point of her mother's life. Her own mother slightly regrets that Nate won't have a sibling; her children brought so much joy to each other and he's missing out on that.

While Terri's, Katie's, and Tessa's mothers would have liked their daughters to have given birth earlier and more often, we found that childbearing isn't a tremendous source of conflict among mothers and daughters. Once a grandchild is born, the grandmother's dreams of being a young grandmother, or a grandmother to many or a few babies, seem to evaporate. Still, the months and years leading up to the birth of the grandchild can be stressful for both generations of women. How can they manage the strain that comes with the daughter's delayed childbearing?

ADVICE FOR MOTHERS

Voice your concerns. If a mother feels her worries are valid, she could tell her daughter, in a gentle way, to consider the difficulties in getting pregnant as she ages, and that she may have less energy as an older mother.

Accept your daughter's choice. Women like Louise worry about being an older grandmother. Still, if her daughter chooses to be an older mother, Louise needs to be on board—if only for the simple reason that she cannot reverse time. "We need to support and accept" the choices our daughters make "even if they're different than what we would choose," Dr. Sanford says. If a daughter has already delayed her childbearing, no good can come of harping on her decision, since the choice can't be reversed.

Every mother and daughter we spoke with had a unique set of concerns, but our team of therapists has offered up some general words of wisdom to mothers and daughters who don't see eye to eye when it comes to childbearing.

ADVICE FOR MOTHERS

Accept that it's your daughter's personal choice, not a reflection on you. In the end, a daughter's choices reflect her own needs and preferences.

She is not making choices to spite her mother or to malign the choices that her mother has made.

ADVICE FOR DAUGHTERS

Ask yourself: Am I fulfilling my needs or my mother's? Daughters need to ask themselves whether they're living their lives as they truly want to, or whether they are trying to carve out a life different from their mother's. It's hard enough to discover what you need in life without confusing it with the needs of your mother, says Dr. Mayerson. Bearing children is one of those core life events that seem to be expected of women. It's difficult to make a thoughtful choice with so many external pressures. The critical factor here is to clearly define the boundaries between mother and daughters. Having children is a lifelong responsibility and that choice needs to stay squarely in the daughter's corner, says Dr. Mayerson. Though it may be difficult for mothers to accept these decisions, maintaining a loving relationship with their daughters is often what is at stake.

When you're on the fence, talking to Mom is okay. There are times when daughters are ambivalent about having children. This may be a time for open dialogue with their mothers. But, mothers beware, the operative word is "open." Be prepared to support your daughter, even if she ultimately decides not to have children.

CHAPTER 5

The Struggle Over Work: Career Choices, Crises, and Compromises

These early years are so precious and you'll never get them back. Is your career really worth being away from your child all day?

Your father and I didn't pay for tuition at a fancy Ivy League school so you could be a waitress!

You girls can have any job you want today. You should aim higher.

After her first child was born, Tiffany Wagner, 27, suffered from severe postpartum depression. She dreaded the nights spent cradling her colicky baby and stared at the clock on the wall each day, longing for the moment her husband would return home to help. Just weeks after giving birth, Tiffany returned to work as a criminal defense attorney. Tiffany's legal work energizes her and bolsters her self-esteem. She believes that working makes her a happier and more secure parent, but her mother, Lois Linney, 56, disagrees. Lois feared her daughter wasn't physically or emotionally ready to head back to work and encouraged Tiffany to take more time off with the baby. Tiffany says her mom seems oblivious to her professional accomplishments and talks to her only about her role as a new mother. "She never really asks about my cases or my clients."

Monica Chalmers, 26, had the opposite problem. When Monica, now a successful political campaign manager in New York, was working in her first job after graduating college, she was miserable. Monica had landed what she thought was her dream job in public relations for a nonprofit organization in Washington, D.C., but her boss was a nightmare: a moody, sullen man who imposed unreasonable dead-lines. When Monica quit her job abruptly and decided to travel for a few months before lining up another position, her mother, Pamela, told her she had made a huge mistake. Pamela Chalmers, 59, is a consummate professional who has worked in career placement at prestigious banking firms and universities for more than three decades. She was dismayed that her daughter would leave what many would consider a great job. Monica was deeply hurt. "She'd rather see me suicidal in a job I hate than unemployed," she explains. When her mother asked her how she could "walk away from a perfectly good job," Monica was resentful because her mother knew how unhappy she was.

Working women today are trapped in a "damned if you do, damned if you don't" quandary. While the feminist movement of the 1960s and 1970s opened doors to career opportunities that women in past generations could never have imagined, it also fueled the belief that women not only *can* but *should* have thriving careers—while also being devoted parents and spouses. While most women feel the pressure to work, mothers of young children also face the pressure *not* to work too much, or too soon after their children are born. That would send the message that they value their careers more than their children—still a major no-no for women, even in the early twenty-first century. Just as mothers of a generation ago often felt trapped by their lack of career opportunities, young women today feel overwhelmed by their seemingly endless options. In our interviews, it was a rare daughter who felt she was "doing it all" and doing it well. Working mothers fret that they're not spending enough time with their kids. Women who turned their backs on demanding professional careers for more low-key yet personally fulfilling jobs, like freelance writing, feel they haven't accomplished enough. Stay-at-home moms question whether they're sending the right message to their young daughters and wasting their education and the skills they acquired when they worked for pay. Single and childless women worry that they've sacrificed satisfying personal lives for fast-paced professional lives.

The pressures on today's working women come from multiple sources. Magazine articles showcase the "Top 40 under 40," women who manage to cure global epidemics while raising perfect children and maintaining a taut size 4 figure. Popular books and op-ed pages caution that women's work choices have an unavoidable dark side. Sylvia Ann Hewlettt's *Creating a Life* describes the misery of professional women who reluctantly found themselves unmarried and childless after ascending the corporate ladder.[1] In *Home-Alone America*, Mary Eberstadt blames middle-class working mothers for everything from the rise in attention deficit/hyperactivity disorder to children's crazed consumerism and the childhood obesity crisis.[2] And in *Get to Work: A Manifesto for Women of the World*, Linda Hirshman argues that stay-at-home moms are doing a tremendous disservice to women by sacrificing "their education, talents and prospects to their spouses' aspirations and their children's needs."[3] Journalist Leslie Bennetts sounded a similar warning in *The Feminine Mistake*, telling women that it was a "willfully retrograde choice" to leave the workforce and depend on a man for one's economic well-being.[4]

But there's one source of psychological pressure that's more intense than even the most riveting *Newsweek* cover story: our mothers. A mother's off-handed comment or doubting glance can turn even the most poised and accomplished woman into an insecure, argumentative adolescent. In our interviews, we found that mothers often disapproved of their daughters' work choices and made sure to let them know about it. What these mothers had in common was they believed they knew what was best for their daughters and their families—even if their daughters disagreed.

It's not just the case that traditional stay-at-home mothers wanted their career-oriented daughters to stay home with their kids, or, alternatively, that trailblazing career-focused mothers wanted their more laid-back Gen X daughters to be more ambitious and directed. We found tremendous variety in the sources of mother-daughter dissent. Some women who cast aside their own career dreams and felt stifled as stay-at-home moms pushed their daughters to accomplish more than they had. Others who worked reluctantly out of financial need wanted their daughters to devote themselves to prestigious, high-paying careers. Still others who were resentful of having to work wanted their daughters to stay home with the children. Each group of mothers wanted their daughters to have lives that they themselves couldn't have. We found that work-related issues were some of the most painful for mothers and daughters to navigate. To convey why this subject is so emotionally charged, we'll first offer some glimpses into the lives of women from the older generation to reveal the personal challenges they faced on the work front.

Peggy Pennington remembers that when she was 22, in 1955, she applied for a position at a public utility company in Michigan. At the time, her husband had just started law school at the University of Michigan. The utility refused to hire her because she was married. Peggy's experience was common back then. Companies assumed that married women were a poor investment because they would only quit work when they got pregnant. Peggy eventually found a job running lunch programs in the public schools, working until she was six months pregnant with her first child. But she was forced to hide her pregnancy so she wouldn't be fired. "I kept ordering bigger uniforms so they wouldn't know I was pregnant. It was a whole different world." Peggy quit working when she had children and happily took on the role of wife and mother.

Doreen Madison, now 74, was raised by a single mother after her father was killed in a plane crash in the Air Force when she was only 6 months old. Doreen's mother encouraged her from a young age to be independent and self-sufficient. Doreen received her bachelor's degree from Vassar in 1956 and wanted to pursue graduate school. But the college dean discouraged her. He told her "they didn't like to waste [an education] on women who were going to get married and have children," she recalled. Doreen married and had children. She returned to school for an advanced degree and started her career only after they were grown.

Betty Mahoney, now 79, was a young woman with big dreams. She was in college and aspired to be a doctor when she met her future husband. But she dropped out before graduation because her fiancé didn't have a high school degree "and I didn't want to put a rift between us by being better educated than he was," she remembered. Instead, she married him and had seven children. They recently celebrated their sixtieth wedding anniversary.

Those who did work when their children were young often were scorned by their peers. Shirley Stein, now 67, resumed teaching when her children were infants because her husband's business was struggling. Although Shirley loved her work, her enthusiasm was dampened when her mother-in-law and friends would say to her, "I could never leave *my* child." They rarely pitched in if the sitter didn't show. "They would say, 'You want to work—it's your responsibility,'" Shirley recounts.

Women just a decade younger than Shirley found that the world was beginning to change. Even though it wasn't easy juggling professional and family responsibilities, women at the forefront of the baby boom generation weren't met with the same kind of overt hostility that Shirley experienced. Pamela Chalmers, 59, had already earned a master's degree and had worked in career placement for several years before she gave birth to her daughter, Monica. Pamela had her daughter when she was 30 and couldn't wait to return to work. She resumed full-time work and a busy travel schedule when Monica was just 3 months old, leaving all child-rearing duties to her schoolteacher husband, Charles. Pamela associated staying at home with "isolation and misery." Her own stay-at-home mother felt trapped in that role, struggling with depression all her life.

Women like Pamela and Peggy can't help but reflect on their own choices when they look at their daughters' lives. They worry that their daughters' careers are hurting their family lives. Or they're worried that they're not working up to their potential, throwing away opportunities their mothers desperately craved just a few decades earlier.

"How Can You Leave Your Children All Day?" The Struggles in Balancing Work and Family

Daughters who work full-time often get the message from their mothers that they're falling short as parents. It doesn't matter whether their mothers were stay-at-home moms, career-focused moms, or something in between. We found that mothers often convey to their daughters the mantra that family should come first. Some daughters stand firmly by their choice to work full-time, as we'll see with Lynn Arnold. But, for daughters like Karen Levi and Terri Romero, who already had lurking doubts about their ability to do it all, a mother's criticism has undermined their resolve and heightened their guilt.

Lynn Arnold, 45, is a genetic counselor whose job involves helping those predisposed to genetic conditions, like Huntington's disease, to manage the medical and psychological consequences of their condition. She provides advice on whether to be tested for a particular disease and how to cope if test results come back positive. She often travels to professional board meetings and makes presentations at medical conferences throughout the United States. Lynn feels energized by intellectual discussions with her colleagues. Taking a break from work to stay home when she had her children didn't appeal to her, since it would have prevented her from keeping up with the rapidly evolving scientific developments in her field. Lynn couldn't imagine staying home with her children like her mother did. Lynn put her oldest daughter in child care at 6 weeks of age and has never stopped working. As a result of her busy schedule, she has little time with her husband, Robert, and her children, Rebecca, now 15, and Joshua, age 12.

Lynn's mother, Beverly, now 71, can't understand why her daughter has chosen such a hectic lifestyle. The gloves come out the moment Beverly leaves her Washington, D.C., home and travels to her daughter's house in Michigan. As she pulls into the driveway of her daughter's stately white colonial, she takes a deep breath before walking in the door to brace herself for the chaos she's about to witness.

The morning after Beverly arrived on a recent visit, her daughter was already headed to work by 6:45 A.M. "I was hoping to have a cup of coffee with her," Beverly says with a hint of sarcasm. Beverly didn't expect her daughter to make time for her on this visit, since Lynn is always on the go. With her crazy schedule, Lynn also has little time to focus on her appearance. She is slender, with short, fine hair. She dresses casually and never wears makeup. Lynn strongly resembles her mother, with the same small, dark eyes and bright smile.

Beverly admits she "comes home exhausted from these visits" with her daughter's family. She thinks the whole family suffers because Lynn is not home enough. Though Beverly now works as a consultant for the federal government on early childhood education projects, she never considered working when her children were young. She felt her place was at the helm of the household, raising her children and taking on the domestic responsibilities. She believes Lynn's career places too big a burden on her husband, an oncologist with a forty-five-minute commute to work, who takes on most of the domestic chores. Beverly says her daughter's work schedule forces the family to lead a life of utter chaos, with late, hastily assembled dinners and a messy house. Lynn and Robert are away from their children all day, so they allow them to stay up late. Yet the kids rise early for school during the school year, or when they go to camp and child care during the summer months. As a result, they're often cranky from lack of sleep, says Beverly. She thinks children grow up with more confidence if their mother is a regular presence in their lives, and she wants that for her grandchildren. She doesn't hesitate to express her concerns to Lynn, urging her to slow down.

She also worries about her daughter and son-in-law's peace of mind. Beverly says they have no time to themselves to unwind from their busy day. "It's hard to watch Lynn go through all this. It breaks my heart to see her racing around," Beverly explains. She fears that her daughter pushes herself too much to be a supermom, baking brownies and volunteering in the classroom during those precious moments when she's not working.

Beverly's life as a young mother, by contrast, was "less frenetic." She worked part-time as a teacher, but only when her children were in school. She had dinner on the table by 6:00 P.M. and her children played outdoors with neighborhood kids while she took care of the cooking and cleaning. She felt her household was far more organized and orderly than the environment in which her daughter is raising Beverly's grandchildren.

Lynn agrees with that assessment, and she knows her mother blames her extensive work hours for the disorganization. Lynn admits that juggling a career in science with parenting is a big challenge. She gets so absorbed in her work that she often doesn't get home each night until after 7:00 P.M., leaving the dinner responsibilities to her husband, who she says is perfectly capable of cooking. But as much as she's devoted to her work, she says, once she walks in the door, she's entirely focused on her family. She feels her contentment with her job makes her a happier, more self-confident person and a better mother. The domestic chaos is a small, insignificant price to pay: "I feel perpetually behind but professionally fulfilled," she says.

Lynn is often overcome by anxiety when her mother visits, anticipating the criticism that's coming. She believes her mother focuses on superficial issues like cleaning and less on meaningful matters like raising content, well-rounded children. During one visit, her mother insisted on immediately organizing Lynn's daughter's closet, rather than spending time going to the neighborhood park with Lynn and the kids. Lynn's days are so tightly scheduled she needs to make choices about the best way to spend her limited time with her children—and she often chooses to take them on bike rides rather than clean her house. Lynn knows her mother judges her choices harshly and wishes she could understand how much gratification her career brings.

Despite the challenges Lynn faces in balancing work and home life, she doesn't feel even a tinge of guilt over her choice to work full-time, and her mother's disapproval doesn't shake her resolve to do what's right for her. But when a daughter is already insecure about her choice to work, a mother's disapproval is like salt on an open wound. That's the case with Brenda Sherman and her daughter, Karen Levi, and Louise Goldfarb and her daughter, Terri Romero.

When we meet Brenda Sherman, an active 73-year-old, she is dressed casually in pants and a sweater. Her daughter, Karen Levi, age 39, is in comfortable sweatpants and has a rosy complexion, dark eyes, and raven-colored hair. She greets us in her home in an affluent Midwest suburb as her husband finishes putting the dinner dishes into the dishwasher. It's 8:00 P.M., and she's just tucked her two children, Eytan, age 2½, and Elise, age 4½, into bed after a long, exhausting day. It's one of the rare times she has for reflection, and she settles into an overstuffed chair to chat. At one point during our talk, her pint-sized son with chocolate brown eyes bounds down the stairs in his footed pajamas, seeking a nighttime cuddle from his mother.

Karen's mother, Brenda, starts the conversation, recalling her years raising her four children. She says being at home with them was the happiest time of her life. Though she resumed teaching when she divorced her husband, she has no regrets about postponing her career. And she made it clear to her daughters that her way of doing things was best.

For Brenda's three daughters, a college education was a given. "I wanted my kids to get the best degrees, but I wanted them home with their kids," she says. "Parents should be home with their babies." Her oldest two daughters followed their mother's advice. Eileen, now 47 and living in Indiana, and Diane, now 43 and living in Illinois, both received degrees from top-notch universities. Diane earned her law degree and said her mother thought it was great that women of her daughters' generation could become lawyers. Speaking by telephone, she said, "The problem is, when we had kids, she said, 'Oh, you'll quit your job now.' She was absolutely rabid." Brenda is adamant that good mothers should be home with their children. "What was law school for? I should have just played tennis," Diane joked. Even so, Diane felt she was "a much better mother than a lawyer," so she quit working after her first son, Jonathan, was born. Both she and her older sister, Eileen, married men with substantial incomes, so they could afford to stay home.

But Karen, the only one of the daughters who lives in the same town as her mother, didn't have that luxury. She needs to supplement the income of her husband, a purchasing manager. After working in marketing for several years, Karen wanted a new challenge. A year ago, she started her own business. She's now an importer and wholesale distributor of fashion jewelry. The business took off beyond her wildest expectations, requiring Karen to work 9:00 A.M. to 5:30 P.M. on weekdays and five hours on the weekend. She also travels five days a month to jewelry shows. Karen works from home but has a full-time nanny who handles everything from child care to running errands and buying the kids' clothes. She admits her days are hectic and regrets that she only has a couple of hours in the evening with her children.

Karen is so preoccupied with running her business she often forgets details of her children's lives. After returning from a recent business trip, she arrived at her daughter's dance class only to realize her daughter didn't have dance shoes: Karen had misplaced the paperwork on the shoe requirement. In Karen's mind, though, this type of misstep is a small price to pay for the prospect of developing her successful business: "It would drive me crazy being home full-time. I don't know how other mothers do it."

Even so, she feels guilty for the time spent away from her children. Compounding the problem is the fact that her mother doesn't support her choices. "She's critical of my not being a full-time parent," Karen says. Even though Brenda says Karen is a great mother, Karen feels her mother's frequent questions and uninvited comments imply she's not with her children enough. Business trips are viewed by her mother as a "grave parenting mistake. There is no understanding or sympathy for the fact that I have other responsibilities that are important to me," Karen says.

Because Karen runs her own business and works out of her home, her mother doesn't recognize that Karen has to protect her time and boundaries. Just because Karen is physically at home doesn't mean that she's on call for her children. Brenda stops by her daughter's house unannounced on a regular basis, often when Karen's working and the nanny is there. When the children need something, like a diaper change, Brenda will suggest to Karen that they need their mommy to do it instead of the nanny. "I'd love to, but I don't have the luxury to tie every shoe, wipe every nose, comfort every cry," Karen responds. Nonetheless, Karen often complies because her mother makes her feel like an "evil mommy" if she doesn't.

Karen is also annoyed that her mother repeatedly calls her to have lunch on a weekday even though she always turns down the invitations. Since Karen has her own company, her mother thinks she has the freedom to ditch work and take a leisurely lunch break. "It's about not being in touch with how busy I am," Karen gripes. Her mother doesn't understand that "if I don't do it, it doesn't get done. She has little respect for the commitment I have to my business." Karen says she can't afford to waste her working hours on lunch with her mom and likes to save those precious hours when she's not working for her children.

"She never goes to lunch with me. I would like her to," Brenda tells us. She also questions why Karen can't pick up her kids at school instead of having the nanny do it. School pickup times were an opportunity for Brenda to meet other moms. Brenda thinks her daughter doesn't have enough adult interaction. Karen says socializing isn't a priority right now, and she turns down almost every invitation to social events. "I'm just too busy—I've got this deadline and that deadline," she says, adding, "I don't meet other moms for playdates or go to lectures with other moms. I am a working mom."

Brenda defends her actions. She thinks Karen's life is unnecessarily difficult, and that she's just looking out for her daughter's own good. "I think women now have a much harder time than we did when we were just focused on the home." The women's movement and the idea that girls can do anything was a breakthrough, "but it made life harder for women. It was easier when we all stayed home. No one expected us to make a living," she says. She found so much joy in raising her children and she doesn't want Karen to miss out on that experience. "I think she's giving up a lot," Brenda worries.

Ironically, Brenda's concern for her daughter's well-being has only served to heighten Karen's feelings of self-doubt. "The whole thing has been one big bag of guilt. Every time I work, I feel guilty. Every time I do something for myself, I feel guilty. It's like I'm doing something wrong," she said. "Every time I try not to feel guilty, my mom will say something that makes me feel guilty again."

Karen is not alone. Terri Romero, 44, also feels conflicted and guilty about her time-consuming work demands, and her insecurities aren't helped by her mother, who regularly tells Terri that she needs to be home more with her twin 7-year-old daughters. Ironically, though, Terri's mother, Louise Goldfarb, 72, worked full-time as a schoolteacher when Terri was young, and Louise tells us that she felt guilty about being one of the few women in her neighborhood who relied on a babysitter to watch her children. Still, she thinks Terri's job as a marketing executive in Manhattan takes her away from her children too often, and she regularly tells Terri that she should be a schoolteacher so she'll "have afternoons and summers off." Louise's advice is particularly painful because Terri already is wrestling with conflicting feelings. She staunchly believes that women should pursue their career dreams and be strong role models for their daughters, yet at the same time feels "that tug of wanting to spend more time with my girls."

Louise married in her early twenties and had five children. She returned to school for her master's degree in teaching after her second child was born and taught high school theater classes at an inner-city school for three decades. She loved her work and Terri praises her mother for sparking her passion for theater and literature. Louise explains how she got into teaching: "I'm a very active person. I was going kind of crazy at home with the babies; they were not very good conversationalists." One day, a friend visited and told her about a program to get a master's degree in teaching at a local university; Louise signed up right away.

Louise knows she was out of step with her peers and says she was the only one in the neighborhood who worked full-time. "There were times when I was really torn," she says. She would take her two youngest children to a sitter's house before school. "Leaving them there with someone who was almost a stranger, and picking them up after school—that ripped me apart." She got out of school about 2:30 P.M. and "raced to pick them up." Terri remembers that she was one of very few children with mothers who worked full-time.

Terri says her mother inspired her to believe that she could do anything she wanted and that's one reason why she finds it so hurtful when her mother tells her to cut back on her work. "My mother worked, so I assumed it was normal. I just grew up thinking that women worked and that was totally natural," she says. Terri never thought she was just going to get married and stay home with the kids.

Like many of the daughters we interviewed, Terri experienced two equally strong feelings. On the one hand, she enjoyed her work and was very committed to seizing all the opportunities afforded to women today. "I work because I love what I do, and I think it makes me a better parent," Terri says. On the other hand, she wants to be there for her girls "and I know it will just get harder as they get older," she says. She may make some career concessions because of that, "but I won't give up my own dreams, either."

Terri says she has considered taking her mother's advice to become a schoolteacher, but decided she wanted to tackle a more powerful, traditionally male-dominated job. "I need to make it in a man's world." But that means working whatever hours are necessary and traveling wherever and whenever duty calls. Terri recalls with some regret the time a business trip was scheduled on her twin daughters' first birthday. "The first few times I went away after the girls were born, I felt horribly guilty." She planned their first birthday party for the weekend, but she didn't realize she'd be in another city on their actual birthday, which fell midweek. Even though her girls, then a year old, were too young to know she missed their birthday, Terri still felt awful.

Although Louise regularly tells Terri that her job takes her away from her girls, she says she's her daughter's biggest supporter. "I'm very proud of Terri," Louise says. Though they don't always see always eye to eye, she applauds what Terri has accomplished and the way she lives her life. "I believed in women's liberation for a long time, and she's a prime example of it."

Mothers like Louise, Brenda, and Beverly are proud of their daughters' successes, but their notions about the ways mothers "should be" often lead them to condemn rather than praise. Their daughters admit that they can be curt and impatient with their well-intended mothers. Our team of therapists offers constructive advice for how the two generations can heal their differences when the mothers feel their daughters' career choices are hurting their family lives.

ADVICE FOR MOTHERS

Recognize that times have changed. Women's opportunities have changed drastically in the past five decades. A daughter's choice may be right for her, even if it wouldn't have been right for her mother thirty years ago. For example, Karen doesn't have the luxury of staying home like her mother did and is building her own business, partly out of necessity and partly out of personal desire. Each should respect the choices that the other has made.

Treat your daughter like a grown-up. Trying to tell a daughter what to do or how to do it will only backfire, says Dr. Mayerson. It's often difficult for mothers to hold back, since their instinct is to parent and tell their daughter what they believe is right. In earlier eras, daughters who married young and made marriage and parenthood their career often turned to their own mothers for advice, hoping to follow their parenting model. By asking their mothers for all of the answers, daughters essentially continued their childhood role of being the dependent and deferential child. But things are different today. Daughters often postpone parenting to establish their careers and seek to parent in an entirely different way, without soliciting their mothers' input. If mothers like Beverly push their own agendas rather than trying to understand the issues their daughters are facing, that may interfere with their ability to support their daughters.

Understand that unsolicited advice can appear judgmental. Advice-giving mothers are trying to be helpful, but they're inadvertently creating feelings of inadequacy in their daughters, suggests Dr. Sanford. "A lot of mothers don't know how to relax. They're very goal-directed." By offering advice or doing things for the daughter, mothers may subtly transmit the message, "You're not good enough. You're falling short." Dr. Sanford suggests that rather than giving advice, mothers could say, "Honey, I'm really worried about you. What would you like me to do to show my love and support?" That type of message isn't threatening and asks for a daughter's suggestions instead of telling her what needs to be done.

ADVICE FOR DAUGHTERS

Talk it out. Experts agree that the key to a harmonious relationship with your mother—and getting her to accept your choices—is open communication. But confrontation is often difficult for both generations of women because the issues at stake are so important, explains Dr. Mayerson. Working women today say their mothers don't understand their passion for their careers. That's quite different from disagreements between earlier generations of women. A mother may have faulted her daughter for not keeping the house immaculate or not paying enough attention to her husband. Today, the disagreements are far more complex. Dr. Mayerson says young women today are often wary of sharing their struggles with the very person who can help them most and instead seem to convince themselves, "They won't understand my way of doing it, so I need to figure it out myself." Mayerson says that's going about it the wrong way.

Make your mother aware of the impact of her words. Mothers like Beverly and Brenda may be disappointed because their daughters are implicitly rejecting the way they were raised. At the same time, their daughters feel hurt because they think their mothers are criticizing and judging them. Daughters should convey their hurt feelings to their mothers, says Dr. Julia Davies, a psychologist and certified psychoanalyst based in Ann Arbor, Michigan. She suggests daughters use words like, "I know you don't intend this, but when you say things about my parenting, I often feel criticized." If a mother feels she's being helpful and is unaware that her messages come across as critical, a daughter's gently worded request might open the door to a constructive conversation.

Set aside quality time with Mom. When a daughter is overwhelmed with work and family responsibilities, quality time with her mother often gets thrown out the window. For example, Brenda is craving time and attention from her daughter and feels neglected. Daughters should try to schedule time for some regular visits or phone calls with their mothers at a mutually convenient time, says Dr. Davies.

Brenda should stop asking her daughter to lunch, to avoid reliving the same battles. Dr. Davies suggests that Karen might acknowledge her mother's hurt feelings and say, "You know, Mom, I would love to have a meal with you, but lunch is not possible. How about dinner?" An evening appointment, after Karen's kids are tucked in bed, might make more sense for her.

Admit that Mom can be right. Daughters should try to keep an open mind and not be judgmental when their mother gives advice, suggests Dr. Diane Sanford. Mothers often give advice out of concern and do not intend their words to be a criticism of their daughters' life management skills. Plus, the older generation has more experience than their daughters. Dr. Sanford says that the younger generation shouldn't presume that since their mothers led a different life, they are incapable of helping them cope with the pressures of work, an ill-behaved child, or feelings of inadequacy as a mother. The older generation can provide empathy and assistance if their daughters give them the chance.

A Mother's Unfulfilled Promise? Daughters Who Fall Short of Their Mothers' High Hopes

One of the most surprising things we discovered was that many mothers felt their daughters weren't fulfilling their potential when it came to work. Mothers from all backgrounds—reluctant stay-at-home moms, trailblazing career women, women who were happy to be homemakers despite their Seven Sisters bachelor's degrees, and women who reluctantly worked when their husbands couldn't support them—often said their daughters take their work lives too lightly. Either they didn't put their hard-earned college degrees to work or they took their careers for granted and failed to recognize that their mothers had to fight to get a foot in the door at many workplaces

From Wharton to Waitressing: When Working Daughters Defy Stay-at-Home Mothers' Dreams

If the women's movement promised choice for a generation of young women, that choice could include leaving the fast-paced rat race for a low-key and personally rewarding career. That's what Stacy Fines, 44, tried to do, but it caused an almost irreparable rift between her and her mother, Jean Kaplan, 68. Jean and her husband were ecstatic when Stacy decided to attend the Wharton Business School at the University of Pennsylvania. For Jean, this was a proud moment. She had spent her twenties and thirties as a homemaker, and was delighted to see that Stacy was going to do bigger and better things. When Stacy later dropped out of the business world and became a waitress, it was a horrible blow to Jean, who viewed her years spent raising a smart, self-assured, intelligent daughter as wasted.

Stacy, now living in the Midwest, was raised in New Jersey, where her mother still resides. Her mother, Jean, met her husband at age 16, married at 20, and willingly gave up her teaching job when she had her first and only child at 24. "Almost everybody was a stay-at-home mom," she recalls. "There was always something to do . . . some class, some book, cleaning. I was never bored." Jean actively discouraged Stacy from becoming a nurse or a teacher, the only choices available to her when she herself was a young woman. "I lived in a very narrow world," she says. She saw the education profession as "limiting" and pushed Stacy to take advantage of new opportunities for women in the business world—the choice she would have made for herself. Jean has worked for several large companies in recent years and believes it's given her the opportunity to meet "many different people and expand my horizons." She designed an entire maternity wardrobe for herself when she was pregnant and would have enjoyed launching her own clothing business, but few women were entrepreneurs at that time. Since Jean received no career guidance from her own mother, she decided it was her job to guide and encourage Stacy's professional aspirations.

At first, Stacy lived up to the goals her mother set for her. Initially, she got good grades at Wharton, but by her senior year she had plummeted to a 2.2 grade point average. "I wasn't self-aware enough to know it was because I wasn't interested in my courses, and that I should not have been in business school," she says. Even so, after graduating, she accepted an offer to work for a major accounting firm. She lasted nearly a year there and quit because she was so miserable. As she ruminated about her decision, Stacy realized, that she "really needed to find something that made me happy. That's the one thing I never heard out of my mother's mouth—'Do what makes you happy.'"

Stacy, then 23, took a job waitressing while she figured out what career was right for her. "You would have thought I had committed a triple murder," Stacy complains, describing her mother's reaction to the news. Jean told Stacy that since she and her husband spent so much money on Stacy's education, she should be working in a more challenging job. When Stacy visited her mother, Jean cried about Stacy's decision. The two barely spoke for two years, until Stacy got a "real job" working for a graphic design firm. "It was not what you'd expect from a parent," Stacy laments.

Jean told us she didn't want her daughter's high-quality education to go to waste and if she wasn't going to pursue a serious career, she could have attended a less expensive state school. "I was disappointed in her because she is brilliant. . . . They say a mind is a terrible thing to waste and she was wasting her mind." Jean says she suspected the choice to waitress was something Stacy was doing to get back at her. "I was very, very upset. I just cried. I couldn't believe she could do this." She reasons that Stacy could have opted for a more middle-ground alternative, working in a different field, instead of lowering her standards and becoming a waitress. Jean says the dispute created a rift between them that still exists today. A few years ago, when Stacy was visiting, Jean asked Stacy if they could be friends. According to Jean, Stacy told her that she hated her because of her lack of support during that time. Jean says, sarcastically, that Stacy wanted her to say, "You be the best little waitress that you ever can be, honey." But Jean never felt comfortable doing that.

After her stint with the graphic design firm, Stacy married and took time off to raise her four children. Then, in 1999, when her youngest was nearly 2, she returned to school to get her teaching degree and for the past four years she has been a math teacher. After all her years of soul-searching, Stacy feels she's found her passion in teaching—the same job her mother had, and a career option her mom discouraged her from pursuing. Jean now believes it's a good choice for Stacy, since it offers a great pension that Stacy, a divorcée, will need if she doesn't remarry. The pension wasn't the main motivator for Stacy, however, who says she loves teaching "because I feel I am making a difference in kids' lives."

The dispute over Stacy's choice to be a waitress was the beginning of a downward spiral that caused an icy relationship between mother and daughter. Stacy says her mother maintains she did nothing wrong. Jean retorts that Stacy rejects her advice at every turn. "Stacy doesn't need a mother. She doesn't need anybody, including me," she said. Stacy says their relationship is cordial but strained, and that she could never imagine confiding in her mother, despite her overtures toward friendship.

Like Jean, Helen Ingersoll, now 69 and living in a suburb of Washington, D.C., wanted her daughter Janet, 42, to take advantage of the career opportunities she had been denied. Helen felt stifled as a homemaker and stay-at-home mother. She lived a life typical of many women of her generation: raising her three children while her husband worked as a doctor. Her parents were both immigrants who did not attend college. Her father told her that women couldn't go to college, but Helen was determined and attended Vassar, majoring in psychology.

College courses sparked Helen's intellectual curiosity. Even so, Helen says her mother's plan for her was to get married and have someone "take care of her." Helen ultimately fulfilled her mother's goal. She met her husband when she was a freshman in college and he was in his first year of medical school. She married at 22, had three children over the next seven years, and stayed home to raise them. They moved around often because of her husband's schooling and career as a surgeon. In each new town, Helen was lonely, since her husband worked long hours. "It was terrible. It was very isolating," she says. She had no friends or family nearby. She jokes that she never said no until she was 40. "It was an expectation that the husband made the decisions and the wife followed along and made it work," she says.

Even when she was home all day with her children and supporting her husband's medical career, Helen says she was always "trying to find a life in addition to being a mother." As her children grew older, she found her niche, volunteering at an art museum, then as a production assistant at a television station. Her quest for personal fulfillment didn't come easily, however. "It was very hard. On my hand I had a nice diamond ring. They knew I was married to a doctor. They'd ask why I needed the work." Ultimately, she went back to school for two master's degrees, including an advanced degree in social work. Now, still married to her husband, she is a social worker specializing in couples and individual therapy. "I feel a sense of self about it, using resources I didn't know I had," she told us. But, she adds, she didn't have the chance to find herself until she was 45. "There was always a piece of me looking for roots, peace, and belonging," she said.

Helen wanted to make sure her daughter didn't suffer the same inner turmoil she did, the restlessness and the search for an identity outside the home. Helen urged her daughter not to marry until she was 30 and to "get to know who she was." She says her daughter is extremely bright and a very pretty woman with "a lot of gifts" and she encouraged her to be independent and find a job worthy of her talents. Helen pushed her daughter to take the Law School Admission Test. Helen boasts that Janet scored "phenomenally well," but decided she didn't want to become a lawyer. Helen was shocked, as she wanted her daughter to have a respected, lucrative profession, one that wasn't available to her years earlier. Helen says if she had scored as high as her daughter on the LSATs, she would have "had the applications in the mail."

Janet, now 42 and living in a small Massachusetts town with her husband and 7-year-old son, decided to become a writer instead of a lawyer. Her initial stint as a freelance writer troubled her mother. "It was a risky life. You get all those rejections," Helen says. She was happier when Janet went to work for a company as an editor and received a steady paycheck.

Janet tells us her mother "was determined to see me play out her ambitions." She adds ruefully, "I think she is still disappointed I haven't achieved more." Janet says her mother continues to tell her daughter she would have made a wonderful judge, but Janet relishes her work as both a writer and an editor, even though it doesn't pay as well as a career in the legal profession. Since her husband is also a writer, they both need to work to make ends meet, but Janet is content with the sacrifice. She loves her work, but she would prefer to cut back on her hours so she could volunteer in her son's classroom and spend more time with him during the day. The irony of the situation is not lost on Janet: "I feel like my mother had time with her kids and didn't enjoy it, and I wish I had it and I think I'd really enjoy it."

Janet also feels her mother is trying to live out her ambitions through her daughter. It's a tough burden to carry, Janet says. She doesn't like it when her mother nags her about achieving more professionally and she feels like she has to constantly justify her career choice, which is a huge source of stress in her already busy life.

Helen and Janet's situation isn't uncommon. Many women who raised their children a generation ago were restless; they wanted more challenging opportunities than doing laundry or organizing a school bake sale. For women like Helen, who attended college, the emotional toll of staying home and raising kids was particularly high. It's not just Helen who felt this way. A study by Deborah Carr, one of the authors of this book, verifies that many women were feeling this way.[5] She focused on more than five thousand women who graduated from high school in 1957 and followed their work and family experiences over a span of fifty years. Those women who failed to live up to the career goals they had in high school were more depressed and had a lower sense of purpose than women who had met their goals.

This regret and sadness affects the ways mothers interact with their daughters. Their daughters have access to opportunities their mothers lacked, and when they throw those opportunities away, it's a bitter pill for their mothers to swallow. Our therapists give advice on how to repair a relationship that's been damaged by a daughter turning her back on an opportunity her mother would have cherished.

ADVICE FOR MOTHERS

Don't be afraid to open old wounds. Women like Helen often look back at their lives with some regrets about the opportunities that passed them by. Dr. Renée A. Cohen, a clinical psychologist specializing in families and relationships, based in Los Angeles and Torrance, California, suggests that women acknowledge their disappointments, even if just to themselves. Some women may need to go through a mourning period for the losses they suffered years ago, "whatever the situation may have been that cost her her dream," Dr. Cohen says. She could write it down, using phrases like, "I feel this way because I . . ." or "In choosing to be a homemaker, I lost out on . . ." By acknowledging her past hurts, she will be better able to understand the motivation for her treatment of her daughter. Even better, if the mother chooses to discuss her regrets with her daughter, it could be an opportunity for an extremely beneficial "sharing moment," says Dr. Cohen. The mother should make it clear that "I understand this is my fear, this is my need. I'm just sharing it with you so that there are options out there for you that I didn't have." This type of language indicates why this issue is so important to the mother. At the same time, after hearing this, the daughter may say, "And now you're asking me to give up my dream?" The result could be a mutually beneficial, empathetic exchange.

Don't live vicariously through your daughter. Mothers need to recognize that they and their daughters are autonomous individuals. Some mothers may see their daughters as an extension of themselves, and this makes it very difficult when the daughter tries to carve out her own life. Noncompliance can be viewed as betrayal. If the end goal of parenting is for children to lead happy and productive lives, then mothers need to let go if their daughters take a different path. It's not a sign of rejection, says Dr. Cohen, but rather a reminder that the mother has raised an independent and thoughtful daughter who knows what's best for her.

Don't curtail your daughter's freedom to choose. Women today have many more choices than they did five decades ago. Yet, ironically, when a mother demands that her daughter opt for a particular career, she is replicating the circumstances that she faced as a young woman, when she didn't have choices and someone told her what she needed to do. "While she was told she needed to be a homemaker, she is now telling her daughter what she should do, rather than seeing that there are multiple options that her daughter can take," Dr. Cohen says.

ADVICE FOR DAUGHTERS

Limit the time and place of the discussion. Like many of the other disputes we've discussed, in the case of work conflicts, daughters should set limits to prevent mothers from repeatedly bringing up the same topic of conflict, suggests Dr. Cohen. Daughters should set a specific time frame for having such discussions, perhaps a one-hour slot. They also may want to limit the physical space where these discussions happen and select a neutral spot, like a restaurant.

Understand your mother's true feelings and where she's coming from. Mothers of a generation ago typically fall into two camps. On one side are reluctant stay-at-home mothers who feel like they didn't have a chance to develop themselves and want their daughters to take full advantage of opportunities available today. On the other side are stay-at-home mothers who are validated when their daughter also stays at home with her children. Jean and Helen are in the former category. Daughters can ask their mothers to talk about their own career goals and recount what happened as their mothers tried to pursue these goals. Mothers may feel a sense of relief in sharing stories about their pasts and daughters will come away with a greater understanding of the sacrifices women were forced to make in earlier generations.

ADVICE FOR MOTHERS AND DAUGHTERS

Use "I" messages. Conversations focusing on sensitive issues will work best if the mother "opens it up to discussion rather than being authoritarian or judgmental," says Dr. Cohen. Mothers and daughters are encouraged to use "I" messages, such as, "I feel this would be the best for you," versus a "you" message, like "You should really do this because it's in your best interest." A message like "I realize these are my thoughts and not your thoughts" is better than "You're not thinking clearly." Delivering the message in an empathetic way will lend itself to listening instead of shutting down as soon as they hear an accusatory "you."

Ultimately, try to forgive and forget. Forgiveness starts with understanding and trying to feel empathy for the other person. Communicating openly about what happened may be the stimulus for healing to occur. Again, it will be important to listen and understand each other's point of view. Listening without interruption or judgment is crucial. If it's not possible to forgive or forget, then it may be useful to turn to a third party or a therapist to help foster effective communication.

Squashing the "Starving Artist" Dream: When Mothers Fear for Their Daughters' Financial Security

Helen and Jean desperately wanted their daughters to have the professional and personal fulfillment they craved when they were young women. For Eleanor Kowalski, 56, "the very notion of fulfill-ment" is a luxury. Her goal for her daughter, Megan Harper, 29, is fi-nancial security. Eleanor, whom we first met in Chapter 3, is a Polish immigrant who experienced serious economic hardship when she single-handedly raised her children after walking out on her abusive alcoholic husband. She didn't want Megan to face similar struggles and constantly pushed her to find a stable, if not necessarily glam-orous or fulfilling, job. Although Megan understands why her mother feels that way, that still doesn't make it easy for Megan to accept the fact that her mother "squashed" her dream of becoming an artist.

Eleanor wants her daughter to be financially self-sufficient and not dependent on a man, like Eleanor's abusive ex-husband. She wor-ries that Megan has made a series of impractical financial choices, from her choice of a spouse to her interest in a low-paying career.

Megan counters that her mother has always been very controlling, although she understands her mother's motivation. "She did it out of love, I guess." She says her mother emphasized the importance of ex-celling in school, getting good grades, and obtaining a fine education. "I did all that," Megan said. Art was her favorite subject in school and she took advanced studio classes. Her dream was to go to New York, attend Parsons School of Design, and become an artist, "which didn't sit well with my mother," she says. Megan recalls that when she was 17, her mother told her she wouldn't visit her if Megan went to New York to study art.

"Everybody has some dream. Sometimes, it's not a realistic dream," says Eleanor, in a matter-of-fact tone that bears traces of a Polish ac-cent. She told Megan that she should pursue a more practical career than studio art so that she could be independent and support herself. "I wanted her to go into a higher-paying job," she says. Megan's best friend at the time was attending Pratt Institute in Brooklyn, New York, and ultimately became a studio artist. But Megan listened to her mother and didn't attend art school. "I felt like I had to do what she told me," she says. "She listened to me and I don't think she regretted it," Eleanor responds.

Instead of heading to the Big Apple, Megan attended a small college in West Virginia on an art and academic scholarship. As a freshman, she was still intent on pursuing her artistic dreams. Megan said her mother continued to discourage her from majoring in art by telling her that regardless of her talent, she wasn't going to make any money or be successful in that field. Megan later transferred to a larger school in Baltimore and stopped studying art. "It pretty much went by the wayside after my sophomore year of college," she says. Her mother pushed her to go to medical school, but she refused, since she "couldn't stand" the pre-med curriculum. Instead, she became a social worker, a career her mother endorsed. "I was very happy because I knew she's going to have a secure life," Eleanor says. But Megan maintains her mother deterred her from following her passion. "I can't tell you what would have happened if I had gone to New York," she says, her voice trailing off.

When mothers steer their daughters away from a risky career path toward a more "stable" profession not favored by their daughters, how can the two overcome this difference of opinion? Dr. Cohen provides some direction.

ADVICE FOR MOTHERS AND DAUGHTERS

Make a list of job options. When a mother is worried about her daughter's financial security, she could ask her daughter to make a list of the pros and cons of a particular career choice. Dr. Cohen also suggests that the two brainstorm together and do research to find careers that offer financial security, yet allow the daughter to express her artistic passion, like interior decorating. The mother cannot deliver her message in a judgmental way. If the mother's tone presents her as a compassionate, empathetic parent who is saying "Let's explore this together," the daughter may be more likely to listen.

Set short-term goals. Another possibility is for mothers like Eleanor to say, "I respect your desire to do this. Have you thought about a five-year plan?" That opens the door for the daughter to try something else and not feel ashamed if her first choice doesn't work out. Or, the mother could suggest a supplementary job that will allow the daughter to earn more money.

Know when to let up. If the daughter insists on pursuing her original career choice, the mother needs to back off. Even if the choice ends up being a bad one, mothers need to realize that daughters, whether they are children or young adults, need to make their own mistakes through life experiences. "That's the building of wisdom," Dr. Cohen says.

Taking a Career for Granted: When Mothers Blaze Trails and Daughters Take a More Relaxed Path

Women like Helen Ingersoll, who attended college in the 1950s, often found that career doors were closed to them. They were expected to become wives and mothers rather than corporate executives and scientists. Just a decade later, however, the women's movement started to take hold on college campuses and women were encouraged to pursue majors other than nursing and elementary education. Business, law, and doctoral programs were slowly but steadily opening up to women. Even as late as 1970, women earned just 5 percent of all law degrees and 10 percent of all medical degrees. Today, women earn roughly half of both degrees. Those pioneering women business executives, lawyers, and doctors had few other female classmates and often had to endure both subtle and overt discrimination. But they also had the satisfaction of knowing that they paved the way for their daughters and granddaughters. For that reason, it's hard for career-oriented mothers to accept their daughters' more laid-back approach to work, often taking career opportunities for granted.[6]

Pamela Chalmers, 59, is one of those mothers. She stepped onto the campus of the University of New Hampshire in 1965, exactly the moment that life-altering social changes were starting. Pamela was the valedictorian of her high school and planned to become a teacher, like many young women at that time. Instead, she got caught up in the women's movement and anti-war protests once she started college, and she realized that as a smart, focused, young woman, she could take on any job she set her mind to. She decided to attend business school and earned a master's degree in public administration. While getting her degree, she met her husband, Charles, who was getting his graduate degree in school administration. The two married and moved to New York City after graduation.

Pamela is still happily married to Charles and is the loving mother of 26-year-old Monica, but she admits that the most important aspect of her identity is her career: "I love to work." She has worked in university career placement and financial institutions for the past three decades. Pamela took just two months off work after Monica was born, leaving child-rearing to her schoolteacher husband, Charles. "I took a few months off," Pamela recalls, "but I just couldn't wait to get back to work." In retrospect, she acknowledges that she "had nothing to do with raising Monica. My husband did everything." She says she would have been "terrible" as a stay-at-home mother. And it helped that her husband was a teacher at her daughter's school, so he could be home with her more easily.

Pamela admits that part of her professional drive and aversion to child-rearing comes from witnessing her own mother's depression as a housewife cooped up at home. By contrast, she saw how happy her businessman father was as he enjoyed the respect of their local community. The thought of not working traumatized Pamela. "Home represents entrapment and misery," she says. If she ever loses her job, she plans to volunteer, to avoid the fate of being stuck at home like her mother was.

Her daughter, Monica, is more mellow about work—although she's neither lazy nor lacking in direction. As a college student, she founded a campus chapter of the National Organization for Women. Now, five years later, she is a political campaign manager in New York City and throws herself into her work 100 percent when she's involved in a campaign. But once the campaign ends, she's out of a job, and she accepts that. Monica explains: "Because of the nature of my work, I change jobs at least twice a year. I know that every job I have will end." She enjoys the hectic pace of her work assignments, followed by a month or two of down time, when she can relax or travel. And since she's unmarried and has no children, she doesn't need to worry about supporting anyone else. "As long as I'm making a good enough living to support myself, the down times don't bother me," since she's confident she'll soon find another job.

Monica knows her on again, off again employment status worries her mother. "We both are career-focused and driven, but I'm less concerned with job stability and more comfortable changing jobs frequently," she says. She's optimistic that her mother is finally starting to come around, though. "As I keep finding work—and finding better jobs that pay more money—she's starting to understand."

Pamela admits that she and her daughter think about work in different ways, and that Pamela has a much greater need for the "trappings," as she calls them: the paycheck, the thick résumé, the structure. She says her daughter is different and doesn't want to be chained to a desk. Pamela admits she is petrified about being out of work and projects that fear onto her daughter.

That fear comes from Pamela's own experience of unemployment. Pamela was laid off from a major financial institution in the early 1990s. Following a merger, she and dozens of her coworkers were out of work for almost year. "She's so identified with her work, she was absolutely miserable during that time," Monica tells us. "To her, any unemployment spell is only second to death."

Pamela is finally starting to understand that Monica can survive an occasional spell of unemployment. Even so, for Monica, the memories of how unsupportive her mother was about a decision to leave a job she held six years ago still sting. "I was working at a job I absolutely hated. It affected my whole life." Monica had moved from New York to Washington, D.C., to work in public relations for a nonprofit organization. Her boss made her miserable, often assigning her massive projects to complete at a moment's notice. Her mother's advice was to "just stick it out for six months and everything will be fine." When Monica quit without having another position lined up, her mother said, "How can you walk away from a perfectly good job?" Monica resented that response, since it implied job security was more important to her mother than Monica's happiness.

Our therapist Julia Davies offers her advice for women like Pamela and Monica.

ADVICE FOR MOTHERS

Have faith in your daughter's ability to find work. Dr. Davies reminds Pamela that she and her daughter have very different worldviews, owing in part to their past experiences. Pamela fears unemployment; Monica is more comfortable with uncertainty. Monica's track record has proven to Pamela that she can find a job once she loses one. Pamela should have as much faith in her daughter as Monica has in herself.

ADVICE FOR DAUGHTERS

Ask for Mom's help when you need it. Monica should feel comfortable tapping into her mother's expertise and turning to her for career advice during long periods of unemployment.

When the Apple (Intentionally) Falls Far from the Tree: Daughters' Rebellions

Many young women we spoke with made choices different from their mothers' because they were presented with different opportunities and obstacles. In a number of cases, though, daughters purposefully chose career paths that were diametrically opposed to their mothers'—either because they saw how miserable their mothers were, or because they felt their mothers' choices weren't good for their children. In most of these cases, the mothers and daughters were close and had relatively conflict-free relationships. The daughters recognized their mothers did the best they could, given the many constraints in their lives. Still, when a daughter actively tries to avoid her mother's fate, that often triggers a sense of regret and self-doubt in her mother.

Frustrated Stay-at-Home-Moms and Career-Oriented Daughters

Many stay-at-home mothers of past generations tried hard to put on a happy face, even if they were filled with pent-up resentment about the career opportunities they gave up when they married and had children. Yet when these façades started to crack, their children were often the first to notice. Even though Betty Mahoney, now 79, tried to convince herself and her children that she was happy raising a brood of seven, her daughter knew otherwise. Tammy, now 44, was determined to have a fulfilling career, in part because she sensed that her stay-at-home mother was frustrated and exhausted by her life. Tammy says her mother longed to be a doctor, but as a religious Catholic, she instead married young and had a large family. Tammy is now married and is the mother of two girls, ages 7 and 9. She remembers her mother as frequently frustrated, overwhelmed, and unhappy. She regained some of her confidence and self-esteem when she went back to school to become a nurse when Tammy, the youngest, was in middle school. "Nurturing my children is a wonderful experience," says Tammy, "but if I don't also do other things, I fear I'd end up resenting them."

Betty would tell her daughters, "You can do anything you set your mind to," but that wasn't the case for her, Tammy says. She was bored being a mother and resented that her husband had professional choices unavailable to her. "I hope not to emulate her anger," Tammy says.

Tammy found herself drawn to the education field and for the past three years has been working full-time as a professor at a large university in the school of education. "I enjoy what I do very much," she says. She took some time off for maternity leave and realized that, like her mother, she was bored at home. She hired a babysitter who also takes care of chores during the day, so Tammy can be involved in "purposeful playing," like board games, puzzles, and reading with her children. Although her life is hectic, she feels her happiness in her profession makes her a better, more engaged mother. "My self-worth is tied to my job more than I realized," she says. Still, she limits the amount of time she spends at work because her family comes first.

Though her mother is very proud of Tammy's Ph.D., she says the most important degree is the "M.O.M." Being there for your husband and children is far more important than any job outside the home, her mother tells her. Betty considers herself a successful mother because all of her children have turned out well. "Sometimes I have moments of doubt, but I look at where they are and am so proud," she says. Though she was satisfied raising her seven children, she regrets not going on with her schooling, which she quit when she met her husband. And, she says, she enjoyed returning to school and work twenty-five years after she got married. However, being a nurse wasn't her ultimate goal, and she would have relished the chance to be a doctor. "I'm ferociously independent and didn't like following someone else's orders and yet being responsible for the outcome." She said she encouraged her daughters to reach higher and become a doctor, dentist, lawyer, or astronaut, not a teacher or nurse. Because of the vast array of career choices available to today's women, Tammy feels she has created a satisfying life for herself that protects her from the discontent that her mother suffered.

Daughter of Free-Spirited Mother Seeks a "More Domestic Path"

Marla Beech, 59, spent her young adult years rebelling. She grew up in a small, conservative town in Iowa in the 1950s, but in her college years she was swept up in the political activism of the 1960s. Her life started off as fairly traditional, but quickly spiraled into a series of cross-country adventures. She married during her junior year in college after she became pregnant. Much to her husband's disappointment, Marla decided to stay in college and go to graduate school, even though she had a toddler and another baby on the way. The marriage lasted just four years.

As the single mother of two preschoolers in the early 1970s, Marla continued to find adventures for herself. She relocated her children to Boston from Iowa "on a whim," says her daughter Cassie Woodley, now 38. Marla, now a director of sales and marketing for a large engineering firm in the Bay Area, feels that her children were well cared for, despite their peripatetic upbringing. Although she was busy with graduate school and work, she recalls that she relied on the support of friends to raise her kids. "When I was in graduate school, I lived in a large house with about eight other people, so I had access to babysitters. The girls were in co-op day care. It wasn't a difficult time for them."

Marla fondly recalls her days as an adventurous mom, yet Cassie looks back with a mix of regret and embarrassment. Her mother wasn't like other mothers, and that often brought a sense of shame to Cassie. She recalls one time that her mother forgot her house keys when she went to work, so she dropped by Cassie's third-grade classroom to get Cassie's keys. Cassie recalls that none of the other kids had keys to their houses, because most of their mothers didn't work and stayed home. To make matters worse, Marla had been working as a welder in a ship-yard and entered Cassie's classroom decked out in her work clothes, welding mask in hand. "I was mortified at the time, although it's now become something of a family joke," Cassie laughs. She remembers that when she went to play at other kids' homes, "people would give me snacks because Mom wasn't there to take care of me."

Cassie, like her mother, has rebelled—but she's done so by taking a traditional path. While her mother cherished her education, her ca-reer, and her freedom, Cassie has simpler goals: running a day-care center out of her home. Cassie knows her career path is a disappoint-ment to her mother. Marla is pleased that Cassie runs her own busi-ness, boasting to friends that she's an "entrepreneur," but Cassie thinks her mother has little regard for child-care workers. She's not sure if that's because Marla views it as a low-prestige, female-dominated field or because it doesn't pay well.

Marla knows she could be more supportive of her daughter's choices, yet she grapples with the pain of knowing her daughter has purposely chosen to take a path that keeps her closer to her kids. Marla says when Cassie first started the day-care center, "there was a part of me that felt like rejection. She was choosing to do the opposite of what I had done." Marla and Cassie say they're very close, yet they both have the nagging feeling they can't get each other's approval for their life choices. Dr. Davies offers advice to mothers and daughters who have purposely made divergent career choices.

ADVICE FOR MOTHERS

Realize your daughter may be trying to fill voids left in her childhood. Mothers need to recognize that their choices may have created distress for their daughters even if that's not what they intended. "Cassie clearly felt abandoned and unprotected by her mother," says Dr.

Davies. "She doesn't want her children to feel the same way." The more difficult a child's experience was in a specific area, the more urgent the need to do it differently for her own children. Rather than feeling hurt, mothers should feel heartened that their daughters are resourceful enough to bounce back and make choices that work for them.

ADVICE FOR DAUGHTERS

Recognize your mother did the best she could, given her options at the time. Dr. Davies tells us there are at last two major themes at play here. One is generational and cultural, and the other is more individual and psychological. Daughters could tell their mothers directly that they understand why they did what they did years ago, just as they hope their mothers will understand their current choices. She suggests daughters say something like: "I respect the decisions you made and understand they made good sense for you. Now I would like the same respect for the decisions I'm making now, in this culture."

Following in Mom's Footsteps, but Feeling Like You Can't Fill Her Shoes

Some of the daughters we spoke with viewed their mothers as inspiring role models—such positive role models, in fact, that the daughters didn't believe they could achieve all their mothers had. But we often found that the pressure to be a super-careerwoman and a supermom didn't necessarily come from these high-achieving mothers. Rather, it comes from what author Judith Warner, in her book *Perfect Madness,* calls the culture of "high-intensity parenting."[7] While professional women of a generation ago were happy to let their kids entertain themselves, working mothers today feel compelled to supply their kids with a steady stream of attention, love, warmth, and intellectual engagement. As a result, women like Natalie Mendel, 42, are running themselves ragged—and that worries their trailblazing mothers who didn't have the same sense of anxiety that today's mothers experience.

Natalie comes from a family of strong women. Both her mother and her grandmother balanced medical careers and families in an era when few women went to medical school. Natalie's mother, Barbara Mendel, now 65 and living in Chicago, Illinois, began medical school when Natalie was 12; she was the only mother in her medical school class. She eventually became a radiologist. Natalie's grandmother, now 95, was a pediatrician, one of only three women in her medical school class and the only one to actually practice medicine. Natalie views her mother's and grandmother's professional accomplishments as a source of inspiration. "I looked to the experiences of my mom and grandma as models," Natalie says. Her mother, Barbara, adds, "The life you know becomes what is possible for you."

Natalie proudly told us that her grandmother advocated for improved prenatal care and the regulation of abortion providers in New York City, while her mother concentrated on finding the best ways to screen for and diagnose breast cancer. "They were and are committed to using their talents and their intelligence in their careers," she says.

Natalie was beginning law school around the time her mother finished her residency. Now a tenured law professor at a large midwestern university, she's living up to the standards of her family's high-achieving women. She looks every bit the scholar, with thick glasses, no makeup, and a long skirt. She talks frankly about what she liked about her upbringing and how her life as a professional working mother differs from her mother's.

Unlike most of the children in her neighborhood who grew up having their mother at home most of the day, Natalie was instead left with a babysitter, though her father, a professor, was often home. She always knew she would have a career, even after she had children. Natalie wanted to make a "positive difference in the world at large." Even though Natalie admires her mother's and grandmother's ambition and professional success, she's raising her two children, Lauren, age 9, and Edward, age 7, differently. Though her mother worked at a very demanding job, Natalie says, Barbara didn't feel the same pressure to be entirely focused on her three children.

Natalie says she misses her children when she's away from them during the day and feels guilty about leaving them in child care for so many hours. She deliberately chose the career of an academic, like her father, because she believes it gave him more flexibility to balance his career with home life. She purposely avoided her mother's field of medicine because she thought it demanded too much time away from home. She also learned an important lesson from observing her mother's and grandmother's careers: "Significant career contributions can be made at many stages of life, and often, it will work out fine to take a break from a career." Her grandmother took a brief hiatus from medicine to stay home with her children; her mother didn't go back to medical school until Natalie was a teen. Natalie followed their leads, and took lengthy maternity leaves. She cut back to part-time hours when her children were young, but she never left the workforce entirely. "It's difficult to reenter the workforce after extended time away," she says.

Natalie's job is demanding and often keeps her up late grading papers after her children have gone to bed. Still, she loves earning a salary and not being dependent on others. She also enjoys teaching and research and helping students discover "how they might use their talents to contribute to the world." Above all, Natalie appreciates the flexibility of her job, which gives her control over when her work gets done. That permits her to occasionally pick up her children from school or accompany them on field trips.

Even so, Natalie feels slightly cheated that she can't spend more daytime hours with her children. To compensate, she and her husband insist that any moment away from work be spent engaged with her children in so-called quality time. "We lead a very child-focused life," Natalie says. She and her husband, Ron Watkins, a lawyer, insist on sparing their children from mundane tasks like shopping when they're home with them. Instead, Natalie and Ron put off chores until the kids are in bed. They even prepare dinner for the next day—simple meals like chicken breast and a salad—in the evening, after their children have gone to sleep. It's ready as soon as they walk in the door from work the next day and their children don't need to entertain themselves while Natalie and her husband prepare dinner. Natalie doesn't feel comfortable allowing the children to play on their own and wants to make the most of her time at home. "The best way for my kids to feel loved and supported when I'm away from them all day is to put them first at all times," she says. She would prefer to "read to her kids than take them furniture shopping or have them play while I deal with practical matters."

Even though her mother also worked full-time and had three children, Natalie says, "my style of parenting is more involved." Barbara, Natalie's mother, worked in a demanding profession in an era when many women stayed home to raise children, yet she tells us she didn't feel any of the guilt her daughter experiences. Barbara says it's ironic that in a time when women are free to pursue any career they like, working mothers like Natalie often feel they're inadequate parents if they don't make their children their top priority at all times when they're with them. Barbara feels it was healthy for her three girls to play on their own or with each other, and they often did while she fixed dinner.

Barbara says she was relaxed with her children in a way her daughter is not. She feels that Natalie has made parenting a second career in itself and is so busy trying to compensate for time away from her children that she can't enjoy being a mother or a wife. "Life shouldn't revolve around your children to the exclusion of everyone else," she tells us. "That makes it easy for children to think they're the center of the universe." Barbara also worries about the toll Natalie's high-intensity parenting is taking on her physically. "She's exhausted. She's my child. I don't want to see my child exhausted."

Barbara's and Natalie's experiences point out an interesting paradox. Career women of a generation ago had it tougher. Child-care services were in scarcer supply. Most husbands had inflexible jobs and weren't particularly helpful with a Crock-Pot or a vacuum cleaner. Women had more children. Human resource managers rarely uttered words like "flextime" and "job sharing." Yet today's working mothers complain of high levels of anxiety and self-doubt and their mothers are worried about the toll it takes on their daughters' well-being and their grandchildren's adjustment.

ADVICE FOR MOTHERS

Realize that a child-centered universe is now in vogue. Natalie's child-centered lifestyle has become more common, meshing with today's cultural expectation that when you're not on the job, you should commit most of your time to your children. What Barbara sees as excessive, Natalie views as normal. This is one of the greatest differences between the moms of yesterday, many of whom were content to let their children entertain themselves to ease their at-home burden, and many of today's mothers, who feel the need to make up for time spent away from their children.

Accept the fact that family time has become social time. Some experts say that if the cultural norm is spending more time with your kids, it probably isn't harmful and Natalie's mother shouldn't worry about it. This is an area where women may need to accept their daughters' desire to spend leisure time with their children, instead of taking time alone with their spouse. Dr. Tom Sullivan, a pediatrician based in Alexandria, Virginia, and a member of the American Academy of Pediatrics Committee on the Psychosocial Aspects of Child and Family Health, says that while Barbara was accustomed to having friends from her adult social circles and work, and making social outings adult-only affairs, "that's what people did then." Just because it's not as popular an option now doesn't mean it's wrong for families to spend more time with their children, he says.

Choose soft words. Dr. Donna Mayerson says the choice of language in this situation is crucial so that it doesn't sound like Natalie's mother thinks her daughter's priorities are misguided. Barbara shouldn't come across as saying that Natalie is "neglecting" her husband or "spoiling" her kids—that she isn't doing enough for her family or that Barbara's way was better. That type of language is likely to be hurtful to Natalie, and she won't listen to the advice. Barbara's concerns should not come across as criticism. She shouldn't say to her daughter, for example, that she's "somehow responsible for creating selfish little monsters." Instead, she could say, "Honey, I understand you are doing everything you can to make certain your kids are raised well, but one thing I know from my own experience is that it's very important for you to take care of yourself and your marriage."

ADVICE FOR DAUGHTERS

Lighten up. Experts tell us we need to stimulate children intellectually and play with them extensively. "But that's not necessarily in their best interest," says Dr. Diane Sanford. She agrees with Barbara that children need to understand they're not the center of the universe. They should learn to be self-sufficient and entertain themselves without their parents doing that job for them, she says.

Examine your feelings—and their role in how you act. Dr. Ellen Berman suggests that Natalie ask herself why she doesn't feel comfortable taking time for herself and feels the need to spend every leisure moment with her children. She says that as an academic with flexible hours, Natalie shouldn't have a problem finding time for herself and her husband, as well as with her children. Natalie should ask herself why she has such difficulty carving out this adult time. "That's not traumatic for most adults. Why is it for her?" she asks.

Take the kids grocery shopping. Don't hesitate to take your children on errands, says Dr. Julia Davies. Natalie could kill two birds with one stone and have some quality time with her children by taking them on errands she considers mundane. While Dr. Davies doesn't endorse dragging them around for hours, she says that children often enjoy selecting food at the grocery store for the weekly meals. "The sharing of daily life is a bonding experience for a child and also teaches them about reality," she says.

CHAPTER 6

Breast-feed or Bottle?
Time-outs or Spankings?
The Rules of Parenting and How
They've Changed

How can you trust a stranger to watch your child all day?

You let your son walk all over you. You need to be firm with him.

If Madison can lift up your shirt and ask to nurse, she's too old for breast-feeding.

B reast-feed or bottle-feed? A day-care center or a nanny? Chicken fingers or tofu? *Girlfriends' Guide to Pregnancy* or *What to Expect When You're Expecting*?[1] Mothers today agonize over every child-rearing choice they make, egged on by daily news stories and "expert" advice on how to parent. We can't turn on the television or computer without being bombarded by yet another new path-breaking study touting the pros and cons of a particular stroller, child-rearing tactic, or Baby Genius DVD. A generation ago, mothers didn't obsess as much about things like baby formula and sleeping arrangements, which are now considered benchmarks for determining whether one is a competent parent.

With endless new information come endless choices, however. Young women are turning their backs on the tried-and-true child-rearing tactics used by their mothers, and are turning to science, the Internet, or their peers for cutting-edge child-rearing advice. Their mothers often feel slighted as a result, because they want dearly to pass along their child-rearing know-how and experience.

Mother's Milk or Factory-made Formula: The Tussles Over Breast-feeding

For many new mothers, the breast-or-bottle decision is the most important choice they make early in their child's life. While formula feeding was the norm a generation ago, most mothers today are sold on the health benefits of breast-feeding. Their mothers may not fully understand why their daughters want to endure the rigors of pumping their milk or being on call all day to nurse their baby. Some women from the older generation didn't get the appeal of breast-feeding because it was not part of their cultural heritage. Others questioned whether it was wise for a young mother to be physically tethered to her child around the clock, as breast-feeding often requires. Others supported their daughter's decision to breast-feed, but only during the baby's early months. In all these cases, though, the daughters wished their mothers were more supportive of their nursing choices.

Deirdre Hamilton, age 41, says her Korean-born mother, Yoon-Ji Hamilton, age 73, didn't nurse her children and had no interest in breast-feeding. Deirdre suspected her mother would condemn her decision to nurse, so she turned down her mother's request to visit her the first month after her daughter was born. She explains, "I didn't want the pressure of her saying, 'Oh, just drop it.' " Yoon-Ji thought breast-feeding was unnecessary: her children were formula-fed, and they all turned out to be healthy. She couldn't understand why her daughter was willing to go to the trouble and worried that her grandchildren wouldn't get the important nutrients they needed during their formative months.

Like Yoon-Ji, Marla Beech, 59, also bottle-fed her two daughters when they were babies in the late 1960s and early 1970s. While many women in the 1960s relied on formula because it was recommended by doctors as the best nutritional source, Marla Beech, age 59, rarely followed convention. She participated in the anti-war protests in the 1960s and was a graduate student during the 1970s while single-handedly raising her two young daughters. She even ran for public office on the Socialist Party ticket while in graduate school. Given her hectic schedule, Marla relied heavily on day care and couldn't be on call to breast-feed her children. She admits that she feels a tinge of regret over this decision, but didn't realize this until her own daughters started breast-feeding their babies.

Her daughter, Cassie, 38, is now the mother of three children ages 11, 13, and 16. Cassie breast-fed her children, and is still a bit miffed that her mother sneered at her decision to do so. Cassie recalls her mother didn't have a problem when she nursed her firstborn, because she thought Cassie was doing it to save money: formula can be pricy. But when Cassie nursed her youngest daughter, Mariah, until she was 18 months old, her mother took great issue with it and perceived that as a rejection of the way she fed her babies. According to Cassie, her mother said, "You're just doing that because I bottle-fed you." Marla admits her opposition to breast-feeding stems from her insecurities about not breast-feeding: "In my mind, the question was, did my daughters feel I did a bad job?"

For the other mothers and daughters we spoke with, the practice of breast-feeding wasn't necessarily a problem. However, nursing the children until they were old enough to ask for milk was a point of contention. Vivian Kleinschmidt, now 77, nursed both of her children for roughly a year. "I was the only one of my friends who did that," she recalls. Though she's supportive of nursing babies, she believes her daughter, Mary, now 46 and a divorced mother of three children, went overboard, nursing each of her children for two and a half years. Mary's youngest two are only two years apart, so Vivian believed that when the third baby was born, Mary should have weaned the other so the youngest could have all of her milk. "I have a photo of her with one baby at each breast," Vivian tells us. Mary remembers that picture. "I think my mom thought it was a bit bizarre," she says. Mary says she liked the "closeness, warmth, and convenience" of nursing and also was a vocal advocate of the family bed concept. All of her kids slept with her until they were 7 years old. Mary belonged to La Leche League, an organization that encourages mothers to nurse until their children are ready to stop on their own. Mary says said that by 18 months old, her children nursed only in the evening, before nap time, or when they were ill or insecure. "So, I basically let them decide when to be weaned. Ironically, the kids have been calling the shots ever since," she jokes.

Although breast-feeding seems like the most natural act in the world, it has become a hot-button issue for new mothers in recent generations.[2] Throughout history, women have nursed, but the popularity of breast-feeding started to decline in the 1920s, when evaporated cow's milk and infant formula became widely available. Throughout much of the 1940s through the 1960s, mothers turned to formula, spurred on by aggressive marketing campaigns by formula companies. Breast-feeding became associated with uneducated or poor women who didn't have the means to purchase baby formula. Since the 1970s, though, breast-feeding has once again risen in popularity, as doctors, nurses, and public health advocates have trumpeted the nutritional value and other health benefits of mother's milk.

The popularity of breast-feeding has even waxed and waned in popularity during the lifetime of the daughters we interviewed. Data from the Ross Laboratory Mothers Survey found that in the late 1960s and early 1970s, just 30 percent of mothers breast-fed their newborns, although this figure climbed to more than 60 percent by the 1990s. By 2004, 70 percent of women breast-fed their babies, at least once. The proportion of women who breast-feed their infants drops off steadily as the baby gets older. According to the Centers for Disease Control, 36 percent are still breast-feeding at 6 months, 18 percent at 12 months, and just 6 percent at 18 months. While breast-feeding is much more common today than it was a generation ago, it's still uncommon for women to breast-feed as long as Mary did. Given how personal the decision to breast-feed is, how can mothers and daughters like Mary and Vivian make peace on this matter?

ADVICE FOR MOTHERS

Accept the data: breast is best. Hundreds of medical studies show that breast-feeding is beneficial to infants, says Dr. Barbara Howard, an assistant professor of pediatrics at the Johns Hopkins University School of Medicine. She believes that nursing a child for the first year of life is the "best possible form of nutrition" and provides antibodies that protect against a host of illnesses. Breast-feeding into the second year provides immune system benefits as well, she says. Dr. Howard agrees with Vivian that Mary's long-term breast-feeding may be taking things a bit far if it's done for reasons other than just providing nutritional benefit, for instance, to satisfy a mother's need for intimacy. Mothers could talk honestly with their daughters about what the benefits and costs are of breast-feeding so long. Dr. Howard says that if a child is allowed to nurse at will, mothers may be similarly lenient in other ways that stunt development, so "it's a marker to watch out for."

ADVICE FOR DAUGHTERS

Let Mom in. The period following the birth of a child is the most exhausting time for a mother, so it's wise to let your mother help you adjust during this emotionally and physically challenging time. Dr. Pamela High, professor of pediatrics at Brown University Medical School and director of developmental-behavioral pediatrics at Rhode Island Hospital, says keeping her away is "a sad way" to deal with a mother's lack of support for breast-feeding. Having Mom around to help with household tasks, like cooking and laundry, could really ease the load. If moms try to impose their advice on their daughters, daughters could simply reply, "I've made a conscious choice to nurse my baby and I'd really appreciate your support."

Talk to your mother about her experiences bottle-feeding or nursing her children. Feeding one's baby in the early 1960s wasn't nearly as politicized and hotly debated as it is today, so mothers of a generation ago may fail to see why breast milk is such a big deal. "They don't think about it," says Howard. So it's "really worth the conversation" to ask how her own experiences shape her positions on her daughter's breast-feeding choices. Moms might have had a good reason for the choices they made. Perhaps they didn't have proper training in breast-feeding, as in Yoon-Ji's case, or maybe the demands of being a working single mother made breast-feeding impossible, as in Marla's case—especially without today's electric pumps to retrieve and store breast milk. That may not change the daughter's view, but it could make her more empathetic and understanding of her mother's position, Dr. Howard says.

Food Wars: Picky Eaters and Family Dinners

Once children are weaned, new battles between mothers and daughters emerge over food. A generation ago, food was a common way for mothers to show their love for their families. They might spend a good part of their day preparing nutritious meals from scratch, featuring dishes like pot roast, vegetables, and potatoes, along with homemade pies and cakes for dessert. Families would sit down together at the dinner table at 6:00 P.M. sharp, and children would eat—often grudgingly—whatever was served to them.

For today's mothers, however, especially those who work outside the home, family dinners frequently are prepared by the local takeout joint or Trader Joe's. Exhausted mothers don't have the energy or patience to demand their kids clean their plates, so they indulge their child's finicky tastes. This practice frustrates grandmothers, who believe dinnertime should be an opportunity for the whole family to gather for conversation and a nutritious meal. They feel their daughters are breeding a generation of unhealthy, unadventurous eaters by catering to their children's food demands. Some think it's ridiculous that their daughters go to such lengths to satisfy a child's picky palate. At the same time, many daughters can't fathom why food generates so much drama for their mothers.

When Food Is More Than Just Food . . .

For Rebecca Marshall, 36, food has been an emotional topic for as long as she can remember. Rebecca's mom, Joan Miller, 72, grew up in Germany during World War II, when food was scarce. To this day, the thought of wasting a mouthful is unthinkable to her. Joan was just 12 years old when she and her family fled Germany for the United States. "It was a difficult life," Joan says of her upbringing during wartime. "Of course there was rationing." Joan has vivid memories of going hungry in Germany and admits she "has a problem throwing food away." Joan vowed that her children would have a happier childhood than she did, and as a young mother she took full advantage of the bountiful food available in the United States. She worked from home as a piano teacher and cooked dinners that the family ate together every night. Despite the idyllic new life Joan created in the United States, one part of her past lingered: the unwillingness to see food wasted. "My mother could get slightly psychotic about that," Rebecca says.

Rebecca has vivid memories of her mother force-feeding her. Her mother would stick a forkful of food into her mouth and then threaten to hit her with a large wooden cooking spoon if she didn't swallow "on the count of ten." Rebecca usually managed to swallow on time. One time, however, her mother forced her "to eat runny, scrambled eggs that made my stomach turn." Rebecca swallowed and then threw them up on her plate. "I remember my mother being very angry at me, acting as if I had done it intentionally," she says. Rebecca says the food battles were power struggles, and she remained a picky eater until college. She didn't try many foods until she was an adult and waited until she was 19 to taste Chinese food. Rebecca has always been thin, so much so that her mother worried she was anorexic when she was a teen. (Rebecca says she wasn't.)

Like many of the daughters we've talked to, Rebecca feeds her children differently then the way she was fed. "There are choices she made as a parent that I have consciously decided not to repeat," explains Rebecca, now a research editor at a magazine and the mother of two girls, ages 5 and 2. She deliberately makes food a low-key affair. "My painful memories of mealtimes have led me to go the other way with my kids. If they want only two bites, that's fine," she says. "I do ask them to take one bite of a new food when it's introduced, but if they don't want more, that's it," she adds. But her mother sometimes tries to take the same approach with her grandchildren as she did with Rebecca. "She'll say, 'One more bite' to the girls and I'll give her that look," she says.

Rebecca says dinnertime at her house is "so different" than it was when she was growing up, where the family sat down together every night. She hardly cooks. Her husband does most of the cooking, while she does the dishes. Also, "the girls almost never eat with us." She says she feels guilty about not taking part in that "hallowed family time," but she "doesn't feel like having arguments with the kids about eating." Since her kids eat only seven or eight different types of dishes, her husband prepares what they like and serves them around 5:30 P.M. Once the girls are tucked in bed, she and her husband have dinner "and then we can eat in peace," spared of food wars, she says.

"I know Rebecca recalls food problems and there probably were some, but I didn't notice them," Joan admits. Just recently, she attended a barbecue where a large amount of chicken was going to be thrown away. "I couldn't stand the idea of throwing it out. I took it home. It's just the way I am," Joan says. She says Rebecca is "more relaxed" about food than she was. She sees her daughter on a daily basis, since she lives upstairs from Rebecca in a two-family house in a small Massachusetts town. When Joan babysits for her granddaughters, she feels she has to make sure they eat. She was babysitting during one recent weeknight, feeding the kids dinner. "I was the one who had to see to it that Lily ate a piece of pizza," she says. Her granddaughter, Lily, wasn't eating, but ultimately agreed, after Joan promised her a reward of "another video" if she did. Joan says her daughter is "less firm" about getting her children to eat.

For Joan Miller, a well-stocked kitchen represented security for her family. For Eva Cohen, 79, dinnertime is more than just a time to eat, but an occasion for the family to get together and enjoy each other's company. Eva, like Joan, is concerned with how her 45-year-old daughter, Susan Greene, feeds her children. Eva's father was a butcher, so she made meat-heavy dinners for her family, even though she also worked outside the home as mayor of a working-class town in Michigan. Her daughter, Susan, who now lives in New Jersey, works full time as a marketing consultant and doesn't cook. Instead, the family's nanny prepares meals for the children, making only those dishes they request. Susan admits her daughters, ages 12 and 9, are picky eaters "because they get whatever they want." She says the children usually eat early, while she and her husband have dinner later.

Eva wishes they would all come together for dinner each night, as her family did.

Eva says that instead of stating, "Here's what we're having for dinner," Susan asks the children what they want. Since they're allowed to call the shots, they have a very limited list of acceptable foods, nixing beef, chicken, and fish. "They won't eat anything," Eva told us. When Eva was raising her children, she believed that if the children were hungry enough, they'd eat whatever was served to them. But Susan, like Rebecca Marshall, feels it's not worth the battle of getting her children to try new foods, and she'd rather have her nanny indulge their finicky tastes. Having them eat a varied diet simply isn't a priority.

The Crusade Against Junk Food

Many working mothers admitted they don't have the emotional energy to battle it out with their children every night at the dinner table, so they feed them chicken fingers or macaroni and cheese if that's what makes the kids happy. But women like Lois Linney, 56, believe that indulging kids' preferences for unhealthy foods is the first step on the road to obesity. Her daughter, Tiffany Wagner, a 27-year-old criminal defense attorney living in Texas, knows there's some truth to her mother's words, but the thought of preparing well-balanced meals is too overwhelming for her right now.

Tiffany describes her own childhood as idyllic. Although her mother was a schoolteacher before she had children, she was a devoted stay-at-home mom when the kids were young. Lois made homemaking a true profession. She had been a home economics major in college, and she prepared her own baby food, sewed her children's clothes, and cooked nutritious, balanced meals. She even belonged to a dairy co-op where she purchased milk fresh from the cow. Lois breast-fed her children for a year at a time before it was fashionable; she was convinced it was the healthiest option. "She did everything a good mom should do," boasts Tiffany.

Although her mother was a wonderful role model, Tiffany says she has chosen to follow in her father's footsteps. Her father, now a consultant to a school district, is driven and career-oriented, like Tiffany. While Lois relished being home with her young children,

Tiffany suffered from postpartum depression when her daughter, Lauren, was born eight months ago and was eager to return to work as soon as possible. Lois reluctantly supports her daughter's choice to work, yet she worries about her daughter's hectic lifestyle and the toll it takes on her health.

Tiffany's daughter is in a Christian child-care center from 8:00 A.M. to 6:00 P.M. every weekday, so by the time Tiffany or her husband brings her home, they're too tired to cook. Tiffany and her husband, a computer programmer, go out to dinner with their daughter five nights a week. "I don't cook at all. I'm a horrible cook and my husband hates doing the dishes," Tiffany says. The baby is accustomed to restaurant food, since that's all she eats. Tiffany says her mother is concerned this isn't a healthy choice and admits her mother's probably right. "But we both work so late, so it's hard to find time to cook meals," she says.

Lois worries about the longer-term consequences of her daughter's unhealthy eating habits. She's especially concerned because Tiffany and her husband are both overweight—Tiffany by twenty-five pounds, and her son-in-law by one hundred pounds. On Lois's recent visit to her daughter's home, she found that they had no food in their refrigerator. They don't eat breakfast and they eat out for both lunch and dinner. "I worry about the effect it will have on my granddaughter nutritionally and weight-wise," says Lois. She also fears that her daughter and son-in-law are at risk for diabetes, especially since Lois's husband has it.

On Lois's most recent trip to visit her daughter, she saw Tiffany giving her daughter a Popsicle. As the baby was sucking on it, Lois looked at the ingredients and noticed it contained a large amount of sugar. She told her daughter, "That's an awful lot of sugar. She shouldn't have it." Tiffany realized her mother was right, but nevertheless let her daughter have the Popsicle. "She just ignores me," Lois sighs. During that same visit, Lois helped her daughter cook a meal at home. "It was very basic— spaghetti—but at least it had a vegetable," Lois says.

Lois doesn't think her daughter will change, and, in fact, she believes things will get worse with time. Her daughter's extra weight tires her out, and her demanding job and child-care responsibilities won't let up any time soon. "Eating healthier would give her more energy to withstand her busy life," her mother says. Lois does her best to keep quiet, typically making only subtle suggestions about a switch to healthier eating. She hopes that as the baby gets older, she won't have the patience for restaurants and that will force Tiffany to make some changes. In the meantime, though, "I just have to bite my tongue and not say anything, since that makes her angry. Now that Tiffany is an adult, I have no business saying too much," she says.

The food wars were one of the most emotional issues that mothers and daughters discussed with us. Food is more than just an emotional issue, though; it's a health issue. Roughly 60 percent of American adults are now classified as obese, and most experts attribute this to our unhealthy diets, often eaten on the run, as well as to a lack of regular exercise. Children, too, are heavier. While just 6 percent of children were considered overweight in the late 1970s, 18 percent of children ages 6 to 17 are overweight today, according to the National Institutes of Health. While mothers may try to hold their tongues when their daughters maintain unhealthy diets, most know their silence could do more harm than good in the longer term. What should mothers and daughters do to resolve tension over the food wars? Dr. Barbara Howard confronts the issue below. We've also collected some healthy lifestyle tips from our experts.

Tips for Raising a Healthy and Well-Nourished Child

Never force-feed your child. Force-feeding prevents children from recognizing the physical cues that tell them when they're full. It also takes away their sense of autonomy. Dr. Howard suggests letting children over the age of 9 months feed themselves.

Don't reward children for eating. Rewarding children for eating a certain food conveys the message that the food isn't tasty, yet those foods are likely to be the healthiest ones.

Don't give kids free rein on the food front. Parents today are so afraid their kids will get upset that they're not willing to insist they eat healthy meals, says Dr. Howard. Part of a child's development is to get upset and learn how to get over it.

Out with the chicken nuggets, in with the fresh veggies. The foods kids elect to eat are typically high in fat and sugar. Dr. Howard suggests that parents offer healthy foods at every meal, while providing at least one food that the child likes. If children make a fuss, they could be dismissed from the table, with no food for one hour, and then, only a healthy option.

Simplify your life to make family dinners happen. The routine of a family dinner, held at a reasonable hour, along with a regular bedtime, can bring a sense of calm to a child, says Dr. Howard. Family dinners also may help improve language and cognitive skills of younger children, who learn by listening to adult conversations.

If family dinners are impossible, impose mealtime rules. Dr. Howard suggests explicit rules for children when they're at the table—regardless of who is with them. Adults should sit down and talk with the children even if they're not eating the meal. That way, you can retain parts of what occurs during a family meal if the family can never gather, or when the family does get together, children will be in the rhythm of the arrangement.

ADVICE FOR MOTHERS

Don't stay mum. Health and nutrition are critical issues. When a daughter's health is at stake, it's perfectly appropriate—even essential—for the mother to express her concerns. This is one area where a mother may be timid in speaking her mind, even though it's the right thing to do. For example, Lois is so afraid of raising the topic, her daughter doesn't realize that the family's diet upsets her. "If the daughter thinks the mother is totally supportive, the mom has been too quiet," says Dr. Ellen Berman. She says families can dine out regularly and not be overweight. The real issue here is eating habits, not the location of the meal.

Offer to help. Dr. Diane Sanford says that in the case of bad eating habits, the mother could help her daughter discover simple ways to obtain healthier meals. She suggests purchasing ready-made meals at grocery stores like Whole Foods or Trader Joe's or recommending TV shows or cookbooks that show how to make healthy meals in under thirty minutes. Lois could offer a consultation with a nutritionist or an objective third party who can guide Tiffany's food choices, suggests Dr. Roni Cohen-Sandler, a psychologist based in Weston, Connecticut, and the author of *Stressed-Out Girls* and *I'm Not Mad, I Just Hate You!*[3]

Use gentle words. Advice should be kind and constructive. As with all instances of mother-daughter conflict, the mother shouldn't suggest her way is better. That approach will backfire, since it comes across as insulting, says Dr. Cohen-Sandler. She suggests language like, "I support you fully in choosing any way that works for you and your family to have dinner, but since diabetes runs in the family and a huge risk factor is weight, I'm concerned about all of you. Have you thought about this?" If a mother uses nonjudgmental language, the daughter might be more receptive to her message.

Pave the way for revisiting the issue. Dr. Sanford suggests that mothers try to keep the lines of communication open, so that if a daughter ever decides to improve her eating habits, she won't feel sheepish or embarrassed turning to her mother. She suggests saying, "If you ever want to talk about this or if I can do anything to help, just let me know." If that message is delivered in a positive, nonjudgmental, helpful way, daughters like Tiffany may better accept it.

ADVICE FOR DAUGHTERS

Understand why food is so important to Mom. The battles over food seldom are just about food and nutrition. For Joan Marshall, food represents security and safety, reflecting her childhood years in wartorn Germany. She's terrified her children and grandchildren won't have enough to eat. Dr. Howard points out that her daughter Rebecca presumes her mother's insistence on cleaning her plate is a control issue or a power struggle. "People blame everything on control issues and that's really a big mistake," Dr. Howard says. By assuming food is a turf battle, Rebecca feels compelled to fight back instead of being empathetic. The real issue here is Joan's deep-seated fear of food scarcity. Rebecca could talk openly with her mother about her childhood, and together they can come to understand the roots of Joan's food concerns.

Put it in writing. If a face-to-face conversation is too painful, mother and daughter could each write a letter to the other, sharing their stories and their feelings, suggests Dr. Howard.

Flatter your mom. In many cases, mothers may be more knowledgeable about food preparation than their daughters. Daughters can use this as a starting point when trying to win their mothers' support. For example, Rebecca could say to her mother, "You had a tough life, but look how healthy you are. You understand a lot about nutrition and have a lot to teach me. I want to listen to what you have to say." That could be followed with, "I've been reading about these issues and learned that you can hurt a child's ability to recognize when they're full if you force-feed them." In doing so, she's conveying her true emotions but also is taking care to protect her mother's feelings.

Don't be afraid to ask for your mother's help. Mothers who care about their daughters' (and grandchildren's) health will be flattered if their daughters ask for help. Educated, independent daughters are often reluctant to ask for assistance because asking for help is viewed by them as a sign of weakness or incompetence. Tiffany should feel brave enough to ask her mother for assistance with meal preparation when needed.

Set ground rules. Daughters can benefit from their mothers' advice without being steamrollered into doing something they don't want to do, Dr. Howard says. She suggests that daughters clearly convey to their mothers what the house rules are at dinnertime to ensure that their mothers don't overstep the boundaries. For example, Rebecca can diplomatically say, "My husband and I make certain our kids have one bite of every food they're served and leave the rest up to them." Spell out your rules to Mom, for example, requiring the kids to sit at the table for fifteen minutes before they're free to go.

Humor her. Since food is an important way grandparents show their love to their grandchildren, indulge them a bit. If there is something Grandma wants to do that makes her feel like she's providing nurturance and nourishment, don't fight her. Dr. Howard admits that she accepts vitamins from her children's grandmother, even though she doesn't always administer them and or think they're necessary. She says, "Thank you for the vitamins. It's wonderful that you care so much about us."

Parenting Advice: Following Tradition or Turning to Science?

A generation or two ago, young women typically turned to their mothers for parenting advice. In the 1950s and 1960s, women often married young and lived near their mothers, aunts, and sisters, who eagerly shared their wisdom on topics ranging from diaper rashes to discipline. Few parents had any formal training, other than an occasional consult with a dog-eared copy of Dr. Spock's *Common Sense Book of Baby and Child Care.*[4] Most were happy to rely on the know-how that others acquired through real-life experience, and even first-time mothers didn't hesitate to go with their gut in deciding what was right for their child.

But these days, new mothers are generally older and more educated. College-educated and professional mothers often feel most comfortable turning to books that base their child-rearing advice on the latest scientific study or a hot new child development theory. They're turning to experts, rather than their mothers—who they feel may be out of touch with contemporary child-rearing issues. With the explosion of Internet Web sites devoted to parenting issues and a seemingly endless spate of parenting advice books, many women today are shunning instinct and embracing science as they raise their kids. Ann Hulbert, author of *Raising America,* estimates that five times as many parenting books were published in 1997 as in 1975.[5] But as women turn to books, they often end up ignoring their mothers' parenting advice. Mothers want to feel needed by their daughters, and their daughters' refusal to consult them can be hurtful and a source of friction. The generational divide is all the more pronounced for daughters of immigrant women, who feel that both their advice *and* their culture are being rejected.

Parenting by Instinct Versus Parenting by the Book

Cheryl Brand, the 34-year-old mother of 8-month-old Morgan, recognizes the value of her mother's parenting experience now that she's become a parent. Cheryl, an assistant professor of psychology who lives in Vermont, often phones her mother in New York, seeking parenting advice. But to her mother's dismay, Cheryl routinely ignores what her mother says. Her mother "seems hurt and confused that I want to do things differently," she says.

Cheryl says she and her mother are very close and that she had a wonderful childhood in a small rural town in New York. "My mother had a real open affection for children that I wanted to replicate," she tells us. Cheryl secretly rejoiced when she gave birth to a girl, so she could pass on the close mother-daughter bond she had with her mother.

Once Morgan was born, however, it became clear that Cheryl and her mother, Carol Brand, now 53, had divergent views on how to parent. By contrast, Cheryl's two younger sisters follow their mother's parenting advice happily and without question. Both still live in the hometown where they were raised; neither went to college and they had their first children when they were 17 and 19, respectively. Cheryl, on the other hand, waited until she was in her midthirties to have her first child, after her career as a psychology professor was secure. Her sisters' compliance makes Cheryl's independent child-rearing approaches all the more painful to her mother, Carol.

Carol relied on her own mother, maternal instinct, and common sense when raising her children, and she is hurt that Cheryl turns to books. "My mom thinks I read too much about baby care and takes it personally if I don't take her advice," Cheryl says. Carol tells her daughter, "Put the book down. Don't always go to the book." But Cheryl believes that as an academic, she's most comfortable learning about parenting by consulting data and theories. Her sisters, by contrast, don't have access to, or interest in, that kind of information and are more comfortable going directly to their mother for advice.

Cheryl and Carol routinely disagree on parenting issues. Their biggest spat has been over Cheryl's practice of sleeping with her baby. Morgan was a colicky baby and having Cheryl near her at night was the only thing that seemed to calm her. Cheryl says it's a great bonding experience. "It's good for her to be that close to my body because she doesn't see me all day." Even though they're both sleeping, Cheryl feels a real connection with her baby. Cheryl says her mom "doesn't get that at all." Carol has told Cheryl that Morgan is old enough to be sleeping in her own room. She says that even though Cheryl is breast-feeding, there's no reason why she can't put the baby in her own room, going there to feed her when necessary. "She needs to have her own space away from the baby, just with her husband." At the same time, the baby needs to learn to be self-sufficient, Carol says.

The conflict doesn't stop with co-sleeping. Carol also believes Cheryl is overprotective, picking Morgan up at the first sign of tears. Instead, she suggests that Cheryl let Morgan "cry it out" in her own room so she can learn how to sooth herself. But Cheryl says she can't stand to hear her baby cry and sees no reason to leave her in distress.

The quarrels came out in full swing when Cheryl, her husband, and her daughter recently visited Carol in New York. Morgan had been having stranger anxiety, so she cried when she was in Cheryl's sister's arms. Cheryl immediately snatched her back. Cheryl remembers her mother giving her "that look." Carol admits it was hard to watch. She says Cheryl could have calmed Morgan while she was in her sister's arms, saying, "It's okay. Mommy's right here." Instead, she took her back because she didn't want her to feel scared. Carol says that crying it out worked for Cheryl, who has always been secure and independent. "I don't think it hurts them to have a cry," Carol says. Cheryl replies that she wants her baby to feel safe at all times. Carol fears that her daughter's parenting style will ultimately stifle the baby and cause her to grow up feeling insecure.

Cheryl understands that her mother uses what's in her parenting tool kit, and that kit includes ideas that guided mothers thirty years ago. Cheryl, by contrast, is guided by the attachment parenting philosophy, advocated by husband-and-wife pediatricians William and Martha Sears.[6] They encourage parents to sleep with their children. The belief is that a strong emotional bond with parents during childhood leads to secure, empathic relationships in adulthood.

Cheryl regularly phones her mother on the pretense of asking for advice, yet she admits she's just looking for a sympathetic ear so she can vent about being up all night with the baby. Carol thinks Cheryl wants her to fix the situation and is frustrated when her daughter doesn't take her advice. Cheryl says her mother was so young, only 19 when she had her, that she followed the advice of her very controlling mother and doesn't understand why Cheryl won't do the same.

Carol agrees that being such a young mother accounts for much of their differences in parenting style. She grew up with her children, so she didn't hesitate to let her own mother help raise them. "I was fine with that. It didn't bother me," Carol says. However, Carol wasn't committed to a demanding career; Cheryl is. Carol thinks her daughter feels guilty for being away from Morgan all day, leading her to compensate in unhealthy ways.

After a recent phone call with her mother, when Carol again chastised Cheryl for being overprotective, Cheryl was particularly distressed. Her mother had compared her parenting to that of a relative whose daughter was so dependent on her overprotective parents that she couldn't bear leaving home for college. Carol told Cheryl she shouldn't smother her daughter so much, because then she "can't flourish like you and be self-sufficient in the world." The comparison to a relative who Cheryl says is clearly emotionally unbalanced really stung. The next morning, she sent her mother an e-mail. She told her that she listens when her mother gives advice, but new information and new situations have caused parenting practices to change. She told Carol she was grateful for the fine job she did in raising her, but she also let her know that her criticisms make her feel like she's failing as a mother. "I was nervous about sending it to her, but she hurt me and I wanted to express my feelings," Cheryl recalls. "It would be nice to hear there are some things I do well." She says Carol has never told her she's a good mother.

Cheryl's mom was stunned by the e-mail. She replied to Cheryl, "I think you're a great mom." She never meant to imply that Cheryl's mothering fell short. But she wanted Cheryl to know she could do some things differently to help herself and Morgan. "I try to say what I say for her own good," Carol says. "I think it's helpful for you to hear you're being overprotective," she told Cheryl.

Cheryl feels the e-mail was a good way to let her mother know that all she hears from her is negative feedback. She says it also was effective in telling her mother that her opinion is valuable. "Of course I want her to think I'm a good mother even though I won't take her advice. I want her to know her opinion of my mothering matters."

Both Cheryl and her mother agreed that the e-mail cleared up some major misconceptions. Despite their conflicts, Cheryl says she values her relationship with her mother and occasionally takes her advice, like when Carol told Cheryl that she didn't need to change her daughter's diaper every time Cheryl awoke in the night because it ends up waking the baby. "Mom said, 'Don't do that' and I stopped and things improved. It's little stuff like that you can't get in books," Cheryl admits.

"We have our moments when she can get snippety and holler at me and I snap back. But then we're apologizing to each other," says Carol. She believes she has a great relationship with her daughter and the two have always been open with each other. "We're able to talk through the issues," she says. Cheryl agrees. "I've always had a really close bond with my mom," she says

Does Rejecting Advice Mean Rejecting a Culture?
Cheryl and Carol are fortunate; they have a strong relationship and are able to overcome their differences in child-rearing attitudes.

It's more difficult to make peace when the relationship has been strained through the years, or when the mother and daughter were raised in different cultures. When we spoke with immigrant women and their daughters, we discovered that conflicts about parenting strategies often escalated into larger conflicts about the value of one's culture.

Bridging the Cultural Divide: How Immigrants' Daughters Can Merge Old-World Customs with New Parenting Ideals

When daughters are born and raised in the United States, and their mothers grew up in other cultures, the generation gap is all the more pronounced. With 12 percent of Americans now born outside of the United States, more mothers and daughters will need to grapple with cultural, generational, and possibly language differences. Mothers may feel their culture is being rejected when their daughters turn their back on simple things like a favorite food or a type of baby carrier. How can mothers and daughters raised in different cultures navigate this often painful divide? Dr. Cohen-Sandler and Dr. Berman offer their advice to daughters of immigrants.

Find parts of your heritage to embrace. Daughters should try to accept at least some aspects of their heritage, whether it's holiday traditions, a favorite dessert, or a special folk tune. Everyone benefits: the children, their mothers, and the grandmothers, who feel valued and get the chance to develop a deeper connection with their grandchildren.

Try to understand the larger values behind your mother's cultural practice. A mother's specific attitudes and practices, like monitoring a child's phone call, often reflect a larger cultural value. Women like Libby Chang, whose mother emigrated from Taiwan, should recognize that some key Confucian values are respect for family and promoting the good of the collective (the family) rather than the whims of the individual. By understanding the larger cultural values behind a parent's disciplinary tactics, daughters may be more accepting and understanding of why their mothers have done what they've done.

These conflicts were painful for women like Yoon-Ji Hamilton, whom we met earlier in this chapter. Yoon-Ji wanted badly to share elements of her Korean heritage with her daughter and grandchild, yet her daughter snubbed practices she viewed as dated or inappropriate. Yoon-Ji was raised in North Korea; her daughter, Deirdre, grew up in the United States and fully embraces the American way of child-rearing, much to her mother's disappointment.

Yoon-Ji, now 73 and living in California, came to the United States when she was 21, along with her mother, during the Korean War. She dreamed of studying in the United States and says "coming here was like heaven." Within two years, while a student at the University of Southern California, she met an American man who later became her husband. They married in 1957. The two worked full-time, running their own printing business, while Yoon-Ji's mother cared for their children.

Deirdre, age 41, is a staff scientist at a university in northern California. She now lives a six-hour drive from her mother, and has been butting heads with her ever since she was a teen. "The conflict with my mom is like a three-legged stool," she says. "One leg is generation, one leg is culture, and the third leg is language." Since her mother's native tongue is Korean, Deirdre says she can't often express her emotions as precisely as she'd like and her words come across as curt and critical. That's particularly hurtful when it comes to Deirdre's child-rearing choices.

This tension boiled over when Yoon-Ji came to visit a month after Deirdre's second baby was born. At Deirdre's request, Yoon-Ji brought her a Korean-style baby carrier—about three yards of fabric with a strap "and no instructions," Deirdre says. Since Deirdre's mother never used the device with her children, she had no idea how it worked. Yoon-Ji suggested hoisting it on Deirdre's back, and she would try putting the baby in it. Since the baby was so small and had no neck support, Deirdre was worried and suggested they first practice with a sack of potatoes. "I said I need to get a feel for this first." Her mother said, "No, you don't." Her mother was offended that Deirdre didn't want to give it an earnest try. Her mother told her, "Everyone in Korea does it." Deirdre cautioned that since they weren't sure how it could be used safely, it might not make sense to try it. "She was angry with me and eventually she put it away in her suitcase and we never talked about it again. I really didn't think it was safe for a month-old baby," she adds.

Shortly after the incident, Deirdre heard her mother speaking in Korean to her sister, Deirdre's aunt, on the phone. Amid the Korean words, she said, in a sarcastic tone, "isn't safe" in English, conveying her disappointment that her daughter didn't think the Korean device was good enough for her granddaughter. Deirdre says the irony is, now that her daughter is a year old, she has her on her back all the time in a backpack. But her daughter's spine is now well developed, so it's safer than it would have been for a month-old baby. Recently, someone approached Deirdre on the street and said the backpack reminded her of a baby carrier she saw in Korea. Deirdre replied, emphatically, "Well, it's really different!"

Yoon-Ji was upset that Deirdre didn't use the carrier: "I wish she did it because it's a custom and culture," says Yoon-Ji. She was hurt that Deirdre rejected a baby carrier that has been used successfully by many generations of mothers in Korea. But, she says, the choice is Deirdre's, so she held her tongue. She's afraid that if she shared her feelings with Deirdre, the two would just get more upset with each other, "so when she hurts my feelings, I just don't say anything."

Yoon-Ji says she rarely gives advice to her daughter because "everything is her way. She acts like she knows more than I do." She says Deirdre reads more than she did and thinks she's more educated, so she doesn't listen to her mother's advice. She'll typically cut her mother off when she makes a suggestion and say, "I already know that," or "You already said that," which Yoon-Ji thinks is disrespectful. "In Korea, we have more respect for the elderly," she says. "I think the duty aspect is a difficult one," Deirdre responds. She says her mother expects unquestioning obedience and deference to elders, "but we weren't raised in the [Korean] culture, so there are things we don't catch that we should about how we treat our relatives."

Deirdre also says that these conflicts are often swept under the rug. "We're definitely a family of not talking about it." She frequently finds out her mother is upset with her by talking to her older sister, Sally Crain, since her mother often complains to her. Sally, age 46, lives in another California town. Unlike Deirdre, she's good at letting her mother's comments roll off her back. And Yoon-Ji says she has a far easier relationship with Sally than with Deirdre. "My older one listens and doesn't cut me off when I try to say something, but the younger one is a little bit different," she says. One reason for this difference is that Sally doesn't have children, so she's not subject to parenting advice in the same way that Deirdre is.

When Yoon-Ji talks about how she raised her children, Deirdre reacts in a hostile way, saying, "Look, Mom, I know everything I need to know, so don't tell me," Sally explains. Sally agrees with her mother that Deirdre's reaction can be extreme. Since she and her sister turned out well, her mother must have done something right and that it wouldn't hurt Deirdre to listen to her. Sally says her mother complains that Deirdre "snaps at her" and doesn't give her the chance to help with cooking when she visits, while Sally happily turns over her spatulas to her mom.

Sally wishes there was a way to mitigate the conflict because it pains her to see two people she loves fight so much. "I think Mom should be more sensitive to the things that bother Deirdre, and I think Deirdre needs to be more sensitive and better understand my mother's quirkiness," she says.

Like Deirdre, Libby Chang, 33, also argues with her mother about cultural practices. Libby says her mother views her child-rearing practices as a rejection of her Chinese heritage. Libby was born and raised in the United States and now lives in Oakland, California, with her husband and 21-month-old son, Edward. Her mother, Alma Chang, 60, migrated to the United States from Taiwan in 1970 when she was 23. Alma and her husband were committed to raising their children in the United States so the kids could have every opportunity for educational and financial success. Although Alma has been in the United States for nearly forty years, she clings to the child-rearing practices she witnessed growing up in a traditional Chinese household. Like Cheryl and Carol, Libby and Alma are constantly at odds over what they consider tried-and-true versus "cutting-edge" child-rearing practices.

Libby showed us a photograph of her mother enjoying a meal with her son. He's wearing a bib with cartoon dogs on it and both are smiling. From Edward's chubby cheeks, he appears a happy and healthy child. But Alma is worried that Libby is relying on illogical, newfangled ideas she gets from modern parenting books.

Libby and Alma have squabbled about everything from feeding Edward to his napping arrangements. Libby likes her baby to take naps, but Alma says he needs to stay up longer so that he'll be more tired at the end of the day. Alma also suggests waking him up from a nap so that he won't sleep too long and will be ready to go to bed at a reasonable hour at night. But Libby says, "I don't like to interrupt his sleep cycle," and she says her arguments are supported by books. "I told her I've read books and she's like, 'Why do you read books?'" When her mother babysits, Libby asks her to put her son down for a nap at a certain time "and I'm almost positive she doesn't follow my instructions."

Libby says her mother thinks that parenting books "fill my head with ridiculous notions, like allowing a baby to try to feed himself when he's one." Her mother, by contrast, parented more by instinct and from her memories of how she was parented. Libby says she's not a "voracious reader" of parenting books and that her background in developmental psychology and child development has made her more relaxed with her son. But she relies on certain books and Web sites as references, and talks with other moms to get advice. Alma wishes Libby would turn to her more than these other sources. Alma says to Libby, "I tell you what I think, but you don't really listen." Libby says that's deliberate because there are certain practices of her mother's she believes are harmful, like force-feeding. Instead of blindly following her mother's advice, Libby likes to research the issues so she can find the best approach to a problem. Alma is troubled when that approach differs from her parenting practices, since she sees that as a rejection of the way she did things.

It's not surprising that different generations of women hold different beliefs about the best way to raise a child, since preferred child-rearing practices are constantly changing. The movement away from a mother's natural know-how and toward professional advice has been evolving throughout the last century, argues Rima D. Apple, in her book *Perfect Motherhood*.[7] Young mothers in the mid-twentieth century followed the gospel of Dr. Spock, while Dr. T. Berry Brazelton became the go-to guy for parenting advice in the 1980s and 1990s. Women today are increasingly turning to their peers for advice, whether through chat rooms or books like the *What to Expect* and *Girlfriend's Guides* to pregnancy, babies, and toddlers. What's different today is the explosion of parenting information.

Researchers at the Center for Health Communication at the Harvard School of Public Health report that over fifteen hundred parenting books are in bookstores today; that's a whopping one-fifth of all psychology books in print. Over two hundred magazines are devoted to parenting and family life, not including women's or general-interest magazines. Child and family beat reporters are now on staff at most major daily newspapers, and child-related stories are a regular feature of the daily news. Even nightly television shows, like *Nanny 911*, offer advice on how to feed, bathe, and discipline one's child. Parents are exposed to information and advice on a daily basis. This tidal wave of information may make daughters feel their mothers' advice is obsolete. How can daughters follow the child-rearing advice they deem best, and, at the same time, show respect for their mothers' expertise and experience?

ADVICE FOR MOTHERS

Realize there's new information on parenting. Mothers of grown daughters need to accept that new information about parenting is published every day, and that new parents want to use some of that advice when they raise their child. Dr. Tom Sullivan says that when a woman insists her daughter engage in practices she used, he tells her that she made the right decisions *at that time,* but says, "Since then we've learned more about a baby's brain and discovered there was a lot we were doing wrong." For example, he takes issue with old-fashioned notions that you can teach your baby to sleep through the night at six weeks, or that letting the baby cry will make her self-sufficient. "That's totally out of step with what today's mothers are told," he says. He'll often suggest a modern parenting book for the mother to read so that she can learn the new information from an objective third party instead of being lectured by her daughter.

Don't take it personally. Daughters aren't rejecting their mothers' advice to be hurtful or obstinate. Rather, most new mothers feel they're parenting appropriately, so their mothers shouldn't feel offended or insulted, says Dr. Cohen-Sandler. Generation X women and women at the tail end of the baby boom generation rely more heavily on parenting books than previous generations.

Dr. Berman says the greatest conflicts between mothers and daughters occur when a mother believes she's a success only if her children turn out like her. The mother needs to accept that her daughter is an adult and she shouldn't try to control her, she says. She should also realize that there are many ways to raise a child; she shouldn't be hurt personally because her daughter isn't following in her footsteps.

Know when to back off. Ultimately, if a daughter rejects her mother's advice, it's her prerogative, Dr. Merrill says. Don't interject.

ADVICE FOR DAUGHTERS

Choose your words carefully. Women like Libby and Cheryl could tell their mothers they don't want advice, but in a less confrontational way, says Dr. Cohen-Sandler. She suggests saying: "I know you feel strongly about that and I respect it. I realize we disagree, but I'm going to do it this way."

Don't shut your mom out. Part of the wisdom that grandmothers have to offer is that they were once mothers themselves, says Dr. Sanford.

As a result, they *do* know more than their daughters about raising babies and should be able to impart that advice without feeling rejected, she says. Today's book-smart women may feel more comfortable turning to parenting guides than calling their mothers, but that's shortsighted, since a mother's valuable experience can be a helpful parenting tool, Dr. Sanford says. Dr. Pamela High adds that women should realize that mothers had a role in shaping some of their positive attributes and may have some experience to offer from having raised healthy, well-adjusted children.

Don't just rely on books. New mothers who rely too heavily on books or other research may find themselves reined in and anxious, says Dr. Sanford. In her practice, she sees many working mothers today who get fixed ideas about scheduling and routines and become "almost obsessed with doing things in a particular way." She also thinks that parenting guides can breed needless worry: "Parenting has become a high-anxiety situation, especially for older, more professionally successful moms, and I don't think that's necessarily positive."

Understand where your mom is coming from culturally. Women whose mothers were raised in different cultures need to recognize that their mothers absorbed very different lessons when they were young. For instance, in many Asian cultures, children are taught to respect their elders, says Sandoz-Merrill. In China, parents may disown children for minor acts, such as not coming to lunch every Sunday. They view the child as "willful" and uncooperative if they don't do what their parents ask. Mothers may not necessarily be trying to control their daughters; rather, they're simply behaving in accordance with their cultural upbringing. Rather than arguing, daughters today can simply tell their mothers "it's my turn" to be a parent now.

ADVICE FOR MOTHERS AND DAUGHTERS

Open communication can bring breakthroughs. Even though it takes courage for mothers and daughters to honestly share their feelings with one another, it's often worth the risk—as Cheryl found when she sent her mother the heartfelt e-mail message. Cheryl laid out her feelings, telling her mother how she felt hurt and judged when her mother likened Cheryl to an emotionally unstable relative. Instead of becoming angry or defensive, Carol told her she was a great mother and only wanted to help. It is this kind of breakthrough—where each honestly shares her fears and concerns—that ultimately will help mothers and daughters get along better. Too often, daughters are afraid that they'll hurt their mother if they express their concerns or that their mother will be defensive and that it won't do any good. But Cheryl's forthright, nonjudgmental e-mail to her mother demonstrates that this method can work.

Tips for E-mailing Mom

Convey your feelings in a clear and straightforward way. Avoid sarcasm or personal accusations, just as you would in face-to-face communication.

After you draft your message, e-mail it to yourself first. Read the message again when it arrives in your inbox, and ask yourself, "How would I respond to a message like this?" If the message makes you upset or angry, then rewrite it before sending it to your mom.

Remember that e-mail is still a novel form of communication for many older women. If your mother finds it impersonal and insensitive, it's best not to communicate via e-mail. Try to make the message more personal by inserting emoticons, like smiling faces.

Reply to your mother promptly. Just as Mom gets upset if you don't return her phone calls immediately, she may be upset that you don't answer her e-mail right away. Never mind that you have 173 yet-to-be-answered messages in your inbox. Your mother is a priority.

Make sure that others don't read your mother's e-mail. If she shares her e-mail account with her husband or other family members, you may want to reconsider the e-mail communication route.

Use e-mail only when it's most appropriate. Sensitive issues should be saved for face-to-face discussion. E-mail is impersonal and lacks nuance, tone of voice, and eye contact. It's best reserved for conveying factual information.

When you're busy, rely on e-mail. A quick message that says, "I'm thinking of you" or "I love you" can do wonders during those busy days when you can't get into a long telephone call. It may not be a fix-all, but can keep the lines of communication open on a regular basis.

Keep an open mind. Dr. Cohen-Sandler says both traditional and book advice have value. The key, however, is not seeing it as an either-or situation. When mothers and daughters feel the need to reiterate their arguments in an effort to convince the other, they become polarized. Instead, they have to see the merits in each approach—and then agree to disagree on the rest. It's wise for parents to have a number of different strategies—and information sources—for dealing with their children, since there's not one right way to raise a child, says Dr. Howard Weinblatt, a pediatrician in Ann Arbor, Michigan, and a clinical assistant professor at the University of Michigan Medical School: "Kids are like tax lawyers. If you give them a specific, carved-in-stone mode of parenting, they'll figure out a way around it."

Spare the Rod, Spoil the Child? Disputes over Discipline

From feeding the kids properly to teaching them the meaning of respect, moms are taking a radically different approach to discipline these days. Some mothers raising their children a generation ago saw the need for a highly structured home environment. Children were required to follow an explicit set of rules. Spanking was often considered an acceptable punishment for violating those rules. Yet we also spoke with free-spirited women raising their children in the late 1960s and early 1970s who wanted their children to find their own way. Their more conservative daughters are imposing far more order than their mothers. These generational differences in attitudes toward rules and punishments have created significant tensions for several mothers and daughters we spoke with.

We found that many daughters are choosing to discipline their children in a way that's the opposite of how they were disciplined. Women who suffered scars from the harsh punishment of their youth are relying on time-outs, talking things through, hearing their child's side of the story, and imposing few, if any, consequences for bad behavior. But their mothers fear that their daughters are raising children who are ill-mannered, poorly behaved, and disrespectful. At the other extreme, daughters of permissive parents want their children to have more order and stability than they had. Yet their mothers feel that this rigid approach makes their grandchildren less creative and independent.

Replacing Spankings with Time-outs

Tammy Mahoney, 44, whom we last saw in Chapter 5, says harsh discipline was the norm when she was growing up. Her mother hit out of frustration and to maintain control of her seven children. If they didn't go to sleep by their 8:00 P.M. bedtime after several warnings, their mother would come into their room and spank them in their beds. Tammy, the youngest, would often pretend to be sleeping so she could avoid the punishment.

Tammy says her mother's no-nonsense approach to discipline was the result of unhappiness with a life that turned out very different from what she envisioned as a young girl. Betty, now 79, longed to be a doctor. But once she married her husband, who was in the Navy, she decided not to pursue her dream. Tammy says that resentment over being cooped up with so many children often caused her mother to lash out in anger against them. She recalls often being frightened of her.

Naptimes were strictly enforced as well. Tammy says her mother forced all of the children to take naps with her long after they outgrew the need for them. They were required to lie still for fear of being yelled at for wiggling. "This was probably the scariest our mom would ever be," Tammy said.

Betty admitted to spanking her children "when nothing else would reach the child," usually when her children's bickering wouldn't cease. She said strict discipline was essential in turning out well-mannered, respectful children. She recalled one frigid winter afternoon, when after an endless day spent listening to sibling quarrels, she bundled up her children and sent them outside to run around the house several times before they could return.

Tammy, now a mother of two girls ages 7 and 9, works full-time as an education professor. She says she approaches discipline entirely differently for two critical reasons: it's easier to control only two children and she's a more content mother. "I didn't want to be angry as often as it seemed like she was. I think she was tired and overwhelmed," Tammy says. Tammy is convinced that with a fulfilling professional career, she's happier than her mother was and that makes her more patient and appreciative of the time she has with her children.

Tammy admits she's not a perfect mother, but she picks her battles and doesn't force her children to take naps, as her mother did. And, now that she's a mother, she understands why her mother imposed the nap rule—Mom needed a rest! When Tammy was pregnant with her second child and exhausted, she tried her mother's tactic, asking her then 2-year-old to cuddle and lie down with her. Just as Tammy was drifting off to sleep, her daughter, Paige, popped up and said, "I want a snack. I'm not tired." Tammy pleaded with her to settle down, saying, "Please, Paige, Mommy is so tired," but her daughter wouldn't relent. At this point, Tammy felt like throwing a tantrum herself. "I wanted to cry because the promise of a nap, almost realized, was snatched away." But instead of forcing her daughter to nap as her mother would have done, Tammy, in desperation, let Paige watch an educational video, nestling in the crook of her mother's legs on the couch while Tammy dozed. She knows that's something her mother wouldn't have tolerated and, as a mother of two, Tammy now understands her motivation. "Now I know the fatigue was hers and that she was the one who needed that nap," she says.

Tammy says her mother had more will to keep order in the house "and she raised us in a different time. We now live in a more child-centered world," Tammy says, and her disciplinary style reflects that shift. While she tries to be firm and consistent, "my personality is not as rigid as my mother's, so I don't mind many of things she wouldn't have tolerated."

Tammy says she has a gentler approach to discipline, using the word "un," as in unacceptable, when she's unhappy with her daughters' behavior. She also gives them time to think and calm down, and asks them what they think would be a fair consequence when they are out of line. She makes her expectations clear and then gives them one warning. She says that while she's more relaxed about discipline than her mother was, her children are bolder than she was. They don't fear Tammy the way Tammy feared consequences for bad behavior when she was a child.

Betty says her grandchildren aren't as well disciplined as her children were. For example, one of Tammy's nieces recently was reaching for a cookie from a bag of groceries. Her mother, Tammy's sister, told her she couldn't have it, but didn't take action when the child reached up and grabbed one anyway. She said the lack of consequence for that behavior doesn't help children to learn and internalize the rules.

Tammy says her mother tries to correct her children's behavior when she is at her house for dinner, insisting her children clean their plate. Tammy doesn't hesitate to "override her" when she feels her mother is overstepping her bounds. Tammy says her mother "reverts to being the mom and trying to teach them," instead of taking on the role of grandmother, the one who gives unconditional love and acceptance. She continues to discipline. "And her choices are different than mine," Tammy says.

Like Tammy, Mary Kleinschmidt, a 46-year-old attorney living in Indiana, takes a more lax approach to discipline than her mother. As a divorced mother of three teenagers, the job of disciplinarian falls on her. Her mother, Vivian Kleinschmidt, now 77, says that a more rigid posture on discipline—and getting her kids involved in helping out with chores—would make Mary's life easier. Mary says she talks to her children about how they need to pitch in because she has to work long hours at the office. Mary admits she falls into an ineffective pattern of telling her children several times to do a chore, like cleaning their room. Mary says she doesn't have the energy it takes to establish consistent rules. And guilt also plays a huge part. "I don't want this little bit of time I have with them to be me screaming for them to pick up their room and enforcing all these rules," she says. So she'll "just let it slide," rather than having the few hours a day with her children be filled with conflict.

"My mom feels I tolerate too much," she says. Mary has memories of being swatted with a wooden spoon or getting soap dragged across her teeth if she used profanity or talked back. Her mother burned cinnamon oil on her tongue to get her to stop sucking her thumb when she was 7. Vivian doesn't think Mary needs to use those same measures on her children. But she's suggested to Mary that she be firm and follow up with immediate consequences if the kids don't listen the first time.

Old-World Discipline: Protecting Children in an Unsafe World

Many of the daughters of immigrant women told us that their parents were particularly harsh in their use of punishment, in large part because they wanted to uphold values of respect and because they wanted to protect their children from American indulgences they viewed as unhealthy. Libby Chang recalls her parents frequently using corporal punishment. "They would use a stick and they would hit our legs. . . . They also made us kneel against the wall," she says. Alma was born in Taiwan, and insisted on maintaining her Chinese values and practices as she raised her children in the United States.

Libby suffered harsh physical punishment if she lied or talked back to her mother. Her mother's preoccupation with controlling her behavior didn't stop with physical punishment. She was worried Libby would be corrupted by what she saw as wild, undisciplined American teenagers, so she tried to limit Libby's contact with her friends, forbidding her from going out with them on weekends. Her mother also gave her no privacy. She didn't hesitate to open Libby's mail, rifle through her backpack, or listen in on her phone conversations. Libby came home once to see her room turned upside down because her mother had gone through it. In an effort to maintain privacy, Libby had her mail sent to her best friend's house. She would also sneak downstairs after midnight when her parents were asleep to talk to friends on the phone. "I think, looking back, I was a really good girl. I tried really hard to be good, but it was never enough," she says.

Alma believes she was only protecting her daughter, because parents are responsible for their children. Keeping close track of who Libby was hanging out with was the best way to raise her, she believes. She valued education and didn't want Libby "to be distracted by people who were a bad influence." She said Libby's friends were shady characters who could have corrupted her. She recalls coming across a note that Libby passed to her friends in class. The note instructed Libby on how to flirt with a lifeguard. "Disgusting," Alma said. "That's why we read your mail, because we had to know who your friends were and what they were telling you," she tells Libby.

Libby says her mother equated tough discipline with love. She proudly tells her daughter that the parents of her middle school friends "did not have parents who loved them as much as we loved you." Alma's concern about her daughter's middle school crowd prompted her to send Libby to an all-girls high school. She wanted to keep her away from those girls who were "passing notes and flirting with boys," she says. "We spent money to put you in a private school because we didn't want you to be around kids who were a bad influence," she says. She has no regrets about that decision.

Libby has adopted a much more lenient approach with her children. As an adolescent, she remembered thinking, "I never want to become this kind of parent" and she vowed not to recreate that environment for her kids. Now in a happy marriage, Libby tries not to be authoritarian with her 20-month-old son. She teaches him appropriate ways to talk and, once he's more verbal, plans to encourage him to question her disciplinary methods. When asked questions, she never plans to respond, "Because I said so" or "Because I'm your mother." She's hoping to facilitate more open lines of communication, where no topic is off-limits. Libby favors time-outs and having natural consequences for misbehavior, such as getting a poor grade if her son doesn't finish a homework assignment. She plans never to use "humiliating forms of punishment" and intends for her son and her future children to "feel that their opinions matter."

Alma thinks Libby's more lax discipline will be tested once Libby's son is older and more headstrong. Libby says her mother remains judgmental of all her actions and has no regrets about the way she disciplined her children. She says her mother is so rigid and stoic, it's difficult to communicate on an emotional level with her. And she doubts relations between them will improve. She feels her mother is "too embedded in patterns from childhood and things she acquired through her culture."

Permissive Parents and Disciplining Daughters

Most of the older women we interviewed adopted much stricter approaches to discipline than their daughters employed. But, in several cases, daughters raised in freewheeling homes badly wanted their children to have the order they lacked growing up. That's the case with Cassie Woodley, the 38-year-old mother of three children, ages 11, 13, and 16. Cassie, whom we met earlier in this chapter, runs a day-care center out of her own home in the Bay Area. She believes it's important to be home with her children and to provide some stability for them. Cassie's upbringing, by contrast, was one of total freedom, and Cassie and her younger sister, Sari, often felt adrift and in need of boundaries. Their mother, Marla Beech, now 59, was busy juggling single parenthood, graduate school, and paid work in the 1970s. She trusted that her children would do fine on their own.

Cassie recalls her childhood in the 1970s as one with no structure. "When I was six, my younger sister and I were allowed to ride the Boston subway alone," she marvels. She tries to maintain a tighter leash on her children and wants to know their whereabouts at all times. Her mother, Marla, thinks her daughter is "overly protective" and wishes she would lighten up.

Marla believes her daughters were fortunate to experience a life of adventure and freedom when they were young, something she always craved. For instance, when Cassie and Sari were 6 and 4, Marla moved her girls from a commune in Iowa to Boston "on a lark," according to

Cassie. Cassie remembers her childhood as a free-for-all, where her mother spent more time protesting the Vietnam War and going to school than raising her daughters. Cassie recalls that when she was 4 and her younger sister was 2 they took the Greyhound bus by themselves from Iowa City to Dubuque. "My mother thought it was fine, because she put us on the bus and my grandparents would meet us at the other end."

Cassie knows her mother disapproves of her disciplinary style. "She's told me many times I'm overprotective." She'll make an offhanded comment like, "They never get to do anything—they're old enough," and then drops it. "I don't think of myself as overprotective, although I am consciously different," Cassie says. For example, she forbids her children to ride their bikes in areas she doesn't think are safe. She feels her children need rules and boundaries to keep them safe, especially because she felt unsafe as a child.

When mothers and daughters make drastically different choices about fundamental issues like child discipline, it's hard for them not to question and doubt themselves. Our team of therapists offers advice for mothers and daughters who disagree on the best way to maintain order in their homes.

ADVICE FOR MOTHERS

Recognize that physical punishment has harmful repercussions. Both Dr. Mayerson and Dr. High, as well as other experts we spoke with, agree that physical punishment is not the way to go. Though it is still commonly practiced, it's based on a power differential and that power is often abused, Dr. Mayerson says. It's very easy to lose a sense of your own strength and become abusive. It doesn't help children learn alternative behaviors or problem-solving skills. It is mostly degrading and can be very harmful to a child's self-esteem.

Accept your daughter's choices; they're her kids. Mothers should trust that their daughters have given serious thought to their disciplinary tactics, and should appreciate their daughters' intelligence and thoughtfulness. For example, Libby has conducted research and thought about the pros and cons of her upbringing before deciding on her own parenting style. Libby feels her "trust-based discipline" is better than "fear-based discipline," since it emphasizes instruction over correction and uses discussion about choices to help the child act responsibly, says Carl Pickhardt, a psychologist based in Austin, Texas, and author of the book *The Connected Father*.[8] Dr. Pickhardt says that Libby needs to be clear with her mother that when it comes to her children, her own approach to discipline will prevail.

Recognize that just because your daughter takes a different path, she's not rejecting you or your culture. Women like Alma and Marla may feel their daughter's choice to parent differently is a rejection of the old traditions or cultural values that they hold close to their heart. Mothers should recognize that while daughters may still share fundamental values with their mothers, they are free to use different tactics than their mothers did.

ADVICE FOR DAUGHTERS

Learn to forgive. Whether one's mother was too strict or lenient, daughters need to forgive. Otherwise, they will parent reactively rather than proactively. By rejecting their mothers' strategies, they're avoiding practices they think are damaging, says Dr. High. She is impressed at how forgiving both Libby and Tammy were of their mother's strict disciplinary methods. They were remarkably empathetic and understanding of their mother's position. They were able to heal and give their parent a break, before moving on and doing what they thought was right.

Try to understand your mother's culture. In some cultures, like China, happiness is not defined by the well-being of the individual but collectively by the family's well-being, explains Dr. Mayerson. Individuals are expected to sacrifice for the sake of the family. A "good" mother is defined by her children's adherence to these cultural norms. Physical punishment is a common strategy for Chinese families to discipline their children. If Alma remained in Taiwan, she wouldn't have to define her children's boundaries so rigidly. But, because Western culture was perceived as a threat to her values, it increased her anxiety and resulted in an even more rigid stance. And Alma can look to her daughter as proof that her techniques worked, since she views her as a good daughter. By gaining insight into Alma's culture, Libby may better understand her mom's motivations—however drastic they seemed at the time—even though she's chosen a different course for herself.

Share your fears with your mother. Daughters who were afraid of their parents when they were growing up should feel free to tell them, says Bobbie Sandoz-Merrill. She suggests that Libby and Tammy let their mothers know how they felt when they were victims of corporal punishment, saying something like, "I was scared of you. I didn't like it," and telling their mothers that arguing about it dredges up the same feelings now.

Take a break from Mom. If the feuds over discipline don't stop, and worse yet, if they generate painful memories of one's past, it may be wise to take a short break from Mom. If the mother doesn't comply, the daughter can say, "I'm going to take a break from you and we'll try again," and then go a couple of weeks without seeing her. The message needs to be delivered calmly, without fighting or dumping on the mother about how horrible her childhood was. If it's delivered from a "high place in yourself" without getting into a screaming match, or even through a letter "to keep it from getting hot," it will be effective, Sandoz-Merrill says. The daughter needs to let her mother know that "this is my time and this is how I'm going to handle it." and "As a child I had no choice. Now I do."

Kids need limits, so set them. Maybe mothers of a generation ago were stricter than their daughters think is appropriate. Still, Dr. High believes that young children, as well as teens, benefit from having routine and regularity in their day. Young children need to know what's expected of them and what to expect from their world. Practices like a regular bedtime routine, a consistent wake-up time, and eating meals together are important for maintaining stability. It's easy for everyone to get off on their own tracks, especially with more independent, busy teenagers, but "children who have no limits" and no predictable routines in their lives "have problems," Dr. High says. Imposing limits is a form of love that parents show their children. And it's critical for parents to set limits if they hope to earn the respect of their children.

Contracting Out Child Care: The Nanny Divide

One of the most sweeping social changes in the past half-century has been the influx of mothers into the labor force. In 1960, just 11 percent of married women with preschool age children were working for pay; this climbed to 30 percent by 1970, and more than 60 percent by 2000. As more mothers of young children spend the day at work, they face difficult decisions over who will care for their children. Over the past three decades, media pundits have debated passionately whether children fare as well in child care as they do under parent care. Results from the longest-running study of American child care, the Study of Early Child Care and Youth Development, released in March 2007, show that keeping a preschooler in a day-care center for a year or more made it more likely he or she would become disruptive in the classroom—a condition that persisted through the sixth grade.[9] But these effects were small. The most important influence was the *quality* of care received, regardless of who was providing that care.

Mothers of a generation ago, many of whom stayed home to raise their children, couldn't fathom hiring someone to care for their own children full-time. Yet most of them understood their daughters were doing the best they could, given their busy work schedules. Many were pleased with the child-care centers their daughters selected; they thought they were well run and provided wonderful enrichment for the kids. The big exception, however, was with at-home care. They're extremely fearful about what goes on with the nanny behind closed doors once Mom heads to work. And many grandmothers, especially immigrant women, feel the nanny is taking on many tasks that should fall squarely on the mother, like picking the kids up from preschool, arranging playdates, and shopping for clothes.

Brenda Sherman, whom we last met in Chapter 5, believes her

daughter's nanny is too rigid with the children. Her daughter, Karen Levi, counters that the nanny does a wonderful job. Brenda and Karen spoke honestly with each other about the issue when we met with them in Karen's living room one crisp autumn night. Karen works long hours running her rapidly expanding business importing jewelry from Israel. She employs twenty designers to provide goods for her business. To manage her long and stressful work days she's hired a 58-year-old nanny to care for her two children, ages 2 and 4½. "She's like a second me," Karen says. The nanny runs errands, makes trips to the post office, and handles grocery shopping and cooking. Recently, Karen sent her to Old Navy to buy clothes for the kids.

The nanny has worked for Karen for the past three years. Karen appreciates her competence and her ability to "take care of every-thing." She also feels that the nanny, a Seventh Day Adventist, is morally sound, shunning alcohol and caffeine because of her religious beliefs. The kids also seem to adore her, crying, "Louise, I want you to stay!" when it is time for her to leave at the end of the day. She often buys supplies for art projects and is "more creative than I am," Karen says. She says having a nanny in her home is a great arrangement, one that allows her to work at home near her children, yet be assured they're well cared for and entertained.

Brenda doesn't mind Karen delegating household responsibilities to the nanny, but she thinks the nanny takes on too many responsibil-ities that should be Karen's. "I don't always think the nanny is wonder-ful," Brenda admits. She feels the nanny is too strict with Karen's children and reprimands them frequently. If one of the kids throws something on the floor, she tells them to pick it up. Karen shrugs, "I have no problem with that."

Karen agrees that the nanny is stricter, and corrects the children more often than either she or her mother. That's fine with Karen. "Well, I never thought people needed so much correction," chimed in Brenda. "I don't think she's doing it as much as you think she is," Karen told her mother. Karen says even though she doesn't insist her children keep their clothes tidy, she's fine with the nanny taking on that job. "I'm not willing to fight with them about everything they throw on the floor, but if she wants to fight with them about it, I don't mind the lessons she's teaching them." Brenda is worried about the nanny's strict discipline style, but she has a much bigger concern with the nanny spending so much time with Karen's children. She wishes Karen wouldn't outsource so much parenting to the nanny, who she feels is a poor substitute for their mother.

Recently, Karen's nanny decided to leave, so she's hired a 19-year-old who wears flashy clothes and has tattoos on her ankle. The kids like her and haven't requested their previous nanny. Even so, Karen says, "I can tell my mom thinks she's total white trash," and she disapproves of the second nanny as much as the first. To Brenda, who feels that the mother should be with the children, no nanny is good enough for her grandchildren.

The belief that there's no substitute for having a mother or father with the children all day is a common view in the United States today—despite the fact that 63 percent of preschool age children of working mothers are in some type of child-care arrangement each week. A recent Gallup Poll shows that 58 percent of Americans think at least one parent should be home with the kids. The belief that family should care for the children was especially important to the immigrant mothers we interviewed. For them, no nanny was an appropriate substitute for blood relatives.[10]

That's certainly true for Alma Chang and her daughter, Libby. Alma emigrated from Taiwan and she, her husband, and children, settled in Wisconsin, where there were very few other Asian families. Alma stayed home to raise her children when they were young since her husband told her she didn't need to work.

Libby has fond memories of her childhood. She helped her mother cook, and they had entertaining after-school outings together. Alma enjoyed being home to teach her children math and Chinese and monitor their television viewing. She particularly enjoyed hearing them practice piano after school. "I couldn't possibly ask someone else" to watch the children, she says. When Libby was 14 and the family moved to California, Alma started a job as a real estate agent to supplement the family income, since the cost of living was so much higher there. She hired a babysitter, but felt that was okay since the children were teenagers and could tell her if something went awry with the sitter in charge.

Libby, now a graduate student and baker living in Oakland, California, has a life that's very different from her mother's. Both she and her husband work, so she's hired a nanny to care for her 20-month-old son, Edward. She shares the nanny with another family and she's extremely happy with her. Even so, she's acutely aware of her mother's feelings on the subject. "She doesn't think that someone outside of the family should take care of my son," she says. Libby says her mother thinks the only option is for Libby to stay home or for her mother to care for Edward. But Libby is uncomfortable having her mother, who she says is an alcoholic, in charge of her son and believes that the nanny she hired is better equipped to care for him. Alma worries that since he is so young, he's incapable of telling his mother if the nanny does something wrong. She'll question Libby, saying, "Why are you sending Edward to the nanny today? Why can't you stay home with him?" Libby says that since her mother couldn't imagine hiring a stranger to watch her children when they were young, she can't possibly empathize with Libby's situation.

Libby has told her mother that she screened the nanny carefully and put her through a trial period. She's also let her know that the nanny teaches Edward so much and loves him. "But it's never enough" to satisfy her mother. "Family is the best," Alma counters. "Nobody will take care of him like family." She says Libby has no way of knowing what the nanny will feed him, and if something bad happens to him, the nanny won't tell her. "I don't know how you can trust strangers to take care of him," she says. Though Libby is pleased with her child-care arrangement, having to endure her mother's criticisms is a constant source of frustration.

Libby, Karen, and nearly all of the daughters we interviewed were pleased with their child-care arrangements. But on a rare occasion child-care arrangements will go awry and the children's grandmothers feel compelled to express their concern. Ten years ago, when Angela Pennington was 38 and working for the Defense Department in Washington, D.C., she had a "nanny emergency," and her mother, Peggy Pennington, 77, of Fort Wayne, Indiana, couldn't hold her tongue about how "appalled" she was.

Angela had a mother's worst nightmare come true when she arrived home from work one day. Her nanny was watching Angela's 6-month-old daughter, Eve, as she did every day. On this particular day, though, she also was supposed to look after Angela's 5-year-old niece, Elise. When Angela arrived home from work, Elise told her that Eve had been screaming in her crib when Elise got home from kindergarten. A confused Angela tried to piece together what that meant, and "it dawned on me," she says. Angela confronted the nanny and asked her whether she left the baby alone at home when she went to pick up Elise from school. The nanny told Angela that the baby was sleeping when it was time to go, and she didn't want to wake her.

"At first, I couldn't believe it," said Angela, who now lives in Vermont. "I went through the roof." Elise's school was a fifteen-minute drive each way, and the nanny often had problems keeping track of her keys, making for a potentially dangerous situation. Angela's neighbor later told her she often saw the nanny leave the baby alone while she went into town to go shopping and wondered why she didn't take the baby with her.

Angela was shocked that the nanny, who came from a highly regarded agency, could do such a thing. Angela describes her as an intelligent young woman from Kenya who was taking classes at a nearby college. Angela understood that, in the small village where her nanny came from, everyone took care of each other, and it may not have been uncommon to leave children alone. Even so, she feels her nanny was in the United States long enough to know that "leaving a child alone just wasn't good sense."

Despite this disastrous experience, Angela continued to use in-home care for her daughter. She felt that Eve was too young for day care, and she preferred to keep her at home. She ultimately opted for a nanny who had a life, "but not too much of a life," and would be more focused on her daughter. She decided to share a nanny with another family so both could "look over her shoulder." She hired an older woman who recently immigrated to the United States from India. The arrangement has worked out well.

Although Angela thinks everything turned out well in the end, her mother, Peggy, disagrees: "You run a risk" when you leave your child with a stranger and "you have no idea" what's going on. Though Peggy is sympathetic, she didn't hesitate to tell her daughter that the nanny fiasco was a good reason to consider cutting back on work. Peggy was a stay-at-home mom, so she never had to deal with child-care issues.

Working mothers like Angela often must rely on child care. Nearly 11 million preschool children in the United States are in some type of regular child care each week. The average preschool child of a working mother spends thirty-six hours per week in child care. The most common types of care are grandparent care or child-care centers, although more affluent families are relying on nannies and other in-home care providers.[11] Mothers who advise their daughters simply to "stay home with the kids" aren't being realistic. Rather, our team of therapists offers some practical ways for mothers and daughters to overcome their differences of opinion about paid child care.

ADVICE FOR MOTHERS

Competence, not genes, matters most. The concept of relying on someone other than a parent to care for a child goes back hundreds of years to when people lived in tight-knit communities and there were "communities of caregivers," explains Dr. Sanford. The notion that a mother should be solely responsible for her child in isolation from the community is a narrow idea that prevailed only since the mid-twentieth century. What's most important is that the caregiver be mature, competent, and loving. Dr. Weinblatt emphasizes that affection is as important as competence. Having a nanny who is "crazy about the kids" is crucial in the child's first and second year of life. Dr. Weinblatt's mantra is that kids need at least one adult figure "who has an irrational attachment to them," and the more they have, the better. A qualified caregiver doesn't have to be Mom, a grandparent, or a family member. It could be anyone who can provide a secure emotional environment for a child.

Like Mary Poppins, the nanny can sometimes be better than Mom. "Being loved by many different people helps children develop confidence and a sense of security about themselves," so multiple caregivers can be good for a child, says Dr. Sanford. What the nanny has to offer won't be the same as the mom, but it can still be very valuable since everyone brings their own unique abilities, talents, and resources to a relationship, she says. Dr. Weinblatt goes a step further, saying that, in some instances, the nanny may be better than the mother at some aspects of parenting.

ADVICE FOR DAUGHTERS

Understand where Mom is coming from. Mothers of adult women today come from a different generation, when it was widely believed that no one could be a suitable substitute for a mother. Many women chose to stay home, even if it meant casting aside their career dreams.

Careful selection and supervision are key. Unlike day-care centers, where no caregiver is left alone and aberrant behavior is caught and disciplined, leaving a child in the care of someone at home is riskier. Daughters (or their mothers, if they're very concerned) could perform spot checks, where they periodically stop in unannounced. Spending time at home when the nanny is there is also important.

ADVICE FOR MOTHERS AND DAUGHTERS

Impose some limits on the issue. Grandmothers who are concerned something is awry with the nanny can tell their daughter, in a delicate way. Daughters can accept the message in the spirit it's intended. But, generally, this isn't a subject that mothers should weigh in on. A daughter can say to her mother, "I feel differently than you do. I'm making a different choice." She can reassure her mother that she plans to keep a close watch on the nanny to ensure it's the best situation for the children.

CHAPTER 7

From Playing Outside to Playdates and PlayStations: Changing Ideas About Children's Social and Emotional Growth

Why do you push them so hard? Does my grandchild really need ballet and swimming and Chinese lessons?

With so many electronic toys, how will they learn to use their imaginations?

My granddaughter has such pretty hair. Why can't she wear it down, instead of hiding it in a ponytail?

Susan Greene lives in a 6,000-square-foot home, situated on two rolling acres in a posh suburb just outside of New York City. She and her husband work full-time, so they rely on a team of household staff to look after their kids, tend the garden, and manage the cooking, cleaning, and laundry. Susan's daughters, ages 9 and 12, have such tightly packed schedules they could probably use their own social secretary. After a long day at their demanding private school, the girls dash off to religious school, tennis lessons, soccer practice, or Girl Scout meetings. Weekends are filled with playdates and elaborate birthday parties, including "goodie bags" filled with T-shirts, tote bags, and soccer balls. Susan says her kids and their classmates aren't spoiled by their lavish lifestyle; it's the only life they know. Her mother, Eva Cohen, disagrees and thinks her granddaughters' fast-paced, extravagant upbringing could make them spoiled and materialistic. She wonders how their overly scheduled, hectic lives will affect them, and Susan, over the long haul.

Parents today are finding that child-rearing is no longer fun and games. Middle-class parents are told their kids need to start building a résumé for an Ivy League college when they're still in elementary school. A generation ago, parents provided their children with love, food, shelter, and weekly piano lessons or Little League practice. These days, many parents feel obligated to nurture their children's potential with a dizzying schedule of lessons, playdates, and tutoring sessions. Their definition of what a child needs is vastly different than their mothers'. What's happening is more than just a shift in thinking about after-school schedules; rather, a shift in values has occurred, with mothers and daughters holding widely divergent views about what makes a happy, well-adjusted child. Whether the topic is responsibility for chores, talking about feelings, or attending religious school, generational differences in thinking about a child's needs are straining mother-daughter relationships today.

Quality Time Versus Quantity Time: Is "Just Being There" Enough?

Mothers who work full-time worry about how they'll spend cherished evening and weekend hours with their children. A generation ago, mothers often were home all day with their children, or at least during the after-school hours. Because they were with their children much of the day, they were less inclined to scrutinize their children's every word, deed, or emotion. What's more, many women like Peggy Pennington, now 77, were busy preparing dinner or tidying the house when their children came home from school, so they couldn't sit down for an impromptu game of Chutes and Ladders. Today, many of their daughters feel they must fill their precious family time with heart-to-heart talks and a slew of enrichment activities. These generational differences raise two key questions: What matters more for kids, quality time or quantity time? And are the two mutually exclusive? We've found that mothers and daughters often don't see eye-to-eye on the best way to spend time with the kids, and that's often a source of strife between them.

Defining Togetherness: Being in the Same Room or Being on the Same Page?

When Peggy Pennington was raising her children in the mid-1960s, she (and most of the mothers she knew) stayed at home in the conservative Indiana town where she still lives today. She believes strongly that there are tremendous advantages to "being there" every day with your children. Her daughter Angela, however, feels it's more important to be there emotionally than physically. On the wall in Angela's historic home, amid dozens of family photographs, there's a picture of her mother, taken when she was a young woman. Peggy looked every bit the quintessential Camelot-era mother, with her short, dark perfectly coiffed hair, and her long dress accessorized by pearls and pumps. In the photo, she's surrounded by her husband and three angelic-looking, tow-headed girls, each with pageboy haircuts, party dresses, and Mary Jane shoes. This glamorous image belies the more mundane activities of Peggy's life. Her days were spent on the tedious tasks of washing diapers, cleaning house, and preparing meals, like beef stew, spaghetti, and hamburgers. Every night, her family sat down to a full three-course meal: two vegetables, a salad, and a main dish.

Peggy's daughters, Angela and Kami, have arranged their lives very differently. Angela has scaled the ranks of the business world, working in various journalism and government positions, while her sister Kami has been a successful consultant. Peggy is proud of her daughters' professional accomplishments, and admits that she's just a bit green with envy. She has often told her daughters that if she hadn't married and had children, she could have been one of the first women CEOs of a major corporation. Still, Peggy is a product of her traditional upbringing and believes that her daughters' professional lives prevent them from witnessing their children's daily milestones. While her daughters retort that it's the quality, not the quantity, of time that matters, Peggy says she has an issue with the "quality time" concept, since "the little ones may run home excited and you may not be there."

She says you can't predict exactly when a special moment will occur: "They change so much in those first few years, and it's sad to miss it." Peggy is gratified she was home with her children, and feels she was there when they needed her.

When her daughter Kami hears her mother's recollections of the past, she chuckles. We met with Kami on a gray, overcast day in Vermont. She and her family had just flown in from their Colorado home to visit with her sister Angela. The two sisters, who are joined by Angela's 11-year-old daughter, Ella, talk about their childhood over lunch at a hotel restaurant, where Angela is attending a conference. The sisters bear a strong physical resemblance and have the identical voice and laugh. Kami and Angela both believe they have good relationships with their mother, and they agree she provided them with a wonderful childhood. But they do take issue with her memories of how they spent their time together.

Kami has vivid memories of at least two occasions when her mother was physically there but not emotionally available to her girls. When Kami was 9, she was walking home from school when she witnessed a school bus slam into a moving car. The teenage girl driving the car was killed instantly. This was particularly traumatic for Kami because she knew the girl who had died. When Kami made it home twenty minutes later, she was horribly shaken by what she had witnessed. "I remember walking in the door and screaming, 'Mom! Mom!'" Her mother's response? "Shhh, honey, I'm on the phone!" She would not get off the phone, Kami says. It seemed like she was "always doing something else."

Another time, when Kami was 5, she and Angela were in the backyard and Angela started putting pussy willows in her nose, seeing how far she could sneeze them out. Kami, eager to mimic her older sister, gave it a try, but they got stuck in her nose. Kami recalls Angela running into the house, screaming, "Mommy! Mommy! Kami's got pussy willows stuck up her nose!" Her mother's response? "Shhh, I'm busy. I'm on the phone." Of course, when Peggy did finally get off the phone, she promptly whisked her daughter to the doctor's office.

Angela has few memories of her mother playing with her and her sisters. By contrast, she says she focuses 100 percent on her kids when she's with them, playing games and reading stories. Kami also says she has "more engaged time with my kids" and takes the time to play with them on the floor, something her mother never did. When she was working full-time, she missed the kids so much that she couldn't wait to play with them when she got home. "When you're there all the time," she says, "it's 'Yeah, honey, I have to do this'" and there's always a distraction. Even though Kami quit her job six months ago and is now home with the kids all day, she says she's making a conscious effort to be more focused on her children in a way that her mother, preoccupied with talking on the phone, cooking, cleaning, volunteering, and other pursuits, was not.

Kami and Angela have pointed out an important distinction: just because a mom is home with her children all day doesn't mean that she's *parenting* them all day. Likewise, just because parents are away all day doesn't mean that they're necessarily neglecting their children emotionally. A recent study by sociologists Suzanne Bianchi, John Robinson, and Melissa Milkie (*Changing Rhythms of American Family Life*) offers data to support Kami and Angela's observations: the actual amount of meaningful time that parents and kids have together has remained fairly stable over the past forty years, even though women are far more likely to be working outside the home today.[1]

Using data from time diaries kept by parents, the researchers found that parents have actually increased the number of hours they devote to "enriching activities," like reading and playtime. Bianchi and colleagues say their study "refutes any notion that quality activities have been sacrificed as time constraints on employed parents have increased." (As we show in Chapter 9, working women are sacrificing personal time and private time with their husbands.) The study also helps to explain why women like Kami and Angela sound a bit defensive when they compare their parenting style with their mother's round-the-clock availability: the standards for what parents "should" be doing have risen exponentially. As Bianchi and colleagues observe, the requirements for effective and good mothering have increased at the same time that "there are expanded opportunities for women to do other things with their time, such as devoting themselves to full-time jobs."

The Importance of a Child's Inner Life

In our interviews, we found that there are two main areas where the "good mothering" expectation has been ratcheted up most: tending to a child's emotional, or inner, life and providing children with the skills, activities, and resources they'll need to survive in an increasingly competitive educational system and economy. (We'll talk about the second issue later in this chapter.) Several daughters we spoke with said they wanted badly to attend to their children's most private emotional needs because they felt they never developed a particularly close emotional bond with their mother.

That's certainly the case with Terri Romero, a 44-year-old marketing executive and the mother of twin 7-year-old girls. Terri works long hours and admits she wants to make her scarce time with her daughters meaningful. Although her mother, Louise Goldfarb, now 72, also worked when her children were school-age, her job as a teacher allowed her to be home after school and in the summer.

Terri believes she's an excellent mother, even though she spends less time with her children than her mother did. Terri recalls when she was growing up, she and her mother wouldn't talk about feelings or emotional issues. Recalling her childhood as one of five children, Terri says "I didn't feel there was an interest in what was going on in my inner life, and every kid's got an inner life. I didn't get that from my mother and work hard to do that with my kids." Terri and her daughters frequently talk about feelings. She says her daughter recently confided in her that she "feels different from other girls" and "gets embarrassed" about things that don't bother her peers. Terri is saddened when her daughter talks about her insecurities, but she's grateful she feels comfortable opening up to her. "That's how you build self-esteem; you go through your feelings and discuss them with someone you trust."

Terri regrets that she and her mother never talked about personal issues Terri experienced growing up. Terri says she hasn't trusted her mother since the time she read Terri's diary and that the two don't have a particularly deep emotional bond today. She doesn't think they ever will. Resigned, she says, "You don't go to the hardware store for apples. I don't go to my mother for that kind of support."

Tanya Sedona, a 36-year-old art teacher at an after-school center and the mother of an adopted 11-year-old son, recalls a childhood very similar to Terri's. However, Tanya's mother, Marianne Platt, died two years ago, so Tanya will never have a chance to connect emotionally with her. As a result, Tanya is now completely convinced that it's important to talk to her son openly about his fears and feelings.

Tanya grew up in a traditional working-class household in Fresno, California. Her mother was a stay-at-home mom and housewife. "She was married to the same man from the time she was eighteen until she was widowed at age sixty-five," Tanya says. Tanya, by contrast, cherishes her much more free-spirited life. She met her husband when she was 20 and he was 19. "We started living together almost immediately. That was really hard on my mom because it was so out of the norm for her generation." They lived together for fourteen years before getting married and decided to tie the knot only when they adopted their son. "I guess we were kind of a modern-day hippie couple. We just never felt we needed a government piece of paper to prove our love." To give their son stability, though, they decided to make their relationship "legal."

Tanya and her husband adopted their son, Josh, when he was 7. Tanya recounts how Josh came into their lives. He was in Tanya's after-school day-care center for three years and had foster parents. One day, his foster mother told Tanya that Josh wouldn't be returning next year because she would no longer be his foster parent. "I raised my hand and said, 'We'll take him!'" Tanya recalls.

Tanya is raising her son very differently than the way she was raised, especially when it comes to sexual issues. Just the other day, Josh asked her, "Mom, why do you have a tampon in your purse?" She was unfazed and explained how a woman's monthly menstrual cycle works. "I'm just really open, and I'll answer his questions," Tanya says. That response wouldn't have come from her mother, who would typically respond, "You'll learn when you're older." Tanya recalls another recent episode where her son had a dream he lost his mom and dad. He held out his hand and asked, "Can you hold my hand for a while?" Tanya told him, "You will never lose us." Then, she hugged her son.

Tanya is saddened that she and her mother never had such conversations. Even when her mother was on her death bed, she never revealed her feelings. When Tanya would ask her, "How do you feel?" her mother would respond matter-of-factly, "Well, I don't like what's happening, if that's what you mean." Tanya tried to get her mother to open up: "I mean, how do you feel in your heart?" Her mother couldn't answer Tanya's probing question. During the five weeks prior to her death, "I never knew how she was feeling or what she was thinking about. It just never came up." Tanya feels she has lost out on something special with her mother—those poignant moments of really understanding each other. She's determined to make sure she and her son have those moments of deep connection.

In the past thirty years, the ways parents think about nurturing their children have shifted drastically. This is nothing new: the rules of parenting are constantly evolving, argues Ann Hulbert in her book *Raising America.* The most recent change has been a shift from a discipline-focused, parent-centered emphasis to a child-centered focus that stresses warmly encouraging a child's emotional and social development. Although it's hard to pinpoint exactly when one approach came into style and the other went out of vogue, Hulbert notes that the "learning-by-loving-and-listening child-rearing ethos" flourished in the late 1970s, when surging numbers of baby boomers became parents.

An undeniable consequence of this shift is that women today are parenting their kids differently than their own mothers did. They often feel the need to defend how they allocate their time and emotional energy with their children. In the process, they may end up maligning each other's choices. How can mothers and daughters come to accept each other's definitions of "quality" time with children, and stop engaging in the criticisms that women like Kami, Angela, and Peggy sling at each other? Our therapists offer a few pieces of advice.

ADVICE FOR DAUGHTERS

Look to ordinary events to bond with your child. If you think back to your own childhood and recall the times you felt closest to your parent, it was probably during an ordinary event, like passing your father tools when he fixed the car or baking Halloween cookies with your mother. "Those are the moments that bond parent and child together, not going to Disneyworld," says Dr. Howard Weinblatt. These seemingly ordinary exchanges can generate an emotional and intellectual connection between parent and child. Mothers of a generation ago who looked to simpler forms of interaction have a valid point, he says.

Take your child to work. Mothers today have a unique opportunity that their mothers often didn't have, to expose their child to their professional world. If doing the dishes with your child isn't your idea of a meaningful bonding experience, then involve him or her in your professional life. For instance, a chemistry professor might say to her child, "Why don't you come to the lab with me today, and I'll give you some test tubes to play with while I grade papers?" The child may say, "I'm cool. I get to go to the lab." That way, you're bonding with each other and giving your child a glimpse into your other world, says Dr. Weinblatt.

Don't use your children to right your parents' wrongs. A grown-up daughter who is still smarting from her childhood wounds is likely to be a mother with a vengeance, says Dr. Elizabeth Berger, a New York–based child psychiatrist and author of the book *Raising Kids with Character*.[2] She may have trouble responding to her children with empathy, because she always has something to prove. Her children cannot simply be themselves—they carry the burden of being their mother's badge of honor, a walking advertisement that she is not a bit like her mother. Daughters should try to mother in the way they think is best, rather than avoiding an approach they believe is the worst.

ADVICE FOR MOTHERS AND DAUGHTERS

Consider whether the issue is truly about time use or about something else. The stories that Kami and others relayed aren't really about "time," says Dr. Berger. Instead, she believes each has to do with a daughter's belief that her mother was not emotionally responsive to her in moments of crisis or uncertainty. Once daughters start reflecting on differences between their child-rearing styles and those of their mothers, they think about their own pasts and focus on those "wrongs" that they feel their mothers have done to them.

Can—or should—debates over child-rearing serve as an opportunity for daughters to revisit emotional issues from their own past? Dr. John Northman says the issue is how to generate emotional intimacy when there isn't a history of one. Instant intimacy "is like wanting to buy an antique made to order. You can't do it. You can't microwave something that needs to be marinated."

Although Dr. Northman believes that some daughters may be setting themselves up for disappointment if they strive for newfound intimacy with their mothers, he recognizes that sometimes a happy ending is possible. He suggests that mothers and daughters ask themselves two key questions: "What are we trying to attain, and to what extent is that likely to happen? And if we do achieve that, what are the possible downsides?" If mothers and daughters both want to grow closer, their efforts at increased intimacy are almost certainly worth it. However, "if they're on different pages, then maybe they want to leave well enough alone."

Treat every day together as if it's your last. If your mother or daughter were to die tomorrow, would you have any regrets about what you've recently done or said? Tanya, for one, is sorry she and her mother never bonded at a deep emotional level. Mothers and daughters should try hard to make every encounter count. When they hang up the telephone or end a weekend visit together, they should leave feeling satisfied about their time together. It's important to have as few regrets as possible about one's relationship as those regrets can't be resolved once the relationship ends.

Extracurricular Activities: Going Overboard or Essential Enrichment?

When today's mothers were children three decades ago, they filled their summer days and after-school hours with bike rides to the park, loosely organized games of frozen tag, and reenactments of their favorite movie scenes—with minimal, if any, parental supervision. That kind of free, unencumbered play is rare today. Houses are farther apart, sidewalks have disappeared, neighborhoods have fewer children, and many parents are away all day at work, so kids are often cared for elsewhere. Parents are focused on helping their children unleash their hidden talents, so they're introducing them to an ever-expanding array of after-school activities: tae kwon do, violin lessons, Irish step dancing, soccer, and so forth. These activities keep the kids—and their parents—busy much of the time when they're not in school. While parents believe these activities will provide a richer childhood than they had and help prepare their kids for the competitive college admissions process, grandparents often think their grandchildren are exhausted, spread too thin, and in dire need of some healthy downtime.

Angela told us that her kids' activity schedule is the major bone of contention between her and her mother. "My mother believes my kids are completely overscheduled," she says. The "average" day for Angela's 11-year-old daughter includes school, followed by play rehearsals from 5:00 to 11:00 P.M., including drive time to and from, four times a week, as well as piano, voice, and skiing lessons on the weekend. "We'd run directly from skiing to play rehearsals on Sunday afternoon," Angela says. Although she says this tightly packed schedule was "the peak" of the activities—her daughter doesn't always have a play in production—she is eager to cultivate her daughter's interests through a broad range of activities that keep her and Ella's two younger brothers, ages 3 and 6, on the go. "Ella's the oldest and that's what she likes. She thrives on it." Ella is a fair-haired, smiling, precocious child, happy to chime in on our conversation with Angela and bolster her mother's argument that she's pleased with this kind of rigorous schedule.

Angela says it's tough to find a quality theater company in her small Vermont town, so she's willing to drive her daughter to the best one in the area, which is a seventy-five-minute drive from their home. She either takes her boys along or drops Ella off and has her husband handle pickup when the rehearsal ends. Angela says her daughter loves it. "What can you say to your kid if she wants to do theater? That you can't be in it because there's nothing around here?" Angela says theater is a huge time commitment, but her daughter loves it, as does her 6-year-old brother, himself a budding thespian, so the efforts are worth it. Angela, a stay-at-home mom who once worked for the government when she lived in Washington, D.C., says there's a trade-off. "I couldn't work full-time and do the driving I do."

Angela's mother, Peggy, says her children didn't spend their after-school hours being chauffeured from one activity to the other. They lived across the street from a park, and they'd ride their bikes there or go to the city's public swimming pool. "They were on their own a bit more. Things didn't move as quickly as they do today," she says. As for her daughter's children, she says, "I think she has them in too many activities." She questioned Angela's decision to send Ella to a six-week theater camp last summer; Peggy thinks her granddaughter is too young to be away from home for such a long time. She understands Ella is very talented and interested in theater, but she believes her schedule takes a toll on the entire family. The parents, she says, "become an extension of the steering wheel, getting them around to all of these things." She also believes such a jam-packed schedule gets in the way of other important family activities, like sharing a simple dinner at home, and she questions whether an 11-year-old really needs to be involved in so many different pursuits. She worries that so much structured activity will stifle her granddaughter's ability to be creative and imaginative.

Peggy is not alone in her worries. Lenore Hopkins, 59, also questions whether her daughter is going overboard by arranging her family's entire schedule to accommodate her granddaughter's theatrical dreams. Like Angela, Felicia Carter, a 36-year-old Michigan schoolteacher, indulges her daughter Monica's passion for performing, recently driving her an hour and a half each way to perform in forty-one performances of a professional production of *Fiddler on the Roof.* Lenore believes this commitment to theater means the whole family must make sacrifices, including Monica's brothers, ages 5 and 9, who are often toted along. But Felicia says that if Monica wants to do something, "I make it happen for her," adding that she seeks out more activities for her children than her mother did—and she thinks they benefit as a result.

It's not just theater that occupies the Carter family's schedule. Monica participates in a swimming program at 8:00 A.M. every day in the summer, even though she is not particularly athletic. Lenore says she wasn't pushed to do much as a child, so she didn't push her own children. While she fondly remembers taking her son and daughter on outings to the museum and the symphony, she didn't feel the push to involve them in extracurricular activities the way her daughter does with her children. "I wasn't so aggressive or assertive with my children and my daughter is much busier with her children than my husband and I were with ours," she says.

For mothers living in affluent communities, like 45-year-old Susan Greene, there's tremendous peer pressure for kids to have a calendar that is chock-full of activities. Since Susan works full-time and has her nanny shuttling the kids, "it's just easier" to keep them busy with formal activities than with informal play. Both of her girls, ages 9 and 12, play soccer and tennis, attend religious school twice a week, and study with reading tutors once a week. Susan fondly remembers her childhood, where her days were spent casually roaming the neighborhood to play with friends. All the neighborhood kids were outside after school until their mothers gave the universal holler to come in for dinner. She says that doesn't exist anymore, at least in her neighborhood. If her children went outside to play, "there wouldn't be anyone to play with." There are only seven houses on her street and they're far apart, with no sidewalks. All the parents are working. So today, kids get their social interaction from the activities, Susan says. She also believes these activities yield very real benefits. Her older daughter, who struggles with reading, found that the more physical activities she participated in, the better she performed academically. Both girls "need the release of being active and running around, and both are good athletes," Susan says. She believes she has a wonderful relationship with her mother, Eva Cohen, but she knows how her mother feels about all this scheduling. "I think the biggest comment my mom makes is that my kids are watched over all the time—between school, their activities, and the nanny—and they never have time to just wander free." Yet Susan concludes, "I don't see how we could have it any other way."

"Those kids are scheduled every minute," complains Susan's mother, Eva. She feels this is terrible; she'd like to see her grandchildren "have more breathing time." But Susan explains that "everything is bigger than it was" during her childhood. It's hard not to strive to keep up with the Joneses when you live in an affluent town. How could Susan's children be the only ones on the block not to play soccer or take tennis lessons?

It's not just well-to-do parents who are signing their kids up for music lessons and sports camps. Latoya Simpson, 38, lives in Oakland, California, and is the single mother of a 9-year-old son, Antwon. She is convinced her son needs structure in his life, so she pays for basketball camp and hip-hop dance lessons on her modest salary as a customer service clerk at a publishing house. Her mother, Cora Porter, 68, grew up in poverty in Louisiana and can't understand why her grandson can't just entertain himself. Latoya says, "I'm raising an African American boy in a society where they get in trouble at an early age. Let me keep him busy rather than having him stand out on the corner."

Latoya says this is a difficult issue for her and her mother. "She thinks I'm too hard on my son and that I keep him too busy." Her mother tells her, "he's a kid" and should rest. But Latoya doesn't want him to spend the day watching television. Latoya admits she does try to give her son a very structured life, but feels she has good reason. Structure, she believes, will help to keep him disciplined and focused.

Latoya recognizes her son's activities cost her time and money. But, she points out, they won't bankrupt her family. Latoya says her father, a member of the Black Panthers, taught her that everyone should have "hustle." She says her son is her "hustle," so she did the necessary legwork to find him free tutoring and a $25 basketball camp.

She's also trying to give her son the opportunities she missed when she was growing up. Her own mother was a workaholic and her job always came first. She didn't volunteer at school, attend Latoya's choral performances, help with homework, or keep her occupied during the long summer months. Latoya is just the opposite. "I'm in the PTA and school council, and I'm a room parent." She's always thinking about how to keep her son busy on weekends and bought him a scooter so he could get to the library on his own.

Latoya doesn't blame her mother, and says working so many hours as a hotel maid and a nursing home attendant—necessary to make ends meet—prevented her mother from being involved in her life. Cora dropped out of school at age 12 and was functionally illiterate; she simply wasn't in the running for high-paying jobs. Still, Latoya wishes her mother would understand why activities are so important to her son's development and engage in a meaningful way with her son. "I get tired of seeing my mother sit around with my son watching cartoons," she says.

With an ever-increasing number of activities available to children today, it's hard for mothers from all walks of life to "just say no." Although there are no formal statistics on how many activities are currently available to children, there's plenty of evidence that the numbers have skyrocketed in recent years, alongside the burst in demand. For example, in 2006, the Web site Mysummercamps.com listed twenty-one hundred sports specialty camps nationwide, five hundred more than in 2003. World Cup Soccer Camp now has forty-seven camps, attended by two thousand kids—ten times as many as in 1992. These days, a casual, local recreation league isn't considered challenging enough for many committed child athletes. Their parents spend hours on the road so their children can participate in more rigorous sports leagues.

Three of our experts, Barbara Howard, John Northman, and Elizabeth Berger, agree with the mothers who raised their children a generation ago: too many activities can threaten a child's self-esteem and imagination, as well as detract from family togetherness. They offer helpful ways for mothers and daughters to diffuse tensions over the kids' activities. A key strategy is for the daughters to heed their mothers' advice and cut back on the activities.

ADVICE FOR MOTHERS

Choose your words carefully. Women should only bring up the issue of overscheduling if they feel they have a good relationship with their daughter, says Dr. Northman. If they decide to raise the topic, they could say something like, "Have you thought about all the activities your kids are involved in? I'm concerned and I just wanted to raise it as a question." Deliver messages that are empathetic in tone.

ADVICE FOR DAUGHTERS

Ease off the activities. Today's mothers shouldn't be dismissive of their own laid-back childhood. Experts agree that children don't need the schedule of a CEO. Dr. Howard suggests selecting one activity that's social—since children crave the company of other children—and one that's athletic. "I see kids who are doing four activities and it's too many. They're stressed out," Dr. Howard says. She's also worried that having children engaged in several competitive activities can take a toll on their self-esteem. Dr. Northman recognizes that participating in activities these days often becomes a necessity, because a child might find herself with no social interactions with peers if she abstains. But he agrees with Dr. Howard that parents need to provide these activities in moderation.

The decision to limit a child's activities may very well have a payoff in the longer term, when the kids start applying to college, says Susan English, the founder of Insiders Network to College, a northern New Jersey–based private college consulting company that has worked with over five hundred students seeking admissions to college. English says that admissions officers from selective schools don't want to see a student with lots of "one-shot deals—newspaper for one year, soccer for one season" or four different sports. Instead, they would rather see a student's passion, commitment and dedication to one or two personally meaningful activities.

Give your kids the chance to be self-sufficient. Kids who are scheduled every minute lack those empty periods of time where they can "create fantasy play and fun and enjoyment for themselves," Dr. Northman says. He feels it's particularly important for groups of children to spend unstructured time deciding, planning, arguing, playing, drifting around, and working out their own problems together in order to grow. Mothers could encourage their children to get a group of friends together and organize their own baseball or soccer game. This would provide them with valuable skills of organization and negotiation as they make up rules and choose up sides, says Dr. Northman.

Resist the urge to keep up with the neighbors. Dr. Berger agrees with Susan's mother, Eva, and sees excessive extracurricular activities as particularly common in affluent neighborhoods. Well-to-do parents feel pressure to give their child every possible advantage, and they also have the means to provide those advantages. Dr. Berger believes that in well-off families, parents often—unintentionally—lead their children to believe they're not good enough. These children often feel compelled to "excel" or "distinguish themselves" by going to the best college, playing the right sports, and having a wide range of interests and hobbies. The result is that children may feel that they're not "good enough" and can't just be themselves.

Realize that too much action is hard on a child. "Sometimes the kid actually loves the special class in paleontology that Mommy drives him to every Saturday at the museum," Dr. Berger says. But sometimes the child gets the idea that he isn't okay following his own interests at his own speed. The need to be outstanding or special, and the corresponding fear of being just an ordinary person, can be part of the lesson a child learns from this kind of environment. And that's not healthy for a child's psyche.

Don't make your child your "project." Dr. Berger says the overzealous focus on activities is a perfect illustration of today's hyperparenting. Mothers today "tend to make a competitive project out of their children, rather than letting them be who they are and responding to them in a casual, natural, and personal way."

Understand that different children have different needs. Don't back off a busy schedule if you and your child truly enjoy it. It's good for a child to get used to scheduled physical activity or growing up with music, says Dr. Weinblatt. However, what works for some people doesn't work for others. Some children are happy to hang around the house and make model airplanes; others like to have every spare moment filled with scheduled activity. They thrive on it. So pick what works best for your family. Whatever makes all of you happy is ultimately the right choice.

Money and Materialism: Spartan Ways Versus Today's Indulgences

It's not just the schedules of today's kids that raise grandmothers' blood pressure. The sheer number and price of the toys, gadgets, and clothes in children's closets also worry a generation of women who learned to live within their means. Three or four decades ago, married couples often didn't own a home when they had their first child; they'd rent until their income and savings accounts were secure. Credit cards were rarely used. Parents told their children, "If you can't afford it, you don't need it." Two-parent families often survived on a father's income only, so parents and children learned how to get by on less. Even though families were larger, homes were smaller, so children learned to share a bedroom with their siblings. Today, the standards for what one should have and when they should have it have escalated to unprecedented levels. Married couples may hold off having children until they can provide them with the best of everything. Vacations are more elaborate. College is viewed as a necessity rather than a luxury reserved only for the best and brightest. Television shows and commercials show children countless images of pricey products they simply "must have." While today's working moms are pleased they can provide their children with many of the items on their kids' wish lists, some of their mothers think these materialist priorities are misguided and that children aren't being raised with the moral grounding that comes from working hard for what you want and need.

Growing up as one of seven children, Tammy Mahoney, now 44, recalls her family's frugality. She remembers Sunday evenings were a weekly washing ritual. Each child bathed, saving the water for the next in line. Hand-me-downs were common, and Tammy was forced to wear a training bra previously worn by three of her older sisters. The bra was ten years old by the time she got it. One day in gym class, the hook broke and her bra popped open. "That was a bit embarrassing!" she laughs. Her family took trips to the local beach only after 4:00 P.M., when parking was free. She and her siblings would scour the sand around the snack shack for pennies and abandoned soda bottles. They'd use their newfound loot to buy Bazooka bubble gum. "Not a thimble was wasted," Tammy says. Tammy's mother, Betty, says they grew their own vegetables in a garden and made homemade jams, getting by on nourishing meals with a minimum number of ingredients. Eating out was rare, and only at a burger drive-through. All this scrimping paid off. Tammy's parents were able to fund half the tuition for all seven of their children's college educations, while scholarships covered the rest.

Peggy Pennington, Kami and Angela's mother, grew up during the Depression era and practiced her mother's thrifty rules when she was a young housewife in the 1950s and 1960s. Whereas her daughters and their husbands all have their own cars, and bought houses in the early years of their marriages, she and her husband didn't purchase a home until they were married for eight years and didn't buy a second car until they were married for ten years. As Peggy's mother would say, those purchases "just weren't necessary." Peggy often wonders whether the quest for so many material possessions may be skewing parents' priorities today, forcing them to work longer to pay for their expensive rewards. "People can get along with a Ford instead of a Mercedes," she says. When she was raising her family, she budgeted and balanced the checkbook. "I don't think young people would do that today. I just don't think they would make that sacrifice." She also marvels at the high-end toys that some of her grandchildren have, including electric gadgets like iPods and Wii games. "I think most of my friends are appalled at the humongous amount of toys and material goods that every child has today," she says.

Eva Cohen, who splits her time between homes in Michigan and Florida, agrees. Eva is a petite, soft-spoken woman. Trim and dressed in a contemporary jean jacket and jeans, she looks far younger than her 79 years. Everything is grander today, she says, and she doesn't believe that's a good thing. Eva raised her four children in a working-class town in Michigan. Eva's husband was a dentist and earned a good living, yet felt strongly that despite his comfortable income, they should not lead a luxurious life and should teach their children the value of a dollar.

Eva's daughter, Susan, describes her childhood as a happy one. Although Susan grew up in a solidly middle-class home, she is raising her daughters with a far more extravagant lifestyle in a New Jersey suburb. She is married to a money manager who works in Manhattan. She works full-time as a marketing consultant from her home, employing a nanny to watch the children. She enjoys her work because it allows her a creative outlet, access to interesting people, and the opportunity to develop exciting new products. Susan also admits her high salary is an important motivator, which she needs to maintain her lifestyle: "I make a lot of money. I've done this for so long, I can do it easily."

Susan also admits she has no qualms about spending her money as she sees fit. She lives in an enormous house on two lush green acres, with a pool and fountain in the backyard. The backyard is every child's dream and has a huge swing set, jungle gym, and miniature playhouse. She employs a staff, including a gardener, a handyman, a housekeeper, and a full-time live-in nanny, to carry out household chores. While her mother had a housekeeper when she was raising her children, Susan says her mother will often remark that she has a whole staff of people.

Although Susan recognizes that her two girls have far more extravagant toys and electronic devices than she had at their age, she views many of these purchases as necessities rather than luxuries. Susan bought her oldest daughter a cell phone when she was 11. At first, she thought she'd need it just for emergencies, but it's now being used as part of a school pilot program to teach students how to use technology for class assignments.

Cell phones aside, though, many families in Susan's affluent neighborhood spend their money in a way that most observers would consider frivolous or excessive. Birthday parties are a telling example. When Susan was growing up, these affairs were simple celebrations at home, with hot dogs, Jell-O, potato chips, and a homemade cake.

Goody bags would be filled with a few pieces of candy and a small plastic toy. The highlight of the party was game time, when kids would bob for apples and play musical chairs and hot potato. Her children's parties, on the other hand, are lavish galas. Her kids attend a private school and are required to invite all thirty children from their class to the party, so as not to exclude anyone. When her daughter wanted a tea party birthday, Susan rented space in a hotel and the girls dressed up in formal attire, complete with elegant hats. They enjoyed a formal tea service and made baskets with silk flowers they filled with candy. Another party featured a backyard carnival, with a Good Humor ice-cream truck, a giant inflatable structure for bouncing, and face painting. "Working full-time and knowing you have that many kids coming to a party, you need something structured," Susan says. Her day job doesn't allow her the luxury of time to plan the party or clean up after. Susan estimates she spends around $1,200 for an average birthday party for the 4- to 7-year-old set. ("Don't tell my mom that!" she says.) Her kids attended one party where the host imported a petting zoo. At another, a professional dance troupe taught the girls a portion of the choreography for *The Nutcracker,* and the girls performed the show with professional dancers when parents came for pickup.

Even simple activities Susan participated in as a child, like Girl Scouts, have become more upscale. Susan remembers working hard for her photography badge, snapping pictures on her Kodak Instamatic. Her daughter and her troop mates, by contrast, learned photography from a well-known photographer who came to teach the girls some tricks of the trade. An upcoming Girl Scout outing is at a professional theater, where the girls will see the Broadway musical *Hairspray,* followed by a backstage tour to meet the actors and a sleepover party in the lobby of the theater. What they do in Girl Scouts "has nothing to do with public service or learning to be self-sufficient," as it was in her youth, Susan says wistfully.

Despite the often over-the-top lavishness that is pervasive in her community, Susan says, "my kids are so grounded that it hasn't had a bad effect." When her older daughter was in kindergarten, she asked her classmates to bring donations for the local food bank in lieu of gifts to her birthday party. They filled their SUV with food for the local shelter. Susan doesn't see a problem with her children's upbringing: "It's the reality of living among so much affluence."

Her mother, Eva, thinks "there's nothing they [the grandchildren] don't have." Although she is a devoted grandmother, she doesn't buy the grandkids gifts because she says they don't need anything. She worries their expectations are so high, it will be hard to satisfy them as they get older, especially if they grow up to earn less than their parents do. Her own children always had what they wanted, but her granddaughters have far more. She wonders how they will fare if they ever have to face a different kind of lifestyle.

Eva and Susan agree that the two share a wonderful relationship, one of mutual understanding and respect. Eva adores her grandchildren and believes they're growing up to be fine young people. But this issue of money is one of the few wedges between them.

How can the two resolve this difference? Psychologist Julia Davies provides her input. She believes that daughters should try to provide more grounded values for their children. In doing so, they'll help diffuse mother-daughter tension.

ADVICE FOR MOTHERS

Don't sweat the excess. Dr. Berman says if Susan is a good person, then Eva should be assured that she'll be a good mother and will raise well-behaved, kind children, even if they're surrounded by wealth. Lots of kids who grow up with an overabundance of toys "turn out to be very sweet people," she says, so the grandmother shouldn't necessarily worry about the situation.

ADVICE FOR DAUGHTERS

Give the kids a mop and broom. Eva is right when she says that outsourcing household responsibilities isn't always the best way to go, says Dr. Davies. On the positive side, parents who are fortunate enough to hire household help are freeing up their time for their children. However, the downside is that children may develop a skewed vision of how a family works together to keep a household running.

Dr. Davies suggests having the kids handle some of the chores that Susan now hires others to do.

Doing housework together can be a great bonding experience and help foster a child's sense of responsibility, competence, and independence. It can also provide an important learning opportunity. For instance, parents could explain how household tasks connect to the wider world, such as where tap water comes from, where sewage goes, how food is grown, and how it gets to the supermarket and their kitchen.

Realize the pitfalls of prosperity. Many mothers today are raising their children with much higher levels of disposable income than their parents had when they were young, says Dr. Pamela High. However, with wealth comes new challenges. It's hard for kids to understand the value of money when everything is handed to them. The most important thing is that a mother impart morals to her children so they don't take what they have for granted.

Emphasize giving back. Mothers who raised their children thirty years ago have valid concerns about the effect of material excess on their grandchildren's character. One way for mothers and daughters to ensure that the next generation recognizes the value of money is to make charity a priority. For instance, Susan encourages her daughter to request contributions to a favorite charity, in lieu of birthday presents. She may want to increase the variety and value of the charitable acts her daughter performs as she grows up, Dr. High says. She could encourage her daughter to volunteer at a homeless shelter when she gets older. Involving the children in meaningful service projects will be a way to counterbalance their experiences as children of affluence.

Raising the Next Generation of Women: Redefining "Femininity"

Attitudes toward money and kids' activities aren't the only things that have changed in recent years. What we think of as masculine and feminine has been reinvented in the past half-century. Men no longer need to be strong and silent; they're now expected to be nurturing and sensitive. Women are encouraged to be assertive and ambitious and are no longer expected to get dolled up to go to the grocery store. Fifty years ago, by contrast, women faced more stringent expectations about their appearance when they left the house. Some wouldn't feel comfortable heading downtown without a dress and proper jewelry. Children were freshly scrubbed and groomed, in ironed clothes, especially for religious services on weekends. A woman was often judged by the way she kept her house, how she dressed herself, and how she styled her children's hair. But these days, busy moms happily cede to their children control of what they wear. And many don't often take the time to make themselves look perfect, considering that a lesser priority. Their own mothers, though, have a difficult time seeing their daughter's sallow, tired faces free of makeup, and kids who insist on wearing sweatpants and flip-flops to Broadway musicals.

Jean Kaplan, 68, and Stacy Fines, 44, have very different visions of femininity. Stacy has her mother's tall, thin frame—they are both nearly six feet. One of Stacy's vivid childhood memories of her mother was that she was very pretty and stylish. She wore white patent leather go-go boots and miniskirts in the 1970s. Stacy, on the other hand, wasn't "girlie" enough. "I think I was not the ideal daughter to her," she says. Stacy wasn't interested in wearing makeup or fashionable clothes and used her height to her advantage—in basketball. Athletics became her passion. Her mother spent a great deal of time "nit-picking about my looks." She would say, "Why don't you wear your hair this way?" Stacy says she "really wanted me to be *her* vision of me, as opposed to letting me become my own person." When Stacy was 11, Jean insisted she attend a Barbizon modeling school, hoping her daughter could use her height to pursue a more traditionally feminine goal. "It wasn't anything I would have asked to do," Stacy says. Consequently, Stacy won't insist upon any activity for her children unless they request it.

Jean says she applauded her daughter's prowess on the basketball court, but felt strongly—then and now—that women need to show their feminine side. She recalled a time after Stacy was married when she didn't wear makeup and wore her hair very short, like a crew cut, "which I didn't like." She has "gorgeous" hair and her new style didn't make her look feminine, Jean says.

Stacy's fashion missteps continued once she became a mother, much to Jean's chagrin. Ten years ago, Jean threw her husband a sixtieth birthday party at a Chinese restaurant. Stacy traveled with her husband and children, then ages 1, 3, and 5, from Michigan to Philadelphia for the celebration. As they walked into the restaurant, Stacy recalls her mother saying, "*That's* what they're wearing?" Stacy says that Jean was far more concerned with their clothing than the fact that they made the nearly six-hundred-mile journey for the party. "I said, 'You should just be happy that we're here and not worry about what we're wearing,'" recalls Stacy. Jean also chastised Stacy's fatigue pants, telling her she looked sloppy and that the baggy pants weren't stylish enough for such a special occasion. Stacy says that even growing up, she rarely wore fitted clothing, and as she became a mother of four children, each two years apart, nursing each one, she was far more comfortable in loose sweatpants and baggy clothes. Her mother would say, "You should show your figure. That's so unflattering on you."

This issue troubles Jean because she believes Stacy should be more of a feminine role model for her daughters who, she also feels, aren't feminine enough. There was a time when Stacy wasn't wearing makeup, so the girls never watched their mother putting it on. Stacy retorts that her mother now is trying to control her children (Jean's granddaughters) the same way she tried to control Stacy as a child. Two of Stacy's four children are girls, ages 15 and 9. They're built like Stacy—thin, quite tall for their age, each with fire-red hair. Stacy says her mother didn't like the way she dressed them, so she would often buy them new wardrobes.

Jean says she has urged Stacy to send her girls to dancing school, since it would give them poise and grace. "I tell everybody, if you have a little girl, send them to dancing school." She suggests to her 15-year-old granddaughter, Kayla, how to wear her long, red, curly hair. Kayla went through a phase where she pulled her hair back in a bun or a ponytail. "That's an old lady's hairdo," Jean would tell her. When Jean asked her granddaughter how she would be wearing her hair for her bat mitzvah, "Kayla just blew up at me, and told her mother I was bothering her about her hair." Now, Jean's concerned that Kayla irons her hair. "It looks awful." She thinks it's too straight and isn't at all attractive, "like straw hanging down." But, Jean says that Kayla brushes off her suggestions, just as Stacy did when she was younger. Jean feels that Stacy has turned her children against her.

Stacy says she wants to give her children the freedom to wear their hair however they want, without having to hear, "That's the way you're walking out the door?" Stacy explains that Jean's criticism of Kayla drove her away the same way it drove away Stacy. Jean noticed this. She said to Stacy, "Kayla doesn't want me around." But Stacy said that wasn't surprising, since Jean would often criticize her.

Although the issue of hair and makeup seems superficial, it came up repeatedly in our conversations with mothers and daughters. Deena Short, 39, a freelance writer based in Berkeley, California, shared similar complaints about her mother-in-law. Deena was raised in Portland, Oregon, and prides herself on being an environmentalist who doesn't fritter away money on designer clothes, hair-care products, and makeup. Her mother-in-law, however, wants Deena and her two daughters to look like they just stepped out of a Cover Girl ad. Deena and her mother-in-law, Mary Smith, recently had a "huge blowup" when Mary was visiting from Maryland. The cause of the feud? Makeup. Deena told us, "For a hundred reasons, makeup disgusts me. I'm trying to brainwash my six-year-old daughter into believing that it's totally unnecessary and people look silly in it." When her mother-in-law visits, though, "she can't stop advocating for the right of my six-year-old to put it on." Deena recalls that her mother-in-law proposed a "makeup evening" to her daughter, telling her how fun it would be to have a makeup party with her older cousins and aunts when they came to visit.

Deena overheard this conversation and tried to put a stop to the plan. "I pulled her aside to ask why she put that idea in my child's head." Her mother-in-law was very defensive and said it would be fun and wouldn't cause any harm. Mary stormed off, but came back a few minutes later to declare that when her daughters were young, they played with makeup all the time and haven't been harmed by it. The "proof" is that one almost never wears it and the other wears very little; both are happy to look "natural" as adults, despite their childhood experimentation with makeup. At face value, conflicts over makeup and straightening one's hair seem trivial. But lurking under these debates are more fundamental issues about what is acceptable, or desirable, behavior in girls and women. Our team of therapists offers advice for how mothers and daughters can accept each other's definitions of femininity, and in doing so, provide positive role models for the next generation.

ADVICE FOR MOTHERS

Acknowledge that views of femininity have changed. Dr. Weinblatt says that the Title IX amendment, which passed in 1972 and removed barriers to gender discrimination in public schools, was a historical turning point. A key consequence of this legislation was that boys and girls were finally given equal opportunities to participate in sports and other activities at school. He believes this law (in addition to the women's movement of the 1960s that swept in the amendment) has had a tremendous impact on the lives of girls and women. Girls coming of age since the 1970s were raised to believe that being outspoken, physical, and assertive—characteristics that were considered masculine in women a generation ago—is perfectly fine for a young woman today.

Dr. Weinblatt believes that today's young women are learning that if you want to wear makeup, that's fine, but if wearing sweatpants is more your style, that's okay too. They've also discovered that dressing casually or going a day without lipstick won't make you less desirable as a woman. "That's the way it is. There doesn't seem to be any value in fighting it," Dr. Weinblatt says. Embrace your daughter, and granddaughter, regardless of how they decide to dress.

Don't try to mold your daughter (or granddaughter) in your own image. The therapists agree that it's affirming to have a child who's a chip off the old block. Women believe that their daughters and grandchildren are extensions of themselves and want them to conform to their ideas about how things are supposed to be. Being imitated can "nourish our self-esteem," says Dr. Sanford.

Although this desire is perfectly natural, it can be harmful for women like Jean and Stacy. Jean is jeopardizing her relationship not only with her daughter, but with her granddaughter, who is picking up on her critical remarks. Dr. Sanford says Jean should ask herself: "Why can't you love yourself enough that you can accept other people for who they are?" Self-esteem issues should be handled internally and should not be dealt with by trying to change others.

Realize that mother-daughter tension can create grandmother-granddaughter tension. Dr. High says Jean and Stacy's difficult relationship is affecting Jean's relationship with her granddaughter Kayla. Jean's concerns about what her grandchildren wear, their hairstyles, and whether they have good posture are coming between the grandmother and her grandchildren.

Don't dwell too much on appearance. In the grand scheme of things, says Dr. High, one's hair and fashion choices are inconsequential, so it's not worth jeopardizing a relationship over such issues. Parents and grandparents who are concerned can set their own limits, allowing teens to color their hair, for example, but banning piercings, which are permanent and can be unsafe. Dr. High urges all three generations of women to concentrate on other, more significant values. "I think that relationships are so much more important than how a child dresses or how they wear their hair," she says. Grandparents who dwell on this are only hurting themselves if it ends up causing the grandchild to reject them. And, they should remember that many choices about one's appearance are just a short-lived phase.

The Importance of Faith in a Child's Life: The Religious Wars

For many women, religion and spirituality are the foundation for all their beliefs and actions. According to surveys by the Gallup Organization, 80 percent of Americans report that religion is "very important to them."[3] Exactly how religion gets passed down to children and grand-children is a source of major conflict for many of the mothers and daughters we spoke to. The two generations disagreed about the importance of religious attendance, marrying within one's faith, and raising a child with a structured religious life. We found it especially heartbreaking for mothers when they see their daughters rejecting religion as they raise their children. In some cases, liberal daughters of fundamentalist mothers abandoned a faith they saw as judgmental and rigid. In other cases, daughters simply wanted their children to make their own choices, without assuming that they would unquestioningly follow the teachings of their parents and grandparents. These battles were particularly painful, because they reflected fundamental differences in values and beliefs, which are difficult for mothers and daughters to resolve.

Lynette Wagner, now 41, rejected her mother's fundamentalist religious teachings when she was a teenager and now fears that her mother will try to foist her views on Lynette's children. Lynette's strategy for dealing with this is to limit contact between her children and her mother, which is heartbreaking for her mother, Nan Wilkes, age 73. Lynette lives in California and works part-time as an investment adviser. She has two children, ages 4½ years and 6 months, who have inherited Lynette's strawberry blond hair. Lynette desperately wants to shield her children from her mother's conservative beliefs, which she feels are close-minded and judgmental.

Lynette was raised in a strict, fundamentalist Christian home. Drinking, smoking, and dancing were prohibited. Her parents discouraged her from having friends outside their church, because they felt that would encourage behavior inconsistent with the church's teachings. "Almost everything was [considered] bad. Our world was very small," says Lynette. When she turned 12, she decided religion was "hooey and I didn't believe it." She says her mother's fundamentalist thinking made her a bigot and unable to embrace other cultures. Lynette wanted no part of this religion or the negative values it imparted.

Lynette recalls that her mother didn't warmly welcome Lynette's first husband to the family, since he was of Mexican American and Portuguese ancestry. Nan asked her daughter what "color" he was. "I'm not used to looking at people" in that way, Lynette replied. Lynnette's mother says, "I did not agree with her marriage to him, only because I discovered that he was Mexican." She says there are simply too many cultural differences to overcome in mixed marriages. She also believes that children with mixed ethnic backgrounds will have a hard time fitting in with other kids, once they start school.

Lynette is now married to her second husband, who is white. She is a practicing Buddhist and meditates daily. For Lynette, Buddhism is "more of a philosophy" than a religion. She and her husband aren't raising her children with any particular religion. She tells her young daughter there are many different religions and beliefs in the world, and "you get to choose what you believe." She says her mother assumed her grandchildren would be raised as Christians and was profoundly disappointed when that didn't turn out to be the case. It helped, she says, that her older sister laid the groundwork and was the first one to reject Christianity, "so my mom fought those fights with her," Lynette says.

"I think it's terrible" that Lynette is Buddhist, Nan says. "I don't agree with it, not at all, because I think it's a lie." She raised her children to believe there is only one God, and "I don't regret that." Nan prays for her daughter and her "wonderful grandchildren" every day and she's sad that they "aren't raised with the truth." Her daughter's failure to embrace Christianity "is my greatest disappointment," Nan says. The two cannot reach agreement on the issue, so they don't talk about it. Despite living just thirty miles apart, they haven't visited each other in two months. Nan's grandchildren have never spent the night with her, much to her disappointment.

When mother and daughter get together, there are very few topics they can discuss. Most are too heated. Lynette is pro-choice, while her mother opposes abortion. Nan worships President Bush; Lynette finds him intolerable. Nan supports the war in Iraq; Lynette is against it. "We're opposite in almost every way," she says. Avoiding so many hot-button topics is difficult, and the result is superficial conversation, Lynette says. "I have to edit what I say, which is not a comfortable thing." Lynette says her mother is such a polar opposite; it's hard to find any common ground. At the root of all this is the fact that Lynette doesn't genuinely like or respect her mother. "She's not someone I would choose to be in my life," she says.

Nan says the two have so little time together they have "more important things than politics to discuss." She says she hasn't "the slightest idea" what her daughter's political views are. She believes the reason she rarely sees her daughter is that Lynette is so busy and makes her immediate family her priority. "We don't even talk to them that much," she says.

Like many of the conflicts we found between mothers and daughters, the issue of religion can also create a divide between young women and their mothers-in-law. For Anna Ringold, a 28-year-old Wisconsin-based mother of two children, ages 6 weeks and 2½ years, religion is a huge sticking point with her 44-year-old mother-in-law, Dina Webster. Dina lives in a small town in Virginia, and religion has been an enduring source of comfort through her difficult life. Anna says her mother-in-law's persistence in urging Anna and her husband, Jeff, to join a church causes friction in an otherwise harmonious relationship. To better understand why Dina feels so strongly, it's important to look back to her early years.

Dina grew up in a traditional Baptist family. Her main goal in life was to marry well. "You always thought back then that Prince Charming would come and take care of you." Unfortunately, Dina never saw that fairy tale come true. She met her future husband at a carnival when she was 14 and he was 21. "It was puppy love." Their infatuation soon developed into an intimate relationship. When Dina found out she was pregnant at 16, it was a shock to her, and she quickly had a shotgun wedding. She didn't go to the doctor to confirm her pregnancy until she was nearly six months along, hoping she could "wish it away." By that time, her mother sensed something was wrong and insisted she get medical attention. Not surprisingly, Dina's religious mother had a tough time with the news of the pregnancy. According to Dina, she said, "What will my friends think?" Her first impulse was to urge Dina to get an abortion, but Dina refused. "It was very hard. I didn't have anybody," she says. After giving birth to a son, she had a daughter two years later, when she was 18. After four years of marriage, when she was 20, she and her husband divorced. She was a single mother until she remarried five years later.

When her children were 5 and 7, Dina joined the Pentecostal Church and says that made her life as a single mother better in every way. "There's a family to help support you." When her children hit their difficult teen years, Dina sought advice from the youth pastor. "I believe our church family held us up and was always there for us. It was a big part of my life," she says. Her faith and the church sustained her and she wanted that for her children as well. "If it hadn't been for God, I would never have made it," she says.

The feeling that the church is essential is something Dina still carries with her today. Dina's daughter-in-law, Anna, was raised a Catholic, and she and her husband have yet to find a church where they can both feel comfortable. Anna explains that Dina "has a very hard time understanding and accepting that." Her mother-in-law is relentless in pushing them to join a church. She remarks on it during her twice-a-year visits to Anna and Jeff's house. On her most recent trip there, she brought a directory of churches in Anna's neighborhood— provided to her by her pastor. Whenever they drive past a church, she'll ask questions about it, like "What denomination is that?"

Anna tells her mother-in-law that they pray at home and they feel God's presence in their lives. "I don't have to be in a church for that to be the case," explains Anna. Dina tells her that a church family is an essential source of support. Anna replies that she gets support from her own family. She's extremely close with her mother, who lives an hour away, so she doesn't see the need for a church family. "She drives me nuts and it makes me angry with her because she doesn't respect our decision." Her husband "lets it roll off his back," which is far harder for Anna to do, because she takes it as an insult. Anna says Dina doesn't bother her son as much about it. She thinks that, in her heart, Dina blames Anna for her son not belonging to a church. Anna says that Dina's worry is that she, her husband, and her children won't be "saved." Early in Anna's relationship with Jeff, Dina quizzed her about whether she had been saved. She replied yes, and that Dina shouldn't worry.

Dina says she doesn't nag her son and daughter-in-law about religion. She might casually say, "This looks like a nice church," as they drive by one in the neighborhood, but, she says, "I try not to interfere." She says she doesn't want to cause any strife and that she has a nice relationship with her daughter-in-law, whom she says she loves. She's pleased Anna believes in Jesus and feels she's a wonderful wife to Jeff, as well as a good mother. Anna retorts that the rift is there already. The church issue is the only major disagreement the two have, "but it really takes over our relationship because she can't get past that," Anna says.

For both Anna and Dina, and Lynette and Nan, the role of religion in their lives—and especially the lives of the next generation—is a tremendous source of tension. For many of the women we spoke with, the debate over religion was only the tip of the iceberg. Religious views reflected one's larger worldviews—about politics, philosophy, racial relations, and gender. Mothers and daughters discussed how difficult it was to love someone, yet staunchly disagree with their heartfelt beliefs. Grandmothers wanted to pass their cherished religious traditions down to their grandchildren, yet their daughters did not want their children to absorb philosophies and ideas that are inconsistent with their belief structures.

When daughters and mothers (or mothers-in-law) are worlds apart, spiritually, culturally, politically, and socially, is there any hope the two can develop a deeper relationship marked by mutual affection and respect? Dr. Berger provides her perspective.

ADVICE FOR MOTHERS AND MOTHERS-IN-LAW

Don't proselytize. Just as daughters should be respectful of their mother's religious teachings, mothers should be respectful of their daughter's decision to embrace or reject religion. Their main goal is to maintain a strong relationship with their daughter and grandchildren. Trying to impose one's own religious ideals will only derail this goal. Mothers should accept that they've raised their daughters to be thoughtful adults and respect the choices of their daughters and daughters-in-law. To do otherwise could mean a permanently severed or strained relationship.

ADVICE FOR DAUGHTERS

Put family above ideology. Dr. Berger says women shouldn't cut off ties with their mothers or mothers-in-law because they adhere to different belief structures. Surely Lynette has met individuals with beliefs similar to her mother's who may have other endearing attributes. Dr. Berger is sympathetic to Nan's desire to spend more time with her grandchildren and doesn't think it's a good idea for Lynette to shut her out of her grandchildren's lives. She suggests that daughters like Lynette take a step back, examine the reasons why they're so vehemently opposed to having their mother in their children's lives, and consider the potential repercussions of keeping them apart. Dr. Berger suggests that Lynette consider what's in the best interest of her daughters and put ideology aside.

Recognize that it's hard to undo one's own influence on children. Lynette worries that her mother could brainwash her children with conservative religious and political views. But Dr. Berger notes the kids are just as likely to hear those positions uttered in the homes of neighbors, at the schoolyard, and on television. These influences are all grist for the mill, and a small child must learn, sooner or later, that the world is full of discord and people with different ideologies than Mommy and Daddy. These influences can never undermine the loyalty children feel for their parents when this loyalty is based upon love, empathy, and mutual respect. By limiting access between her children and their grandmother, Lynette runs the risk of a greater harm: suggesting to her children that people may stop loving you on account of your beliefs.

ADVICE FOR DAUGHTERS-IN-LAW

Call on the hubby. Dr. Berger wonders where Dina's son, Jeff, is when these two important women are duking it out. Anna could ease the tension if she would let her husband know how much his mother's zeal hurts her. The married couple needs to act as a unified front. As a couple, they can brainstorm about ways for Anna to feel more comfortable in her relations with her husband's mother. Jeff could approach his mother privately, and politely tell her he and his wife are taking their time to decide how they want to handle religious matters in their home. He can diplomatically tell her he knows how important church is to her, but he would appreciate it if she would not address this topic with his wife. He can say his wife is sensitive about the issue. He also can remind his mother that she can share her opinions with *him* alone whenever she likes.

Bridging the Geographic Divide: When Grandparents Live a Plane Ride Away

Many women we spoke with very much wanted their mothers to play a role in helping to shape their grandchildren. Yet many grandmothers worried they couldn't be an important influence because they live so far away. American society today is more geographically mobile than ever. A generation ago, it wasn't uncommon for women to marry and raise their families in the same town where they grew up. Once they had children, Grandma was often just a short drive away and a regular part of her grandchildren's lives. She often pitched in to babysit and offer her advice on parenting. Today, families feel free to leave their roots behind for many reasons. This can bring sadness to a grandmother who wants to spend time with her children and grandchildren more than a few times each year.

That's the case for Helen Ingersoll, now 69 and living in a suburb of Washington, D.C. Her daughter, Janet, age 42, lives in Massachusetts. We last met this pair in Chapter 5, when Helen told us that she wanted a more prestigious career for Janet. A far greater source of heartache for Helen—and a headache for Janet—is Helen's constant lament that Janet doesn't live closer to her.

Until recently, Janet, who is married and has a 7-year-old son, lived just four hours away from her mother. Janet worked as an editor for a magazine in New York City, and Helen was delighted with the arrangement; the two were just a few hours' ride away from each other. For several years, Janet enjoyed the ideal work arrangement. She was able to work one day a week from home. Unfortunately her magazine's management decided to yank that policy and insisted she be in the office every weekday. That change in schedule, combined with the high cost of living in the New York area and the two-hour round-trip commute between Janet's Brooklyn home and her Manhattan office, pushed her to seek a less stressful life elsewhere. In September 2005, Janet accepted a job as an editor with a magazine in Massachusetts, while her husband, also a writer, began working from their Massachusetts home.

Her work is now a mile away from home, in a town that is smaller, more relaxed, and more affordable than New York. Her job gives her the flexibility to come into work and leave early a few days a week. Quality of life "was a big factor" in the move, she said. Janet and her husband decided that "if I were to continue working full-time, we wanted as easy a situation as possible," she says. They've found that in their new home.

Helen feels otherwise, however. "Every day I wake up I hate it." She adds that though New York was four hours away, it was bearable. Another one of her children lived there as well, and she looked forward to visiting her family and enjoying the activities offered in the New York area. Janet's child is her only grandchild and she wishes she could see him more frequently. She says it's more difficult to get to Massachusetts. Even though she saw the "wear and tear" on her daughter working in New York, especially after 9/11, she believes she could have found the same comfortable life in another small town closer to Helen, like Charlottesville, Virginia.

It's now difficult for her daughter and son-in-law to visit her, since they both work and have a limited amount of vacation time. She adds, "They're very protective about family time," so they prefer to spend their vacations together and also have to make time to see her husband's family, who also live out of town.

The feeling of loss from not seeing her grandchild is a constant source of heartache for Helen. She says she's extremely envious when she sees her friends with their children and grandchildren who have settled nearby. They are very involved in their grandchildren's daily lives in a way she can't be. Not having her grandson nearby "is the one real deprivation I feel now." She doesn't think her daughter feels the same sense of loss from not having her mother around. "The deprivation is truly mine," she says. Though she recognizes her daughter tries hard to balance competing priorities, "I would like her to live closer," Helen says.

Helen also is upset that her daughter nixes her offers to babysit her grandson for a few days while her daughter and son-in-law go on vacation. They insist on always vacationing with him. Helen recalls that she went to the Bahamas with her husband when their son was a baby. Janet and her husband "don't do anything" without their son. Helen's offers to watch her grandson for a weekend are also rejected, so "I don't get the chance to be with him more," Helen laments. Since being an actively involved grandparent is no longer an option, Helen tries to keep busy with other pursuits, like volunteering, to fill the void left by not having her daughter, son-in-law, and grandson there.

Janet says she sees her mother frequently, roughly twelve times a year. She heads to her mother's house eight of those times. Janet is frustrated that even though a year has passed, her mother tells her daily how upset she is with the Massachusetts move. She understands her mother's sense of loss but says, "I can't live my life for her." She says moving farther away wasn't the ideal option, but the new location has proven to be a perfect place for her and her husband. Janet says they lived near her mother earlier in their relationship, but her husband didn't like working as a journalist in Washington, D.C., so "we moved away, and ever since, my mom has been trying to get us to move back, and we probably never will."

Janet says the long-distance problem is compounded by the fact that none of her siblings live near her mom, while almost all of her mother's friends have at least one grandchild in town. "I think it's been really painful for my mom that none of us live there and we all chose to live away." She's sympathetic, but says "it's not a problem I can fix." She says she has no interest in moving simply to please her mother.

Janet says her mother's view is that a child owes the parent. She doesn't share that view. For eighteen years, a parent is the caretaker, but if the child chooses not to be around after that, it's her prerogative.

"As much as I would love my child to live next door to me when he's older, I will never pressure him to do that," she says. Though it will be painful to be apart from him, "my son is like a gift that I'm going to have to give back." She hopes this attitude will stop her from making her son feel as guilty as she has been made to feel by her mother.

Is there any way to resolve this problem? Given that Janet plans to stay in Massachusetts and is happy there, how can the two reduce this source of tension and sadness, one that is undoubtedly present in many of the lives of mothers and daughters who live far apart from one another?

ADVICE FOR MOTHERS

Work on your relationship with your daughter first. Right now, Helen wants to be completely involved. But the mother hasn't laid the foundation with her daughter to have a close relationship with her grandson, says Dr. Sanford. Daughters won't necessarily welcome their mothers, as grandmothers, with open arms, just because the grandmothers have reached a point in their relationships when they want more connectedness, if that's not what's been cultivated during the years when the daughter was growing up. So the mother may want to put more effort into her relationship with her daughter at this point.

ADVICE FOR DAUGHTERS

Take your mother up on her babysitting offer. Dr. Sanford urges Janet to leave her son with her mother for a few days occasionally while she and her husband have some time alone. It gives parents a break and provides them with some much-needed personal time, while giving grandparents much-appreciated, focused time with their grandchild.

Recognize the benefit of grandparents. It's healthy for children to be around different adults, like grandparents, says Dr. Sanford. Dr. Weinblatt agrees, repeating his mantra that "the more children experience adults who have an irrational attachment to them, the better off they are." It's wonderful to have two people, usually the mother and father, who feel that way, but it's better to have three or four. Being around other adults also allows children to experience healthy differences in parenting styles. Grandparents may spoil them, or be more permissive, or stricter. Kids need natural laboratories to try out different ways of addressing the world. To be sophisticated, they need to learn you have to treat one person one way and another person another way and you can have that experience by being with grandparents. They're also wonderful confidantes for the child when they have difficulty getting along with their parents, Dr. Weinblatt says.

ADVICE FOR MOTHERS AND DAUGHTERS

Devise new ways to "see" each other. The technological explosion means that mothers and daughters have many ways to connect, other than face-to-face contact. Internet and inexpensive long-distance telephone service mean that grandmothers can communicate with their grandchildren on a daily basis, sharing news of the day and jokes. It's easy to e-mail photos to one another, so grandmothers can see their grandchildren's latest Halloween costume or birthday party almost instantly after it happens. Even more high-tech devices, like Skype or other video-based Internet phone services, allow family members to "see" each other in real time while they're talking on the phone. Although these services cost money, they're less expensive than an airplane ticket and are another way to forge close relationships.

CHAPTER 8

His, Hers, and Theirs:
The Changing Terrain of
Household Responsibilities

Your father never lifted a finger around the house. Cooking and cleaning were my jobs.

Your husband deserves a home-cooked meal.

I don't understand why you each need your own bank account. Don't you trust each other?

Beverly Arnold and Gloria Smith both have the same bone to pick with their daughters Lynn and Carrie: their daughters' husbands are *too* helpful around the house. Beverly and Gloria worry that their daughters—both highly respected professionals who work at least fifty hours per week—are unloading too many domestic chores on their doting husbands. They're concerned that if their daughters don't start appreciating their spouses, their marriages will suffer and their husbands will seek affirmation elsewhere.

Marilyn Schultz also worries about her daughter Jenny's relationship with her live-in boyfriend, Greg. Jenny insists on splitting all the household expenses 50-50, even though her salary as a professor is less than half of what Greg earns as vice president of a small manufacturing company. If Greg really loved her daughter, says Marilyn, then he would take care of her financially. Jenny insists that it's her pride that drives her household's financial arrangements, but Marilyn thinks otherwise.

Men and women are reinventing marriage today, and the boundaries between his and her jobs are blurring beyond recognition. This is a tough situation to digest for women like Beverly, Gloria, and Marilyn. Thirty years ago, when they were young married women raising children, their husbands could barely manage to put their dirty socks in the clothes hamper, much less organize playdates or cook dinner. Many married women accepted that their husbands would be the main breadwinner, while they would manage the domestic front, usually single-handedly. It's hard for them to imagine that a man could be happily married if he's saddled with diaper duty or cooking casseroles after a long day at the office. Wrong, say their daughters, who insist that a marriage can work perfectly well when both spouses are bringing home the bacon and sharing the cooking, cleaning, child care, and bill paying. Lynn, Carrie, and Jenny say that they're putting in a dual shift of paid work and housework, so why should their husbands expect to have it easier than they do? This attitude is creating tense relations for some mothers and daughters, though, as the older generation is either envious of their daughters' helpful husbands or fearful that their daughters' desire for equality will drive their spouses away.

Workaholic Wives and Mr. Mom Husbands

When we first introduced Beverly Arnold in Chapter 5, she was concerned that her 45-year-old daughter Lynn's hectic work schedule made her an absentee mother to her two children. Lynn is a genetic counselor at a midwestern university. She spends long hours advising her patients on how to diagnose and manage genetic disorders. She often travels throughout the United States to present her research findings at academic conferences and attend workshops for continuing education. Beverly fears that her daughter's frenetic work demands are taking a toll on her marriage, because Lynn's husband Robert does the lion's share of housework and child-care duties.

When Beverly was raising her children four decades ago, she proudly took charge of the family's home. She always had dinner on the table by 6:00 P.M. and her children happily played kick the can with neighborhood kids while she cleaned house and did laundry. Home-making duties, she recalled, "rested entirely on me." She can't recall a single time that her husband Charlie ever changed one of the babies' diapers. Beverly thinks this was a fair arrangement, because Charlie worked long hours at the office. She also feels her home was much more organized, orderly, and calm than the environment in which her daughter is raising Beverly's grandchildren. In Lynn's home, dinners are hastily assembled by her son-in-law, who arrives home late in the evening since he has a forty-five-minute commute from work.

Beverly says that Lynn's preoccupation with her career places too much of burden on her husband, Robert, an oncologist. Robert oblig-ingly takes on the role of Mr. Mom much of the time, especially when Lynn travels for her job. He cooks dinner nearly every night, handles the grocery shopping, coordinates the kids' social schedules and car-pools, makes their lunches, and takes care of hiring contractors for home repairs.

Beverly feels Lynn should take more responsibility for household chores, especially since she works only a couple of miles from home. She worries that working at a demanding job and taking on the bulk of work at home will overwhelm Robert. "She's very lucky she has Robert," Beverly says. On a recent visit to her daughter's house, Bev-erly recalled with a touch of envy and awe that when Lynn came home late from work, Robert had dinner waiting on the table. She reflects that "it's not all on Lynn's shoulders. It was all on my shoulders."

Lynn is proud that she and her husband have a true partnership and insists that he is just as capable of cooking dinner or arranging a carpool as she is. In fact, his willingness to be an equal partner in the marriage was one of the factors that attracted her to him when they first started dating. "He can do it just as easily as I can," she says. Since she travels so often, Lynn says it's appropriate and necessary for Robert to take on a larger share of household chores. Robert's involve-ment at home also enables her to work at a job she loves, which makes her a happier person and, she thinks, a less stressed-out mother.

Lynn and Robert aren't the only couple we talked to who are try-ing to maintain an egalitarian marriage. Carrie Smith, age 42, has an intense and demanding job as a pediatric cardiologist in the small

Michigan town where she lives with her husband and two daughters. Her zeal for her job is apparent; her blue eyes sparkle as she talks about what drew her to her profession. Being a cardiologist allows her to care for children who might not have had a fighting chance to survive a heart condition twenty-five years ago. She says it's "extremely rewarding" to see a formerly frail child now filled with energy and playing with his brothers and sisters. She proudly shares many success stories with us, and it's clear just how much she believes in the importance of her work.

Her career has a downside, though. Carrie works at least fifty-five to sixty hours a week, limiting the time she has with her daughters, ages 7 and 9. It's not uncommon for her to work nights and weekends as well. Like Lynn's husband, Robert, her 45-year-old husband David often takes charge at home. His extensive hands-on involvement with their daughters allows Carrie to balance the demands of medicine and mothering. "There's no way we could maintain our family without David's input at home," she says. While her own father was loving, he wasn't involved in the day-to-day activities like her husband is. Her mother, Gloria Smith, 71, who stayed home while her father worked long hours as a lawyer, took care of all the parenting responsibilities. By contrast, David is "an incredible father and does do a lot of things that are traditionally considered a mother's responsibility," praises Carrie. David keeps the girls content at home, happily playing make-believe games like school, hair dresser or book store with them. He knows their favorite foods and often makes their school lunches, regularly taking over dinner and laundry duties as well.

David works as a development manager with a commercial real estate firm, and he's made compromises in his career to give him greater flexibility in caring for his daughters. If one of the girls is sick, he's usually the one to stay home. "I hate to admit that. It always makes me feel bad if I can't be there with the girls," Carrie says, recognizing the irony that she is leaving behind her own sick children to care for other ill children. But she takes solace in the fact that David is a wonderful father, with a terrific sense of humor. He's a "fabulous" parent, partly by necessity, because Carrie is not home as much as she'd like to be. Carrie says this situation—where both she and her husband work and manage the home front—is far more difficult to coordinate than it was in her mother's day, when her mom handled family matters and her father worked for pay. Trying to do both, she says, is a constant struggle for David and her.

Carrie is fortunate to have a very warm and open relationship with her mother, Gloria, who lives an hour away, in Ohio. The two have always been close and became much closer when Carrie's father died of a sudden heart attack at age 49. Gloria traces her daughter's interest in cardiology to this tragic event. She said Carrie often wonders whether her father could have survived if he had had a transplant or access to the technology that is available today.

Carrie tells us there are just two issues that her mother hounds her about: not getting enough rest and David taking on too much at home. Gloria says Carrie doesn't make housework her priority; she either ignores it or hands most of it over to David. When Gloria was raising her children, vacuuming was almost a daily routine since Carrie was allergic to dust. But, she says, Carrie can "let things go in her house more than I do. She has plenty of dust." Gloria thinks the world of David and said he's incredibly supportive. "She couldn't do what she does without him. He's a wonderful father, husband, and homemaker." She says David will do anything "that in my day a woman was expected to do, like cooking and cleaning."

Carrie tells us her mother thinks she doesn't give her husband enough attention. "She does worry that David has too much to do, and that I expect too much from him." Carrie admits her mother's only unsolicited piece of advice has to do with "giving David more of a break."

Beverly and Gloria find it hard to believe that their sons-in-law voluntarily do just as much as, if not more than, their wives around the house. This arrangement is a far cry from the days when breadwinner fathers would sit themselves down at the dinner table at six o'clock, exhausted from a long day at the factory or office, waiting for their wives to serve them their dinners. Their wives would quietly oblige, either because they had been home all day taking care of the house and kids or because they were working only part-time and contributing less than their husbands did to the family coffers.

Psychologists say that most healthy relationships are based on a premise of equity, where both partners give and receive in equal amounts. Although exactly what they give may be different, both husbands and wives should believe that there's a balance in how much they contribute to the household. The spouse who earns less and works part-time may do more around the house, for instance, while the spouse who earns more money and works more hours outside the home might coast a bit when it comes to housework. It's hard for Beverly and Gloria to understand that their daughters and sons-in-law are striving for equitable marriages, because the whole playing field of give and take has been transformed in recent years. Carrie works more hours than her husband and her salary is higher than his, so it makes sense to her that David would take on more of the cooking and carpooling. Roughly one-third of women in dual-earner couples now earn more than their husbands, and most hope and expect that their husbands will pull their weight around the house. While most men still don't come close to taking on as much as Robert and David around the house, they're certainly doing more than Beverly's and Gloria's husbands did. In 1965, men handled an average of just 4.7 hours of housework per week while women put in 34 hours each week. By 2000, men had more than doubled their hours, putting in 10.4 hours per week while women scaled back to just 19.4 hours.[1]

Women like Lynn and Carrie also refuse to believe that women are better equipped to parent than men are. Both deliberately married nurturing, kind, good-humored men who are well suited to the role of father. Both women believe a good father is more than just a good provider. He's also a hands-on parent who nurtures his children just as much as a good mother does. Boulder, Colorado–based psychotherapist Dr. Allan N. Schwartz agrees that egalitarian marriages— or even marriages where spouses share traditional his and hers roles—can be good both for the spouses and their children. Schwartz explains, "Families can benefit from the increased earning power and prestige of successful working mothers. They make wonderful role models for daughters . . . and also for their sons who need to value and respect women as their equals."[2]

Dr. Schwartz also believes that women like Beverly and Gloria should have faith that their sons-in-law can accept this arrangement. They wouldn't have married women like Lynn and Carrie if they wanted more traditional wives. Schwartz observes, "The male ego is strong enough to tolerate wives who can bring increased wealth and success to the family. Successful marriages are based on an equal sharing of responsibility and decision making, along with mutual respect and good communication."

The Financially Dependent Mom and the Pay-Her-Own-Way Daughter

Just as couples like Carrie and David shared household chores, couples like Jenny Schultz and Greg Harris are committed to sharing the costs of running a household. Jenny, the 33-year old college professor introduced in Chapter 3, lives happily with her long-term boyfriend, Greg, in Utah. Her mother, Marilyn, fears their decision to live together without marrying is a sign they're not that committed to a future together. Her worries are compounded by the fact that Jenny and Greg have arranged their financial lives entirely differently than Marilyn and her husband, Matthew, did thirty years ago. Marilyn, a homemaker who ran a small arts-and-crafts business from her basement, says, "Truthfully, I just went through life and spent money. Fortunately, my husband saved and was really wise about investing." While Marilyn depended on the salary Matthew earned as a unionized auto factory worker, Jenny and Greg split all their household expenses down the middle, even though Greg earns much more than Jenny.

Jenny says it's very important for her to have her own earnings, and to never be financially dependent on a man. Her salary as a gerontology professor is only about one-third of what Greg earns as a vice president of a small manufacturing company, yet Jenny still insists that they split the mortgage and household bills 50-50. This does not sit well with her mother. "She hates that we share expenses and that I pay half of our bills." But it's important to Jenny, because she's just starting to be financially independent after years of graduate school. "I want to know that I'm carrying my weight financially," she says.

She is quick to point out that Greg "pays for extra things, like vacations and nice clothes." But when it comes to their home, food, and utilities, they both contribute equally. They run their household like a small business, using a spreadsheet to keep track of all their home expenses. Marilyn views this businesslike approach to money as utterly unromantic, and a sign that Greg doesn't want to marry and take care of Jenny. Says Jenny, "For her, love is tied to money, where the man should provide for his wife if he loves her."

Marilyn also believes that love means that husbands and wives should pool all their resources. She can't understand why Jenny and Greg have both personal and joint bank accounts and investments. She fears Greg's separate account is a sign that he may leave Jenny. Jenny explained: "Greg is seven years older than me, and he worked for a long time before we met. He and his whole family have investments. Of course he should keep that separate." Since he's been successful financially and his earnings predate Jenny, this approach makes sense to her.

Still, Marilyn regularly asks her daughter, "Why isn't everything in your name? Why do you have separate accounts?" Jenny has tried to explain that she is Greg's power of attorney and that if anything happens to him, all of his money would roll over to her, and not to his family. "This is just so foreign to her," Jenny says.

Financial experts say that Jenny is doing everything right. What's most important is for young women to be financially literate, open and honest with their partner about their income and assets, and able to support their own lifestyle on their personal earnings. These messages were often lost on women of earlier generations. "Many women are raised to think that a man is going to secure their financial future for them. A woman can either choose to proactively build her financial awareness now, or choose to wait until she is forced into this situation due to a divorce or loss of a spouse," says James D. Schwartz, an Arizona-based certified financial planner.[3]

Marilyn should take heart in the fact that Jenny and Greg have devised a financial plan that they both agree upon—even if it's a system that Marilyn finds unromantic. "You have to know what feels fair. If it feels fair [to the couple], it's right," observes Adriane G. Berg, a financial adviser and author of *How to Stop Fighting About Money and Make Some*.[4] Although Marilyn worries that Jenny may be contributing more than her fair share to the household upkeep, Berg suggests that this arrangement is fine as long as Jenny and Greg are aware of the potential effect of their arrangement. "Keep in mind that negotiating income and payments can emotionally impact the balance of power in your relationship. So listen to each other. . . . Making sure that both of you feel your system is right will go a long way" in keeping a happy relationship.

Keeping separate and joint accounts is ideal for couples where both partners are accustomed to spending as they wish and do not want to give up their autonomy or privacy. In other words, it works when women are accustomed to having a career and income of their own. This wasn't the case for Marilyn, so she has a hard time wrapping her mind around Jenny's situation. "It's pretty clear that everybody needs some money they can call their own, even if it's just to surprise their partner with a gift," says Berg. Financial advisers suggest that couples contribute to a joint account that covers household expenses, as Jenny and Greg do. Jenny insists that it's important for to her to contribute, to maintain her pride. If that's the case, and if she feels the arrangement is fair, then Marilyn should be proud that she's raised a financially savvy and responsible daughter.

House and Garden Mom and *Real Simple* Daughter

Raquel Andrade, a 41-year-old Brazilian native living in California, rolls her eyes when she tells us that her mother "thinks she knows everything. My mom has been bossy as long as I can remember." Raquel usually tries to let her mother's advice go in one ear and out the other, but that was tough to do when her mother and stepfather decided to rearrange Raquel's furniture during a recent visit. Still, she understands why her mother behaves this way since her own mother, Raquel's grandmother, was also bossy and "had her own view of the world and how it should be." Raquel's mother, Maria Cruz, now 62, worked as a schoolteacher when Raquel was growing up, so Raquel was raised by several different maids. Raquel and her husband left Brazil for the United States when she was 29. Six years later, she gave birth to a daughter, Mariana, now age 6.

It's hard to see any strife in a photograph of the three generations of women. Maria has her arm around her daughter and all are smiling. Mariana has a beautiful face and thick black curls just like her mother's. Since Raquel's mother lives so far away, in Brazil, her first visit to her daughter's home lasted for an extended period. This past spring, Maria and her husband, Rafael, Raquel's stepfather, came to visit Raquel, her husband, and daughter, for four weeks. Raquel and her family had recently moved into a new home, so they still had unpacked boxes cluttering the house when her mother and stepfather arrived. Shortly after Maria set foot in her daughter's home, she was ready to get to work on a home improvement project. "She just wanted to put the boxes away and put things in place," Raquel recalled.

Raquel says her stepfather is a skilled carpenter. One morning, Raquel went downstairs to the kitchen and found a small penciled sketch. The sketch showed her parents' ideas for how the furniture should be arranged in the living room. This angered Raquel. Instead of blowing up—often her first reaction when she has a disagreement with her mother—she calmly said, "Thanks so much. That's very nice." She quietly put the sketch in a drawer, hoping that if she didn't discuss it, the idea would fade away. A few days passed and her mother never mentioned it again. "I thought it was crazy. This is my house." Raquel tried to divert her mother's attention to other topics, and suggested they forget about the cleaning for a while and instead do something fun together, like see a movie, "but she never stopped." Since there were dozens of projects to be done in the new home, Raquel came up with tasks to keep her mother and stepfather busy, like changing electrical fixtures. Devising a long enough list of home activities to keep them occupied for a month was a challenge, but in the end, they were helpful, Raquel said.

Still, the unresolved furniture plan upset both Raquel and Maria. Raquel interpreted the furniture plan as a criticism of the way she was managing her home. Her mother, when asked about the situation a few months later, was defensive and felt she was being unfairly criticized. She said she didn't find the house to be disorganized and felt it was a "normal mess," given the fact that Raquel had recently moved there. She said she was only trying to help. She told Raquel, after the fact, "I thought that you and your husband were happy with the renovations and improvements that we had made in the house."

Raquel says the battle about domestic issues is one of many topics she and her mother fight about, and that she "doesn't take it lightly" when she's criticized. Raquel will accuse her mother of trying to control her. Her mother's response is to defend her actions, and then cry, telling Raquel that "she thinks she knows everything." Serious conversations take so long and are so draining that Raquel's response is to talk to her mother as if she's a neighbor, avoiding deep discussions. It's particularly offensive to her that her mother "still tries to do things her way," since Raquel has been thriving on her own, away from Brazil, for more than eleven years now.

Merry Maids Mother and Do-It-Yourself Daughter

Maria Cruz isn't the only mother who wants to help make her daughter's home ready for its close-up on HGTV. Helen Ingersoll, age 69 and living in a suburb of Washington, D.C., thinks her daughter, who works full-time as a magazine editor, should pay for household help, as she had when she was raising her children. Even though Helen was a stay-at-home mom, her husband earned a comfortable income as a doctor, so she always hired domestic help to ensure that her home sparkled. But, she says, cleanliness isn't a priority for her daughter, 42-year-old Janet, and her husband. Helen says that her daughter feels she emphasizes appearances too much, while "Janet doesn't care." Helen says when she visits her daughter in Massachusetts, she'll look at the refrigerator and want to clean it out. "I'll think I'm doing a wonderful thing for her and three months later, she will say her husband isn't so crazy about that." Helen says that comes from her upbringing, where women were often judged by the way their house looked.

Janet feels she doesn't need household help. Her husband, Andrew, does most of the household work, including all of the grocery shopping and cooking, since he works from home. "He's really great about it," she says. She and her husband clean together on the weekends. They'd rather save their money for fun purchases, like vacations, rather than pay someone for chores they can take on themselves. When Janet and her husband worked in New York City and their son was younger, they both had long commutes so they paid their babysitter for light cleaning. But now that their lives are easier, living in a small Massachusetts town, they have the time and energy to handle it themselves. Janet adds that her self-worth doesn't hinge upon the tidiness of her house.

The ways that husbands and wives arrange their finances, their child-care responsibilities, and their division of household tasks has undergone a quiet revolution over the past four decades. Separate spheres of responsibilities are becoming a thing of the past. Even if young women and their husbands today insist that they're content with their domestic arrangements, their mothers often can't fathom that a husband is happy to arrange a child's birthday party while his wife is off at an academic conference, or that a daughter derives a sense of pride and self-confidence from paying half of the mortgage. Still others find their daughters' tolerance for dust buildup and dirty dishes in the sink to be a disturbing sign. How can mothers get on board with their daughters' domestic choices, or at least hold their tongues when they disagree? And how can daughters keep their cool when their mothers only want the best for them and their families? Our team of therapists weighs in.

ADVICE FOR MOTHERS

Moms should stay mum. How a family chooses to divvy up their domestic responsibilities is nobody's business except the two partners who made the decisions, says Dr. Berger. Any mother "who has the presumption to comment on these matters should be handed a bucket and soapy mop immediately and told to get busy," she says. And the division of labor between a husband and wife, like other aspects of their intimate life together, such as sexual habits or financial status, is no business of the mother's.

Break the cycle of treating the daughter like a child. When their daughters were young, mothers had every right to stomp into their bedroom and tell them to pick their jeans up off the floor or to hang up their coat rather than throwing it on the living room sofa. After all, these daughters were living under their parents' roof. But the daughters are grown and maintain their own homes now. When the mother feels entitled to weigh in on housekeeping—be it because of cleanliness or clutter—it's often a sign that she sees her daughter as a "trainee" instead of an independent individual. Even if mothers want to share their hard-earned homemaking wisdom, their daughters may feel like a scolded child rather than a mature and independent woman. If a daughter feels intimidated rather than assisted by her mother's advice, she can't easily heed her mother's suggestions, Dr. Berger says.

Realize that times have changed. Mothers should recognize that what their own husbands might have found distasteful or alien, like baking cupcakes for the kids' homeroom bake sale, is very much accepted by today's dads. If the son-in-law doesn't have a problem with his domestic chores, then the mother shouldn't either.

Examine your motivations for the way you feel. Mothers need to ask themselves why they're so concerned about their daughters' domestic arrangements, says Dr. Sanford. Do they have "unfinished business" about dedicating themselves to their children and family? Did the mother resent having to do the majority of housework? Did she feel taken for granted? Would she have preferred to have more opportunities for fulfillment outside the home? She may be projecting her insecurities onto her daughter's relationship. The mother needs to ask herself whether there really is a problem in her daughter's relationship, or if she's worried because of her own personal experiences and insecurities. Mothers may feel that their husbands, if saddled with the same amount of domestic tasks as their sons-in-law, would have resented it and it could have taken a toll on their marriage. But that isn't necessarily going to happen with their daughters' husbands, who say they're fine taking on cooking and cleaning.

If the marriage seems solid, back off. In the case of Janet and Carrie, having the husband take on domestic tasks doesn't seem to be creating a problem in the daughters' marriages. Carrie's husband, David, in particular, seems comfortable having his career take a back seat to his wife's. Men today are far more at ease in their dual roles as worker and parent. As long as the couple is not having problems with the arrangement, the mother needs to stay out of it, Dr. Sanford says.

ADVICE FOR DAUGHTERS

Politely tell mom to stay mum. For a mother to comment on the tidiness of her daughter's home, or to devise a plan for rearranging the furniture, can't be done without being at least a little bit offensive. A daughter can gently tell her mother that she doesn't like it when the mother makes remarks about her housekeeping. And she can ask her politely and firmly to stop.

Realize that times have changed. Just as moms need to realize that men's and women's roles have changed, daughters need to realize that their mothers were often raised to believe that one of their primary missions in life was to care for their families and maintain a presentable home. Young women raised in the 1970s and 1980s were raised to believe there was more to life than a clean house. Mothers can't escape the messages they learned as young women, and daughters have to recognize that they may simply be trying to help in the best way they know how.

CHAPTER 9

Personal Time:
Caring for One's Body and Soul

Why don't you wear a little lipstick? You look so pale.

Can't you take a day off from work to rest up? You sound exhausted.

That skirt looks a little snug. Have you put on weight?

Once upon a time, Susan Greene, a 45-year-old marketing consultant, had a personal trainer and worked out two hours a day. But as her client list expanded and her growing children commanded more of her time and energy, her daily exercise regime has gone out the window. Susan is now thirty pounds heavier than her ideal weight and wishes she had time to slim down. Her mother, Eva Cohen, isn't exactly helping Susan with her body image. She says her daughter, with her dark hair, petite features, and magnetic smile, "has a pretty face" yet her extra pounds are detracting from her appearance. She wishes her daughter would make exercise a bigger part of her life.

Kim Rodriguez says she's so busy juggling her kids' playdates and full-time teaching responsibilities that she rarely spends time alone with her husband. They're both so tired when they come home from work that sleep is far more alluring than romance. Kim has accepted that her marriage is a partnership of parenting, not passion. Kim's mother, Rose, by contrast, always made her husband and her marriage a top priority. Rose worries that her daughter's marriage may not withstand the test of time unless Kim and her husband, Mike, find ways to enjoy each other's company, as they did when they were newlyweds.

Dinner parties with other couples or "date nights" were a regular part of Rose's marriage. These days, working mothers like Kim Rodriguez feel they owe it to their children to spend nights and weekends watching Disney DVDs together, so their husbands—and romance— often get put on the back burner. In trying to juggle the roles of wife, worker, and mother, women often surrender private time—giving up on sleep, books, exercise, or a night out with their girlfriends. Women like Rose Rodriguez and Eva Cohen feel their daughters need to devote more attention to their marriages and to their own physical and mental health. Yet other women feel their daughters—products of the "me generation"—put their own hobbies and personal avocations like theater or music before their children. They are trying to do it all, yet feel they're doing none of it well. And that creates distress for them and their concerned mothers.

The Death of Romance? Blending Courtship, Careers, and Children

Kim Rodriguez, now 46 and working as a professor at a university in the Midwest, likes to recount the romantic story of how her parents met. Her father, Frank, a Spaniard, was studying to become a priest in Rome, but was wrestling with whether the priesthood was the right path for him. The church sent him to Ireland to take some time to contemplate whether the priesthood was his true calling. While studying there, he took courses in theology and philosophy. In the evenings, he taught Spanish lessons to pay his room and board. One of the young Irish women enrolled in his class was his future wife (and Kim's mother), Rose. Though neither spoke the other's language very well, they fell in love. "Dad wrote her poems," Kim said. Two months after meeting, they were engaged and Frank kissed the priesthood goodbye. They married in 1958 when Rose was 25 and Frank was 30. Looking to start their life together somewhere new and exciting, they moved to California, where Frank got a job teaching high school Spanish.

Rose quickly went on to have three children, but she refused to look like a frumpy housewife and always tried to keep the romance alive in her marriage. Rose's view reflects the European perspective that children should be independent and one's husband comes first, Kim tells us. Kim proudly recalls that her mother always looked elegant when she was growing up, while her friends' mothers often let themselves go once they married—gaining weight, wearing unfashionable stretch pants, and sitting on the couch eating junk food and watching soap operas. "My mom would never leave the house without lipstick on and didn't watch TV," Kim remembers.

"My children used to ask, why did I vacuum the house with heels on or why was I dressed up all the time?" says Rose Rodriguez. Though she's been in the United States for over forty years, she still speaks with a lyrical Irish brogue. She says that even when she was cleaning house, she was always in a proper dress and nice shoes. She routinely wore lipstick and made sure her hair was neatly styled, going to the hairdresser for a weekly "wash and set." Rose never hesitated to take the time to look attractive and feminine. Those moments spent indulging in personal care were a welcome diversion from the daily rigors of raising her three children as a stay-at-home mom.

Rose also made sure she and her husband had private time away from their children. The couple had regular weekend dates and were members of a gourmet dinner club with other European couples. Children were tucked in bed before the evening started, usually around 7:00 P.M. Child care was cheap—just 50 cents an hour for a teenage babysitter. Sometimes Rose would swap her children with a close friend so she and her husband could drive up the coast and stay in a motel overnight and then return the favor at a later date.

Rose and Frank also took extended time away from their children. The family journeyed to Europe every summer. One year when Kim was 9, her brother was 10, and her younger sister, Kelly, was 2, Rose and Frank left them with Frank's father and sister in a small town in Spain for six weeks while the couple traveled to Russia. "My parents just said 'Good-bye, we'll see you in six weeks,'" Kim recalls. While Kim and her brother had a wonderful time with their grandfather and aunt in the Spanish countryside, her 2-year-old sister had a rougher ordeal. Kelly didn't speak Spanish and had never been away from her mother. She cried for an entire week, and when her parents returned, Kelly couldn't be in the same room as her mother. It took a full day before she would even look at her. Kim says her mother still feels guilty about that. Kelly, now 39, has only fuzzy memories of the visit but was told that she "completely rejected her mother when she came back." Rose says she enjoyed her Russian travels, but sat on her bed and cried when her 2-year-old refused to speak to her. "It never occurred to me that she'd miss me that much," especially when Kelly was surrounded by her brother, sister, and extended family.

Now that Kim and Kelly are parents—Kim has two girls, ages 8 and 11, while Kelly has 5-year-old twin boys and a 16-month-old girl—they can't imagine leaving them for an extended period. Kim and Kelly have the same auburn hair and wide smile, along with identical-sounding voices. They're also of one mind when it comes to time away from their children. They don't see their mother as a role model in this regard, and have a much harder time leaving their kids. At her mother's urging, Kelly recently left her children with Rose during a two-week vacation to Europe to visit Kim, who was living there with her family for the year. "The two weeks that we left our boys, I called every single night and missed them so much," Kelly says. "I was really glad we got away, but I can't imagine doing that for over a month." Six years ago, when Kim and her husband had the opportunity to go to China for eight days, her mother offered to watch the girls, then 5 and 2. But Kim was "freaked out" about how her younger daughter would adjust, since she wasn't old enough to understand that her mother would return after being gone so long. She ultimately agreed, but that's the only time she's left her children for any more than a night or two.

Rose doesn't encourage her daughters to leave their children for long stretches like she did, but she is concerned that they don't have enough time to themselves or with their husbands. Kim works full-time. Kelly, who lives near her mother in California, is a public school teacher. The two sisters spend so much time juggling work and children that they have little time or energy left for themselves. "I think you need frivolous down time," Rose says. Kim says her mother liked to use the word "titivate," which means nonpurposeful relaxing, or to "do up" or "beautify," which her mother feels is an important part of every woman's life. Spending every night and weekend on kids-only activities "is an awful mistake" for a married couple, Rose says. If you had good times together before you had kids, you should be able to continue that throughout marriage. If the kids aren't with their parents for a night, they'll survive just fine. Rose thinks it would do both her daughters' marriages a world of good if they had more time with their husbands. "Their lifestyle would not have suited me," Rose reflects.

Kelly says that although she has her summers off as a schoolteacher, she's always five minutes behind schedule and has little time for hobbies or private time. If she's lucky, she and her husband go out alone once every two weeks. After work, "we're exhausted and it's boom, boom, boom, one crisis after another." She says she has no time to talk to her husband about her day or anything that's going on in her life other than their children. "They're what needs to get talked about, so there's no energy left for anything else." Kelly says one of the best aspects of her relationship with her husband is that he's an equal partner in child-rearing and chores. But the worst aspect is that "we don't have much time to be a couple and do fun things like traveling the way we used to before kids." Rose is always willing to babysit, and Kelly says she takes advantage of her mother's offer, but it's usually to make time for "necessities," like haircuts or doctor's appointments. Rarely will Kelly ask her mother to watch the kids so she can go on a date with her husband. Kelly says, "I guess I'm constantly trying to find the right balance, like the rest of the moms out there, to be the best mom and wife possible, while still holding on to what's important to me as an individual."

Though Kelly wishes she had more time for herself and her husband, she can't think of any way to do things differently. She thinks her mother "doesn't get how crazy our lives are. I feel like I'm rushing through everything. I eat lunch standing up," she says. "My mom says 'Take it easy,'" but Kelly thinks her mother doesn't remember what it's like raising three small children—and she didn't have to juggle parenthood with an outside job. Rose says she couldn't have managed a career and family simultaneously the way her daughters do. "I was never much good at doing two or three things at a time. Multitasking never appealed to me," she said.

Kim, who lives halfway across the country from her mother, also says she and her husband, Joe, don't go out very often. Like her sister Kelly and her husband, "we tend to be tired in the evening." Instead of heading out to a nice restaurant or concert, they're more likely to share a bottle of wine and watch a DVD in the family room. "I think our marriage could be better if we had more time together, and that is definitely something that's hard to find time for," Kim reflects. While her mother put her husband first, Kim says that's not what most of her peers do. "You try to pick the right husband and, hopefully, you love him, but I think most people are really focused on their kids, at least when their kids are growing up." She says her marriage feels more like a parenting team than a love relationship. Kim describes her daily life as "You take this kid here. I take this kid there," while her parents were not focused much on their children's activities or even schoolwork.

Even now, Kim says, her mother puts effort into her appearance and her emotional and mental health, attending jazzercise classes every day, eating right, and taking pride in her appearance. In a recent photo taken with her grandchildren, she's sporting her trademark crimson lipstick and is accessorized perfectly with a beautiful gold necklace. "She tries to make an effort and feels like that's something worth doing," Kim says. The sort of purposeful primping her mother advocates "is not even on my list," Kim tells us. If given the choice between sitting around the house and "titivating" or getting some work done, work would always win out. Kim says her mother has never said anything directly about this issue, but "I can tell that she sort of thinks we're crazy. Her view is, why put yourself through this?" She will ask Kim, now a tenured professor, why she tries getting so many articles published. She wonders why, now that she's established in her career, she can't relax a little or take some time off. "I think she feels like both my sister and I try to do too much." Rose's concerns stem from the fact that her daughters may snap at her, their husbands, or their children when they're overwhelmed by their daily responsibilities. "I think her view is, if we were more relaxed, then all those relationships would be easier," says Kim. Kim admits there's more than a grain of truth to her mother's assessment, but she can't see an alternative, at least while her children are still young.

Kim and Kelly are not alone in their struggle for balance. A recent Gallup Poll asked working women and men whether they felt they spent too little time with their children, with their spouse, and alone. The poll found that 66 percent of women said they didn't spend enough time with their husbands. By contrast, just 41 percent of women said they didn't spend enough time with their young children. And, the National Sleep Foundation found when working women were pressed for time, one-third said they cut out sex with their husbands.[1]

Most of the therapists we spoke with shared Rose's concern that her daughters' hectic lives were potentially threatening their marriages and their emotional well-being. While none suggested Kelly and Kim spend their days at the salon and every weekend traveling without the children, they emphasized that a marriage needs as much attention and nurturing as children. How can mothers help, and how can daughters accept this help?

ADVICE FOR MOTHERS

Help your daughter to steal some personal time. If you live near her, offer to babysit for a few hours. Or, if you're out of town, send her a gift certificate for a day of spa services. Even the busiest mom will have a hard time passing up a free manicure, pedicure, or facial. Or, if your daughter turns up her nose at pampering, buy her a gift certificate for dinner for two at her favorite romantic restaurant and offer to pay for a babysitter. If your daughter rejects all of these overtures, accept that, for now, she's chosen to focus more on her family than herself, and don't make a habit of telling her how worn out she looks. It only makes her feel bad.

ADVICE FOR DAUGHTERS

Nourish your marriage. Therapists agree with the older generation's view that it's healthy to spend time keeping a marriage vibrant and healthy. "It's important for couples to carve out private time," says psychologist Julia Davies. In her practice, she sees a common phenomenon among dual-career couples with children. They feel guilty about being away from the kids all day and devote all their nonwork hours to the children. As a result, "the first thing to go is romance. It's a tension so many people live with." The image of a loving couple who truly enjoy one another's company is an essential role model for children as they grow up and establish their own romantic relationships. Children can feel guilty if their parents are stressed, or if they never take breaks for adults-only time. Making a deliberate commitment to couple time helps parents become refreshed and invigorated, so they're more focused on their kids when they're with them, Davies says.

Make a regular date with your spouse. Dr. Davies suggests couples make a weekly date night, or if that's impossible, then go on an overnight trip together once a month and have the children stay with family or friends. The parents could swap with the hosts to give them the opportunity for their own overnight getaway. Regardless of how frequent these respites are, parents should set aside time for activities they can do with each other, minus the kids. Activities should provide the opportunity to really talk and connect with one another—like a quiet dinner or a long bike ride. Don't go to see a movie unless you're going out for a drink together afterward, advises Davies. The point is to pick an activity both spouses enjoy, where you can focus on yourselves and each other, "not on which kid needs a cup of juice or a cheese sandwich." During these outings, couples should try to learn about one another. Busy spouses have the illusion that they know everything about each other, but in reality they don't share meaningful information about themselves or their feelings—especially when they're managing hectic daily schedules. Setting aside couple time will help to keep spouses in touch with each other, even when they're both ministering to their jobs and children, Davies says.

For Busy Women, Exercise Is the First Thing to Go . . .

Eva Cohen can't hide her worries about her daughter, Susan. When we first introduced Eva in Chapter 6, she shared her concerns about her grandchildren's unhealthy diets. Her focus on health and nutrition isn't limited to her granddaughters. Eva tells us Susan's so busy with work and her children, she doesn't take enough time for exercise—and Susan is now thirty pounds overweight as a result.

Susan was once the model of physical fitness, working out two hours a day and perfecting her exercise routine with the help of her personal trainer. That was before work and parenting overtook her waking hours. Susan now works full-time from her home as a marketing consultant and is raising two daughters, ages 9 and 12. Finding time to exercise has been difficult, as her business has taken off and her tween-age daughters have an ever-expanding social calendar filled with playdates and after-school activities. She feels guilty using her nonworking hours to exercise, taking even more time from her girls. While Susan reserves one night each week for a date with her husband, she's finding it impossible to also squeeze regular exercise—or private time—into her schedule. "Our life is hectic," sighs Susan.

Eva is worried about her daughter's recent weight gain because her daughter has been thin for most of her life. Excrcise, as well as some regular rest and relaxation, will benefit her daughter both physically and emotionally. But Susan says there aren't enough hours in the day.

Many working mothers we spoke with said when life got too hectic, exercise was one of the first things to get cut out of their weekly routine. Most were resigned to letting their gym memberships lapse. It was one of the few sacrifices they could make to save their sanity. National surveys confirm what the daughters told us. The National Sleep Foundation found that when working women were pressed for time, most adjusted by cutting back on sleep (52 percent), while 48 percent said exercise was the first thing to go. Another 37 percent said they stopped taking the time to eat or prepare healthy meals.[2]

Eva is right when she points out that working mothers are sacrificing their health. But are their daughters also justified in putting their families and jobs first? Dr. Mayerson agrees with Eva that exercise will only benefit her daughter. Exercise burns calories and helps women to build up their muscle mass, bone density, and physical stamina. It also increases endorphin levels, which leaves women feeling energized and in good spirits. Not exercising also carries serious costs for mothers and their children. An estimated 60 percent of American adults are currently overweight or obese; obesity poses both short- and long-term health threats. Overweight parents may also convey the message that exercise isn't worthwhile, leading their children down the path to inactivity and weight gain. Dr. Mayerson suggests several ways for daughters to heed their mothers' concerns about their physical health.

ADVICE FOR MOTHERS

Help your daughter make exercise a part of her life. Financially well-off mothers could help spring for a personal trainer, who can schedule appointments at times that work best with a daughter's schedule and who can design a time-efficient workout routine. Or, consider buying her a treadmill or stationary bike, so she can have easy access to physical activity at home. If these options aren't possible for you, and your daughter makes clear she still has no time for exercise, hold off criticizing how she looks. Daughters know if they've gained weight and nothing makes them feel worse than when their mothers mention it.

ADVICE FOR DAUGHTERS

Build exercise into your routine. Exercise can be built into ordinary family activities, says Dr. Mayerson. Instead of dropping the kids off at the skating rink, take your skates and join them. Or the family could take an after-dinner walk around the neighborhood. These tactics allow you not only to exercise and spend time with the family, but to show your children the importance of engaging in healthy behaviors.

Start exercising in moderation. We have a tendency to adopt an all-or-nothing attitude when we think of exercising, says Dr. Mayerson. If we can't do it all, it's not worth doing. The reality is that any increase in activity level is beneficial. It's important to set realistic goals. Rather than saying, "I'll exercise for an hour," tell yourself you'll exercise for just ten minutes; after the first exhilarating few minutes, most people are energized enough to continue for another twenty minutes, even if they didn't have that kind of motivation when the exercise session first began.

Mold your exercise routine to your personality. People benefit most from activities that match their skills, personality, and interests. Exercise is no different. If you're a very social person, working out alone is probably not going to be very satisfying. Rather, set up a regular time to go running with a friend, perhaps when your husband is home and can watch the kids. That also allows you some time for adult interaction. If you're a nature lover, try taking walks in the park rather than on the treadmill at the indoor recreation center.

Not a Moment to Herself:
The Single Mother's Dilemma

For Janinc Marks, age 44, whom we last met in Chapter 4, finding private time is an impossible dream. Janine is the single mother of three daughters adopted from China, so she rarely has time to unwind. Reading novels or spending an afternoon at the gym are the stuff of fantasy. Her single-minded devotion to her daughters and her job as a public school teacher worry her mother, Faye Hayman, age 69. "She has the full burden," from working, to driving the kids to soccer, to picking up the dry-cleaning. Faye says she was a working mother as well, a teacher just like her daughter, but she had a housekeeper. Janine can't afford a cleaning service on her meager salary, so "it all falls on her," Faye says. Each time Janine decided to adopt, Faye worried about the toll raising another child would take on her physical and emotional health—especially because Janine has Crohn's disease. "Why is she making life difficult for herself?" she asks.

Since Janine likes reading, Faye thinks she'd enjoy joining a book club. Janine would get intellectual stimulation and an opportunity for adult conversation and companionship. Faye said she enjoyed plenty of adult time when she was a young mother. She and her husband would spend evenings with friends at the theater or ballet, while other times Faye and her friends would play mah-jongg. When Faye needed time alone or with her girlfriends, she'd hire a sitter; or her husband would sometimes look after the children. Janine won't even hire a babysitter for a haircut appointment, and she takes her three girls with her to the salon. Janine says they're content to draw with their crayons while she's with the stylist. "It seems silly to pay somebody to watch the girls when I get my hair done," says Janine, who notes that her daughters are quite capable of entertaining themselves.

Faye also worries that Janine is doomed to a life of singlehood. With such daunting parenting responsibilities and a full-time job, her daughter doesn't have time to meet a potential suitor for coffee, never mind for a lasting romantic relationship. Janine says she has tried the popular Jewish dating Web site J-Date and met a few "strange men" there. She jokes that her middle daughter won't let her talk to men, so she'll put off dating until her children are older. For the time being, Janine is content with her single status, and says she doesn't experience pangs of loneliness. Still, Faye thinks her daughter sorely needs some adults in her life, whether it's a group of women friends or male friends, or one special man. "I think she's too isolated with the kids and that concerns me."

Janine isn't opposed to having a more well-rounded life, but she doesn't see this is a viable option, at least not right now. She wakes up at 4:30 A.M., then showers, gets dressed, and packs lunches for her children. She and the girls are out the door by 6:20 A.M. so she can drop them at early-morning day care and still make it to work on time. The children go to bed by 8:30 P.M. "and I'm right behind them," she says, so exhausted she can't take advantage of the quiet hours in the evening when they're sleeping. Babysitters and cleaning services are costly, so neither is an option. But Janine insists she's not stressed: "I enjoy being with my kids." She says she has her summers off, and during the school year her workday ends at 2:30. She doesn't pick up the girls from child care until 5:00, so she has a few hours each afternoon, though that time is spent running errands and grocery shopping, not indulging in Pilates and pedicures. When her children get a bit older and are more independent, Janine may take time to explore her own hobbies and possibly start dating again. For now, though, that's not on her agenda. Janine wishes her mother could understand that she has no choice but to prioritize family and work over personal relaxation.

In recent years, social critics like Judith Warner, in her book *Perfect Madness,* have argued that working mothers are trying so hard to be "perfect" mothers and workers that they're anxiety-ridden and hovering on the brink of burnout. Survey after survey reveals that working women like Janine are exhausted and the first things to get excised from their busy schedules are rest and relaxation. Sleep and peace of mind are always in scarce supply. A poll taken by the National Sleep Foundation in 2007 found that 72 percent of working mothers report they don't get enough sleep. And their scarce hours of sleep do not come easily; most worry as they are trying to doze off.[3] A recent survey by Braun Research found that more than one-third of working mothers toss and turn worrying about the next day's activities, while one-quarter say they worry about their families while trying to fall asleep.[4]

Faye is right when she says rest and relaxation would improve her daughter's quality of life. A full two-thirds of the working mothers surveyed by Braun said more sleep would "make them happier." How can mothers like Faye adjust to the fact that their single-parent daughters often don't make private time a part of their agenda? Dr. Sanford weighs in.

ADVICE FOR MOTHERS

Accept that your daughter's needs may differ from yours. Janine thinks spending time with her children is currently her most important duty, explains Dr. Sanford. Her children won't be young forever, but for now, Janine is preoccupied with hands-on care. As her children grow more self-reliant, the daily demands will lessen. Faye should take Janine at her own word and rest assured that her daughter is happy with her situation. Dr. Sanford says it's possible Janine is someone who doesn't particularly enjoy adult company, but who takes delight in her children. They love her unconditionally and bring her joy, so she doesn't crave personal time. She's an excellent mother, and it makes her feel confident she's so good at what she does.

Pitch in to give your daughter a break. Single mothers, perhaps more than anyone, could use their mothers' help. But women like Janine, who pride themselves on being self-sufficient, energetic, and capable, may be reticent about asking for assistance. Dr. Sanford suggests Faye figure out the best way to help Janine and then act on it. What's most important is to help in the way *Janine* thinks would be helpful, not in the way *Faye* thinks is most helpful. Once a week, Faye could pick her granddaughters up at school and take them to McDonald's or bring them to her house one evening a month, so her daughter can go to a book club meeting. On the weekend, she could babysit so her daughter can have a few hours to herself. Or she could offer to pay someone to clean her daughter's house once a month or every two weeks. The mom needs to consider whether she is doing everything she can to help make her daughter's life less difficult. "It's one thing to talk about it. It's another to be willing to put your actions toward helping her," Dr. Sanford says.

ADVICE FOR DAUGHTERS

Take your mother up on her offer. If your mother is worried about you and offers to babysit or treat you to a massage, say yes. There's no point in being a martyr. You will get a chance for some much-needed relaxation and it will make your mother happy to know she's contributing to your well-being.

Assure your mother you're okay. If you've chosen to sacrifice personal time as a way to best focus on your job and your kids, explain this to your mother. Reassuring her that you're comfortable with your hectic life and that you won't have an emotional breakdown may be just the remedy for her constant worrying.

Putting Yourself Before the Kids? Balancing Personal Passions with Family Demands

Mary Kleinschmidt, now 46, has been a musical theater buff as long as she can remember. She majored in radio, television, and film when she was an undergraduate at Northwestern University. Although she ultimately became a lawyer, she keeps her passion for the arts alive by acting in a community theater company, which requires rehearsals from 7:00 to 10:00 P.M., Monday through Thursday. Mary now lives in Indiana, far from the bright lights of Broadway, but she occasionally treats herself to jaunts to world-class cultural destinations. She recently jetted from Indiana to San Francisco to see the world premiere of contemporary composer John Adams's *Doctor Atomic,* performed by the San Francisco Opera. Vivian's mother questions whether it's wise for the divorced mother of three teenagers, ages 19, 16, and 14, to devote so much time and money to her personal passions.

"My daughter and I have conflicts," admits Vivian. "I'll say, 'I think you should spend more time with your children,'" and she'll say 'Mom!' in an exasperated tone." Vivian knows her daughter has it tough raising three teens on her own, but she says that's all the more reason why Mary *should* be home with them when she's not working.

Mary says her mother is constantly criticizing her. "She'll say, 'You're never home with your kids.'" She admits that when her mother makes remarks "in a certain tone of voice, I'll be overly sensitive to that." When Mary does take time for herself, like going to see a play or being in a show, "she'll think I'm really bad" and that Mary should either be working or with the kids. "I defend my right to actually have a life or a hobby," Mary counters. She says theater is a great escape and she enjoys the creative process of producing a show with intelligent, artistic people, who are different than her attorney colleagues. Mary would rather be pursuing her passions than "sitting around at home and twiddling my thumbs." She tells her mother she wants her children to grow up knowing it's okay for parents to have a passion for the arts, or sports, or politics "and not just live their lives for their children. . . . It's acceptable for me to be in a play once in a while or to go to a show or listen to live music."

Mary says her mother thinks she should be content to stay at home and dote on her children, "and not want anything more than that." She says it's hard for her mother to relate, since Vivian is content to stay home every night watching television or reading novels. Mary thinks her mother doesn't take enough time for herself. "I think there's some frustration in her life"—because she feels shackled to her home and her garden. "She's always pulling weeds or working around the house. She's never able to sit down and relax. The thing that's so important to her has pretty much destroyed her in some ways," says Mary. Vivian recently had a knee replacement operation, which Mary attributes to her mother's physical toil in her garden. Mary thinks her mother "seems unfulfilled and enslaved by this whole lifestyle," and she wishes she wouldn't work so hard or obsess over "silly things" like maintaining the perfect backyard garden or the sparkling clean kitchen.

Mary sees her mother's devotion to homemaking tasks as a mistake she doesn't plan to repeat. However, Vivian thinks just being home with the kids should be enough to make her daughter content. She doesn't understand why Mary wants so much more. Mary tells her mother she's not on a quest to find a second husband. She'd rather find fulfillment in other interests. She wishes this conflict over personal time wasn't such a big issue and her mother would relax so the two could enjoy each other's company. "I wish we could go out to lunch and have a fun talk," Mary says.

Like Mary, Deirdre Hamilton is devoted to the arts and refuses to accept that parenthood means one's passions should fade away. Deirdre is a talented alto. She sings in a choir and is happy to drive the two-hour round trip to and from weekly rehearsals. Every Tuesday night, she leaves her house at 6:00 P.M. and doesn't return home until 11:00 P.M. Deirdre has sung in the community choir for the past ten years, well before her daughters were born. She loves singing, and choir connects her to the friends and the identity she had before she became a wife, mother, and scientist.

Her mother, Yoon-Ji Hamilton, doesn't think it's appropriate for Deirdre to spend five hours a week away from her daughters pursuing her avocation for music. "My opinion is that it's too hard for her to do that," says Yoon-Ji. "It's too long away from the kids." Since Deirdre, a staff scientist at a large university, is away from her children most weekdays, Yoon-Ji feels she should spend most of her nonwork hours with the children. Yoon-Ji understands the demands of being a full-time worker. She ran a printing business with her husband full-time while raising her children. But, when the workday ended, she was home with her family.

Deirdre gripes that her mother repeatedly tells her, "You don't have time for choir." For Deirdre and her husband, Seth, it's important that they both have separate hobbies. Seth encourages Deirdre's singing; it's only fair, as he plays on a soccer team twice a week. "He feels this is giving back to me the time I make" for his soccer practice, she says.

Deirdre admits her mother's disapproval "completely sets me off because telling me I can't do something really bothers me." She says her mother's comments imply that Deirdre is not capable of managing the different parts of her life—"that I'm not using the time I have wisely somehow and that I'm making bad decisions."

She gets more support from her mother-in-law, Molly Collins, with whom she has a wonderful, easygoing relationship. Deirdre describes her as "helpful without being invasive." Molly, who works as an administrative assistant, thinks it's terrific that Deirdre and Seth can squeeze their hobbies into their hectic work and child-rearing schedules. "I know from experience that a mother needs her own thing. I wasn't critical at all," Molly says. She and her husband routinely step in to help on choir nights, arriving with dinner at 5:30, so Deirdre has a bite to eat, and then staying with the kids until Seth gets home from work. Molly says her own mother's mother-in-law (her father's mother) was so overbearing and intrusive that she caused Molly's mother to have a nervous breakdown. "I vowed I was never going to be like that," she says. At the same time, she is sympathetic to Deirdre's mother, who had a difficult time raising children in the culture of a new country. She says it's easy to be supportive of Deirdre. "I can't say enough good things about her. I think she's great."

Vivian Kleinschmidt and Yoon-Ji Hamilton can't support their daughters' decisions to carve out a little piece of time for themselves and to keep alive their passions for music and theater. One reason for their skepticism is that women like Deirdre and Mary are very rare; dozens of studies show that only a small fraction of working mothers manage to find any time to pursue their own interests. A recent Gallup Poll found 72 percent of working mothers said they had "too little time" alone, to spend on hobbies or rest.[5]

Mary and Deirdre are purposefully keeping up their musical and theatrical interests in part because they viewed their mothers' lives as joyless. Yoon-Ji worked all day at the family's printing business and prepared traditional Korean dishes for her children and husband for dinner. Vivian was tethered to her home and garden, a decision that Mary thinks left her physically and emotionally depleted. Of course, this is just Mary's perception: as Peggy Orenstein observes in *Flux*, her insightful portrait of Generation X women, "daughters are notoriously unreliable narrators of their mothers' lives."[6] Still, many daughters we spoke with tried hard to pursue their personal interests so they wouldn't suffer from what Betty Friedan called "the problem with no name." In Friedan's *Feminine Mystique*, the book many point to as unleashing the feminist movement, Friedan wondered about suburban housewives like Vivian Kleinschmidt: "As she made the beds, shopped for groceries, [and] lay beside her husband at night—she was afraid to ask even of herself the silent question: 'Is this all?' "[7] Mary Kleinschmidt wants to make sure that for her, the answer is no.

Is a daughter spending too much time on herself—or not enough? Are working women like Mary being selfish if they take time for themselves without the children? The therapists we consulted believe it's crucial for women to have an identity outside of wife, mother, or worker, and suggest ways that mothers and daughters can see eye to eye on the value of private time.

ADVICE FOR MOTHERS

Be sympathetic to your daughter's struggles. Mothers should recognize that their daughters are doing the best they can, given the constraints of their own lives, says Dr. Carl Pickhardt. They're oscillating between their desire for couple time, child time, and rest and relaxation. For example, Mary Kleinschmidt is facing the conflicts of acting as a single woman and a parent. Her mother, Vivian, needs to recognize that Mary must honor and take care of both her family's needs and her own needs. If she overinvests in parenting, she ends up resenting the children. If she overinvests in her personal life, she risks feeling guilty. Mary has achieved a compromise between the two roles she can live with, so her mother should applaud that.

Try to retire from active parenting. Dr. Pickhardt reminds mothers that their daughters are adults and will ultimately have to manage the consequences of their decisions and compromises. Mothers who have raised their daughters to be thoughtful and compassionate should have faith in their decisions. To constantly harp on a daughter's behavior may prove harmful to mothers in the end. As Dr. Pickardt posed rhetorically, "Do I want to die knowing that what I have left my daughter is my lasting disapproval?"

ADVICE FOR DAUGHTERS

Consider the future impacts of your decisions. Working mothers today are constantly struggling with the issue of life balance, says Dr. Donna Mayerson. When time and money are scarce, women need to prioritize, and most give top billing to the concerns that seem most pressing *right now*. But, as Eva's concerns with her daughter's health reveal, it's also important to consider the longer-term ramifications of one's choices. Susan let her exercise routine lapse because her job and children posed a more pressing concern. If her health declines, however, that will compromise her ability to be a good worker and mother in the future. When daughters weigh their priorities, they should consider both the short- and long-term consequences of their choices.

Mobilize your resources. Think of the broad base of people in your life—babysitter, mother, husband, friends, neighbors—who can support you in engaging in personally satisfying, health-enhancing behaviors. Perhaps you can swap with a friend, watching each other's children while you exercise, catch up on reading, or schedule a weekly date with your husband. Your family and friends likely value you as much as you do them and want to help you reach your goals, suggests Dr. Mayerson.

ADVICE FOR MOTHERS AND DAUGHTERS

Recognize that it's healthy for kids to see their parents having fun. It's very important for children to see their mothers doing something for themselves and following their passions, says Dr. Howard Weinblatt, who has spent many years performing in his neighborhood's community theater. Mothers who raised their children thirty or forty years ago should realize the benefits of following personal pursuits, even if it seems time-consuming. When children become adults and look back on their mother's life, they'll view her as a more fascinating person, someone who had a beautiful singing voice or was an engaging performer. It's valuable to see the fun side of one's mother—much more so than remembering one's mother as a martyr who slaved for the family. "It's better to model passions for your kids," Dr. Weinblatt says.

CHAPTER 10

Managing Crises: True Stories of How Mothers and Daughters Undermine—or Inspire—Each Other

When I decided to go back to college at 50, my stepdaughter was my biggest supporter.

My mother was a great source of emotional support during my trying fertility treatments.

I could never have juggled teaching and caring for twins without my mother's help.

Mother-daughter relationships are put to the test when a crisis strikes. If the relationship has always been loving and supportive, it may grow even stronger when the two weather a crisis together. If, on the other hand, mothers and daughters have had difficulty getting along, a major crisis could be the breaking point. In this chapter, we share poignant stories about the crises that mothers and daughters experience and show how these events can either bring the relationship to a better, more empathetic level or magnify tensions that have been building for years.

When the Crises of Aging Strikes:
Making a Bad Relationship Worse

Getting old is never easy. When physical health and cognitive abilities start to fade, most older adults understand that they need to turn to their children for support. The loss of autonomy is hard for everyone, especially for those who cherish their independence. The challenges of aging are all the more difficult when a parent hasn't treated her children well through the years; she may find her children offer their help tentatively and reluctantly. That's the case with Sally Handleman, 71, and her daughters Lindsay, 42, and Jill, 41, whom we first met in Chapter 3.

According to her daughters, Sally always cherished her role as the center of the social scene in her upscale Minnesota city. A regal woman who commands respect from others, Sally is now devastated by the sequential loss of her cognitive functions, her physical health, and finally her home. She's particularly distraught because her daughters did not respect her wish to live independently in her own home. Her daughters believe it's dangerous for her to live alone, but Sally doesn't agree, and berates her daughters for putting her in a nursing home. While most aging parents and their grown children must make tough decisions about long-term care, the decision has been particularly difficult for the Handleman women, whose relationship has been strained for more than three decades.

Fifty years ago, when Sally Handleman was a young woman, she bore a striking resemblance to Jackie Kennedy. She had the same jet black hair, olive skin, high cheekbones, and slender figure. Hints of that glamorous style are still apparent, even in a photograph of her sitting in a wheelchair in the kitchen of her assisted living facility. She's proud that she hasn't gone gray. Her hair is the same radiant color it was in her youth. But her eyes also reveal the strain of a life, once grand, that has fallen into disrepair.

Sally once hosted lavish parties in her historic home, which she's lived in since 1977. Lindsay and Jill describe the house as one of Minnesota's finest mansions. Nestled in the woods overlooking a lake, the home resembles an English castle. The 5,200-square-foot, six-bedroom house was recently put up for sale, with an asking price of more than $2 million. Sally is heartbroken that her home will soon be in the hands of a new owner.

Sally's home serves as a reminder of her opulent lifestyle, now gone. Her memories are bittersweet, however. Sally once shared the estate with her husband, who divorced her twenty years ago, after learning of her affair with the family's architect. Her daughters understand how attached Sally is to her home, but feel she is no longer capable of living there alone. Last March, Sally was diagnosed with Lewy body dementia, a variant of Alzheimer's. At that time, she had round-the-clock care in her home because she was falling and improperly administering her medications. Her doctor told Jill and Lindsay that she should not live in the house anymore.

Sally's daughters, friends, and other relatives had been begging her to move into a condominium for eight years, but Sally had no interest, even after getting the mandate from her doctor. A week after she received the diagnosis, she broke her ankle while getting out of bed and was moved to a rehabilitation unit. At that time, she signed over a quasi-guardianship to her daughters.

After the doctor insisted that Sally move, Jill, Lindsay, and their younger sister began proceedings to sell the house. Jill recalls sitting down with her mother in the rehab facility for two hours, with the staff from the nursing home, explaining that they were putting the house on the market. She was "fairly apprised" of the situation, Jill says. But that's not how Sally remembers it. She recalls that Jill visited with her husband and two boys, ages 10 and 11. Sally says she was asking about the condition of the house and Jill told her it was in good shape. She also said she recalled the conversation with her doctor, but she had a plan to stay in the house, revamping it so she could live on the main floor, with railings to prevent her from falling. She felt that with aides to take care of her, she'd be safe there. But, she says, she learned about the sale that day in the rehab center. "They sold my house without my approval," she says. She regrets turning over authority for such a decision to her children. "I said, 'Jill, take it off the market.'"

Moving one's mother from a beloved home she's lived in for over thirty years would be tough under any circumstances. But for the

Handlemans, the stress is heightened, since Sally's daughters have always had difficulty dealing with their mother. Jill, an even-tempered woman who rarely fights with her husband, says, "My mother is the only person in my life I've ever raised my voice to." Jill says on that spring day when she and her family visited her mother, Sally screamed at her as if it was the first time she had heard about the sale of the house. "She had plenty of warning," says Jill. She isn't certain whether her mother's dementia was responsible for her forgetting the conversation about selling the house or whether she was pretending not to remember.

Jill wishes her mother had taken control of the move herself several years ago when her faculties were intact, as her daughters had urged her to do. When she did finally vacate her home, "she was incapable of even throwing away a newspaper, much less cleaning out thirty years of stuff from one house," Jill said. The house sale ultimately went smoothly in spite of her mother's opposition, because the bank, her lawyers, her brother, her doctors, her friends, and Sally's case manager (and the law) all supported the daughters' decision to move Sally.

Sally's daughters also had to be assertive in taking away their mother's car and driver's license. "She was going to kill somebody," Jill said. Jill lives nearby and many times witnessed her mother swerving down the road. There were scrapes all over the car. For more than three years, the daughters took actions to prevent her from driving, including parking a van in front of the garage so she couldn't get out and hiring a lawyer to help take away her car.

Sally is offended that her children attempted to get a court order to limit her driving. "I was stunned and horrified," she says. "I wanted to continue driving." The scrapes, she said, were from occasionally brushing up against pillars. But there was "no real accident." These kinds of arguments have caused Lindsay to wash her hands of her mother. She rarely sees her. Lindsay's "always standoffish with me. . . . She's never been particularly close to me. I always wanted to be close to her," says Sally.

Lindsay says it's hard to have empathy for her mother, who, she says, was an uncaring mother who thought exclusively of her own needs. And now she's "lonely living in a dreary nursing home." Sally never imagined herself in this situation, Lindsay says. But if she were a kinder parent and more involved in her children's lives, the daughters would have made more of an effort to give her the assistance she needed. It's helped that Lindsay, Jill, and her younger sister support each other when it comes to their mother. Lawyers and real estate agents have told the sisters they "deal well and so respectfully with such a difficult parent." Even though she would rather have no inter-actions with her mother, Lindsay says, "We try to do what we can to make sure she's taken care of."

Jill says that as the oldest daughter, she's become the primary care-taker: "I feel a greater sense of responsibility toward her." Sally says that of her three daughters, "Jill is most like me, only sweeter." She feels closest to Jill, who is more like a friend to her. Jill says she could never turn to her mother for emotional support. And, when her mother be-comes unreasonable, she'll take a two- or three-month break from her, skipping her weekly visits. Lindsay and the youngest sister won't return her calls and could go six months without seeing her. "I respect that," Jill says. But she says she feels a strong sense of obligation, as well as compassion. "I still have it in my heart to feel sorry for her. I wouldn't want to be in her place."

Jill and Lindsay are facing a challenge that is common to mil-lions of adult children as their aging parents experience failing health and the need for round-the-clock personal care. Taking away a parent's driver's license or encouraging a parent to move into an assisted-living facility can be traumatic turning points, because they send the message to older adults that they're no longer competent to care for themselves. That causes a role reversal, where the once-dependent daughter essentially becomes the caretaker—a heartbreak-ing transition. These changes also alter the nature of the parents' daily lives.

It's no wonder that Sally is saddened by the many changes in her life: the new home, the loss of her car, and her fading memory. Geron-tologists often advise adult children to maintain as much continuity as possible from their mothers' past—that is, if their mothers were happy with their past.[1] A favorite wall-hanging from one's home can brighten a nursing home room. Finding an assisted-living facility where the residents are old friends or neighbors can ease the transition.

It's good to encourage Mom to sign up for an activity that is similar to the hobbies or job she once enjoyed. For instance, a former school-teacher may want to volunteer to teach fellow seniors how to use a computer.

Although these general suggestions are helpful, they may fall on deaf ears when the mother-daughter relationship has been strained. Daughters may not want to put themselves at risk of being berated by their mothers, while mothers may automatically assume that their daughters' gestures are controlling or cruel. We spoke with Dr. Merrill for tips on navigating the challenges of aging in those cases where the mother-daughter relationship has been troubled for some time.

ADVICE FOR MOTHERS

Recognize that reciprocity rules. Dr. Merrill often sees situations where mothers are abusive to their children and then expect that the children will be around to take care of them. "It's part of their narcissism," he says. The same thing that undermined Sally's relationship with her husband—he divorced her after she had an affair—is now undermining her relationship with her daughters. Mothers who are still in good shape physically and emotionally may want to reflect on how they've treated their daughters in the past and whether they've created a climate that fosters love and support. If not, then mothers may need to alter their expectations for what their daughters can do for them in the future.

ADVICE FOR DAUGHTERS

When dealing with an unhealthy or aging mother, try to be empathetic. Dr. Merrill agrees with Jill that compassion is what's needed most in this situation. You can have compassion even for people who are narcissistic, he says. Women may cut others slack for their shortcomings, but not their own mothers. Much of that comes from a mother's failure to fulfill her daughter's needs; this can lead to deep-seated resentment, says Dr. Merrill. Sally's daughters, now in their forties, "need to grow up." They should see their mother as a person with shortcomings who has messed up her life, but they have to stop blaming her for messing up theirs.

Don't let your mother run your life. Dr. Merrill suggests setting ground rules and limits on the relationship, in a very loving way, regarding how often you'll see your mother. Make sure it's an arrangement that works for both mother and daughters. The daughter can withdraw, and, like Jill does, take a break from the mother, if she steps over the limits.

When Silence Causes Pain: How Mothers Manage Daughters' "Secret" Crises

Nearly every daughter we spoke with has kept a crisis in her life secret from her mother: a job loss, an abortion, or a failed romance. The explanation was always the same: "I didn't want her to worry." But when we delved closer, we often found that daughters didn't want Mom to *judge*. That was the case with Johanna Jones.

Johanna, now 48, is often likened to a turtle by her sister, Jesse Slater, 51. "She looks like she could draw her head into her chest," Jesse says. "Withdrawing is her main coping mechanism." Even though Jesse and her mother, Genevieve Canvasser, 74, always knew that Johanna kept things to herself, they were shocked when they heard, for the first time, about a secret Johanna had been keeping from them for three decades.

We first introduced Johanna and Genevieve in Chapter 3, when Genevieve shared her concerns about Johanna delaying marriage until she was 46. But Johanna's midlife marriage pales in comparison to her big secret. After graduating high school and learning about holistic medicine, Johanna opened a chain of spas. At 19, overwhelmed by the work, she began feeling weak. Ultimately, she says, she was diagnosed with breast and cervical cancer. Tears well up in her eyes as she reveals the news. Johanna's mom and sister were hearing this for the first time, thirty years after the diagnosis, during our conversation with them.

Johanna concealed her illness all these years because she had decided to use alternative therapy and feared that her mother would disapprove. She was chemically sensitive as a child, so she had no intention of undergoing chemotherapy. She also was vehemently opposed to any type of major surgery: "I didn't want my breasts and other organs removed." She knew that Genevieve, a nurse, would not approve of her radical decision. She sought a peaceful change of venue, so she moved to a remote jungle in Hawaii and began a self-administered regimen of fasting, praying, and a diet that included wheat grass. "I didn't want to be a burden to anyone and I didn't trust that people could honor my choice," she says. Her mother was overwhelmed with her work and her difficult marriage at that time, so Johanna didn't want to tell her about her situation and add to her stress. Shielding her mom from bad news was a pattern for Johanna. "I only called my mom when I was okay." She was concerned that if she shared something unpleasant, her mother would worry. Fortunately, the treatments worked, and Johanna says she is healthy today.

Upon hearing the news of Johanna's cancer for the first time, Genevieve cried. She was "very sad" her daughter couldn't turn to her. But she understands where Johanna is coming from. Genevieve says her daughter's independent, headstrong nature stems from her parents' divorce when she was 7. She says that children who experience divorce grow up quickly and feel responsible for protecting their mother. Jesse, though equally stunned by the news, says it's in Johanna's nature to keep her worries to herself and try to solve problems on her own. Johanna agrees with this assessment. "I don't like you wanting to help me when I'm not feeling well," she tells Jesse. But Jesse understands Johanna's concerns about her mother. She agrees that Genevieve can be very emotional and easily set off by bad news.

The tables were turned last year when Genevieve had surgery and Johanna came to care for her. Since Johanna has experience in health care and was available to come to her mother's house, she was an ideal caregiver. "It was a big turning point and we had more sharing," Genevieve says. "I really appreciated it." Johanna felt gratified providing the care that she could never accept from her mother when she was ill.

Just as Johanna wanted to shield her mother from her cancer di-
agnoses, Janet Ingersoll, age 42, tried not to burden her mother, Helen
Ingersoll, age 69, with her fertility problems. Like Johanna, Janet
feared her mother was too emotionally fragile to provide strength and
support. She also worried her mother couldn't understand what it was
like to go through fertility treatments. After all, Helen married at 22
and had her first baby at 24. Janet, by contrast, married at 29 and tried
to start a family at 31. To her dismay, she had difficulty conceiving, but
eventually gave birth to a son when she was 34. She said that initially,
she would tell her mother about the steps she and her husband were
taking to get pregnant, but Helen got so anxious for her daughter that
Janet stopped discussing it, keeping her mother in the dark. She said
the ordeal was emotional enough for her; she didn't want to have to
handle her mother's emotions as well.

Janet says her mother is "not good at being unselfishly supportive"
and often reacts to others' news by focusing on what it means for *her*.
For example, Helen was upset when Janet and her husband stopped at
one child. She couldn't accept that she wouldn't have any other grandchildren. "There are many issues I avoid discussing with my mom,"
she says.

Helen says she couldn't wrap her mind around the fertility treatments. When she was a young mother, infertility wasn't an issue
women talked about, and most of her friends got pregnant easily since
they married so young. It never occurred to her that her daughter
would have any problems. "It was painful to watch her," she says. She
says she can relate to Janet's feelings of pain and loss better now. She
feels a pang when she sees her friends spending time with their grandchildren who live nearby. Helen lives in the Washington, D.C., area
while her daughter's family lives in Massachusetts. She says she is
more emotional than her daughter, and that Janet doesn't verbalize
her feelings as much, which "sometimes causes misunderstandings between us." The fact that her daughter lives far away now makes communication even more difficult, she says.

Although Johanna and Janet ultimately shared news of their health
travails with their mothers, withholding information from loved ones
can be hurtful and seen as a betrayal. Fortunately, Johanna and her

mother managed to pull through and grow even closer after Johanna's secret was revealed. What about other mothers and daughters who try to shield one another from crises in their lives? Dr. Pickhardt gives his advice on when, and what, to share.

ADVICE FOR MOTHERS

Recognize that empathy may bring complications along with benefits. For most women, empathy is both a strength and a liability. When Helen got "anxious on Janet's behalf," an empathetic response became more burdensome than supportive. Janet doesn't want to "have to handle her mother's emotions as well." Mothers should take care to silence or at least muffle their own anxiety and focus instead on their daughter's emotional response to crisis.

ADVICE FOR DAUGHTERS

Let Mom in. If Johanna and Janet were being honest, they would admit they weren't only trying to protect their mothers; they also were trying to protect themselves from managing their mothers' emotions. A daughter who is determined to be independent of her mother may not be willing to regress and once again depend on her mother's care. She may underestimate her mother's ability to help during a tough time. She should recognize that shielding her mother from difficult news could harm their relationship in the longer term. Daughters should weigh the pros and cons of silence versus honesty, and assess which path brings the least harm to them both.

Take the opportunity to give back. Psychological studies show that people feel better about giving care than receiving it. It makes them feel competent, useful, and valued. That's certainly true for Johanna, who cared for her mother after surgery. When a daughter gives back to her mother, the parent-child roles are reversed. This act of reversal may set the mother and daughter free of old entanglements that have kept them apart, so it's a beneficial development.

Realize the value of Mom's input. Dr. Sanford agrees that a wonderful bond was forged during Genevieve's health crisis. But she hopes that Johanna will seek her mother's help in the future if she needs it, since mothers can be one's greatest source of support. "I hope we reach an age when we're grown enough to have heart-to-heart conversations with our mothers," she says. Just because you had one type of relationship with your mother growing up or in early adulthood doesn't mean things can't be different now, she says.

Branch out for support, if necessary. In some cases, a mother may not be the best confidante. For example, if her daughter's troubles overwhelm her, then the daughter should feel comfortable turning to friends, sisters, aunts, or colleagues. Even the most self-sufficient woman shouldn't have to undergo a health crisis alone.

When Crises Bring Us Closer: Strong Mother-Daughter Relationships Triumph over Adversity

It's no secret that daughters often take their mothers for granted. Daughters *expect* that their mothers will be their protector during difficult times. But many of the daughters we spoke with were profoundly grateful when their mothers went above and beyond the call of maternal duty. These triumphant and loving interventions made healthy mother-daughter relationships even stronger.

For Erin Inges, the turning point came when she was 19, unmarried, and unexpectedly pregnant. Although she feared her mother would condemn her, she turned out to be her best confidante and helpmate. For Kelly Rodriguez, the revelation came when she was confined to eleven weeks of bed rest before giving birth to twins. Her mother was her savior, temporarily moving in with Kelly and helping out with cooking, cleaning, and infant care. Erin, Kelly, and dozens of other daughters we spoke with said that the petty squabbles over breast-feeding and Burger King, haircuts and housekeeping, evaporated when the daughter faced a serious crisis.

Mothers Help Daughters Through the Baby Blues

When Erin Inges was 19, she decided to break up with her fiancé, whom she met at college during the one semester she attended before leaving to work full-time. The emotional devastation of the breakup was bad enough, but she suffered another unexpected blow. She learned she was three months pregnant. "I stared at a wall for about a week and kept saying, 'Okay, God, you don't give me more than I can handle, so I must be able to handle this.'"

The most frightening part was telling her mother, a devout Christian who often cautioned her daughter against premarital sex. Despite her mother's conservative views, the two have always talked openly, especially when Erin was 16 and her mother got a divorce. "That's when we became really close." She mustered her courage and told her mother about the pregnancy. "She was a little bit in shock but handled it very well," Erin said. She didn't scream at Erin or kick her out of the house, which were all possibilities. Her mother calmly asked her what she wanted to do. She didn't suggest that Erin give up the baby up for adoption or get married. "She didn't tell me how I should live my life, but she did help me to see I had a very large decision to make," Erin said. She considered giving her baby to a cousin, who was looking to adopt a child, but in the end, she and her ex-fiancé decided to get married and raise their child together. "My mom was completely supportive." She said, "If that's what you want to do, do it."

That decision was made just over six years ago, and Erin, 26, and her husband now have a wonderful relationship. They live in Texas with their son and 2½-year-old daughter (the result of a planned pregnancy). Erin is now going back to school to earn a degree. Even though Erin was just a teenager when her son was born, she and her mother never argue about how she raises her children, and her mother often tells her how proud she is of Erin and her husband.

Erin's mother, Maureen Sampson, 50, lives in Baton Rouge, Louisiana, the city where she raised Erin. "When she told me she was pregnant, I was surprised," she says. She recalls that Erin hadn't been feeling well and had been to the doctor, so Maureen assumed her daughter was ill. "Pregnancy didn't cross my mind," she said. Upon hearing the news, she said, "I sort of took a deep breath and said, 'Is there going to be a wedding?'" She was devastated at the thought of Erin giving her baby up for adoption. "I vividly remember sitting at a traffic light one morning and just bawling at the thought of having a grandchild and not knowing him or her." She knew she had to stop thinking about herself and her needs, since the decision was ultimately her daughter's. Maureen spoke with her mother (Erin's grandmother) about a cousin who wanted to adopt a baby, but they both started crying at the thought of giving away the baby.

Two days later, Erin told Maureen that she couldn't give up the baby. "And I said, 'Now what do we do? What's the plan?'" Although she supported Erin emotionally, she also knew she had to help her daughter to be self-sufficient. She told Erin she needed to move out and live on her own and that she and her boyfriend would have to deal with the pregnancy like adults. After that discussion, he and Erin decided to marry. Four months after their wedding, the baby was born. Once they decided to marry, Maureen met her son-in-law's family. "I didn't know him very well and getting your daughter pregnant is not the best sort of introduction." Even so, as she was leaving their home, she gave him a hug and said, "You're a part of my family. I'm going to be there for you and I'm going to be watching out."

Maureen says Erin's husband has been a "pleasant surprise" and that both Erin and he are focused on doing what's right for their children. She tries hard not to interfere. "I feel like she's doing a good job and doesn't need me to tell her how to do it." She admires her daughter's determination, especially her commitment to making her marriage work despite the unplanned pregnancy. Maureen lives by the mantra "Don't sweat the small stuff."

Erin says her mother's support during her pregnancy and shotgun wedding helped her to form a loving family of her own. "My mother is my best friend," she says. The two regularly go shopping and have lunch together. Even though she was afraid to tell her about the pregnancy, she was confident that her mother would support her. "I always knew my mother was going to love me, regardless of what I did." She hopes she can be similarly supportive if her daughter finds herself in a similar situation.

Kelly Rodriguez, who has been married for eight years, also discovered that her mother was her best supporter. When Kelly was twenty-six weeks pregnant with her boys, she began having contractions, so she was put on full bed rest. "I was fearful that I was going to lose the babies," she says. Her parents worked two days a week and lived an hour and a half away at the time. For the entire eleven weeks that she was on bed rest, they drove to be with her on Thursday mornings and then returned to their home on Sunday nights. "Every time they'd come down for those four days, I remember instantly feeling a peace of mind and calmness." Her mother cooked meals and helped with the laundry.

Kelly delivered the babies full-term, at thirty-seven weeks. At one point, she suffered complications and had to return to the hospital for three days and her mother took care of the babies round the clock. Her parents stayed with Kelly and her husband for the first month after the births, and then returned for their four-day stint every week for the first eleven months of the babies' lives. Kelly says they helped enormously, since the babies had to be fed every two hours and it took forty-five minutes to feed each one. Her husband, a software engineer, lost his job when the babies were 3 months old. When he started a new job, he felt pressure to put in a full day's work and make a good impression on his new boss. As a result, he wasn't able to provide much assistance.

When the babies were 11 months old, Kelly's parents moved nearby. Kelly wanted to go back to work part-time as a teacher, but couldn't find reasonably priced day care. Her mother stepped in and cared for them until they were 3½ and ready for preschool. Kelly is infinitely grateful to her parents and says this experience has deepened her relationship with her mother.

While several of the daughters we interviewed "banned" their mothers from visiting during their baby's first few weeks of life, fearful of their mother's criticism and judgment, Kelly doesn't know how she would have survived without her mother's help during those early weeks. "That whole period for me was so stressful and Mom handled it all so well and never made me feel guilty." She says that when she was sleep-deprived, she was inclined to feel depressed, but her mother kept her upbeat. "She'd just say, 'Look at these beautiful babies.' She was always positive and she definitely helped my mood." Kelly admitted she had no idea how to care for her babies and her mother was an enormous help. "I don't know if she was doing things right or wrong. I was just so happy that someone was doing it." She also doesn't think that she would have had her third child if she couldn't count on the help and support of her mother.

Rose says that pitching in was simply a matter of motherly instinct. She felt horrible seeing her daughter on bed rest. She thought, "Oh my God, poor woman. This is supposed to be a wonderful nine months." She says she willingly cut back on her job to be there midweek for several weeks. "It was a joy," she says. She cooked dinner every night and it was a "lovely" time. "We never seemed to fight or have arguments." Since Kelly's husband had lost his job, Rose says that she and her husband, Frank, felt it was their obligation to help out. When Kelly seemed exhausted after the babies were born and needed help, they didn't hesitate to stay. "I don't think you should have children unless you're going to be behind them right to the bitter end, through school, going through college, and afterward." Rose says she's "very close to those boys" as a result of all the time she spent with them in their early years. Even today, if Kelly tells her mother she's tired and needs a rest, Rose immediately volunteers to babysit.

Mothers' Inspiring Models

As long as Isabella Gomes, 39, can remember, her mother, Gina Gomes, 68, has been a progressive woman, ahead of her time. Gina, who speaks with traces of an Italian accent, grew up in Italy. Gina's grandparents lived in the same apartment building as her and her parents. Gina moved from Italy to Brazil with her family when she was 10. She met her husband while attending a university there. After the two married, they moved to Albany, New York, in 1965, when she was 27, after her husband was offered a job as a physicist.

Gina wanted to ensure that her daughter, Isabella, would have every opportunity to challenge her intellect while growing up in a small, conservative town in upstate New York. When Isabella was in high school, her mother pushed her to take an industrial arts class, which ended up being her favorite class, instead of home economics, which she had initially wanted to take. She insisted that Isabella attend a top-notch four-year college and "hit the ceiling" when her high school guidance counselor suggested she instead apply to a two-year vocational school, despite the fact that she was at the top of her class.

Gina worked in the library of a small women's college and always urged Isabella to support herself, since "you're a heartbeat away from poverty." She campaigned for women's rights, used birth control to limit her family size to two children—though she was raised a religious Catholic—and breast-fed her babies and pumped her milk, despite the lack of support for it at the time. Isabella saw her mother as a pioneer—a strong role model for women's rights and helping others. Her mom always pushed her to achieve in a town where the goal for many young women was to become a cheerleader and get married after high school. When Isabella decided to become an engineer, it was heartwarming to Gina. "She really has fulfilled what my generation worked for," for women to have the same opportunities as men, she says.

Listening to the casual banter between Gina and Isabella, it's clear they have a comfortable, warm relationship—similar to a friendship between peers. They live near each other in Michigan now, where Gina and her husband settled after Isabella finished her undergraduate education at a college in New York. After graduating, Isabella wanted to save money, so she moved in with her parents. She lived with them for five years, from age 22 to 27, when she was working at a printing business. At 27, she decided to attend graduate school in Wisconsin to get her master's degree in industrial engineering. Gina recalls the astonishment of people who would remark, "Oh, your daughter is living with you?" Gina would respond, "Yes, I love it. I love to have my daughter home." She says she and her daughter "had a grand time together."

What's nice about her relationship with her mom, Isabella says, is that "I feel like, if I have an issue with her, I just tell her." She'll say, "Mom, I think you shouldn't have done that in this situation," and her mother communicates the same way with her. For example, it drives her mother nuts that she's often late and she'll tell Isabella. Isabella tries to be prompt, but her mother accepts that's the way Isabella is and they move on. When her mother gives her opinion, Isabella can say, "That's great, Mom, but I'm not going to do that." Her mother might bring the issue up a couple more times, but eventually she'll drop the subject. Being open and not holding things back from her mother has been a key element in their harmonious relationship, Isabella says. "I feel very accepted in my relationship with my mom."

While in graduate school, Isabella met her future husband, who lived near her parents. She moved back to Michigan when she graduated and the two of them decided to raise their family there. Gina and her husband often babysit and help out with child care, since Isabella and her husband both work full-time while raising their two young children. Isabella's children now enjoy the same type of extended family that Gina had when she was a child. "My husband and I joke that they're better parents to our kids than we are," Isabella says. She says her children can't wait to head to their grandparents' house, since they get so much love and attention. Her father climbs trees with them. Gina swings on the swing set. The kids run under the sprinklers and read books with their grandparents. Gina says that when you're a grandparent, "you have the time to do things that you didn't do when you had young kids" and are preoccupied with household chores. "You can be dedicated to playing with them." Isabella says it's not uncommon for her to stay for dinner at her parents' house after work, since she enjoys their company.

This picturesque scene almost didn't happen, though. Around the time that Isabella was starting her family, Gina and her husband had contemplated moving to a warmer climate. As Gina talks about their decision, tears well up in her eyes. She pauses while she removes her glasses, dabs her eyes, and says she decided to stay in Michigan because of her daughter. She says she so enjoys her grandchildren, she realizes that was a wise decision. As she says this, tears begin streaming down her face and Isabella reaches over to give her a comforting hug. Before long, Isabella starts to cry as well as she talks about her father's recent diagnosis: stage four stomach cancer. Isabella has applied for a medical leave from work so she can spend one day every two weeks helping her father and supporting her mother during this difficult time. "I take time off and try to help," she says, crying. As the two embrace, Gina says "it helps a lot" to have her daughter there for her. Isabella says it's her chance to pay her mother back for all she's done for her.

For Isabella and Gina, a late-life crisis brought mother and daughter even closer. For Emily Rogers, the crisis came much earlier, when she was just 5 years old. That's when Emily's mother, then seven months pregnant, roused her out of her bed just after midnight and put her in the station wagon while she told her husband, an alcoholic, that she was leaving him and wouldn't come back until he got sober. "I remember him running after the car calling for us and telling us how much he loved us," Emily says. She clearly recalls the motel they stayed in that night.

Emily's mother, Doris Foster, now 50 and living in Indiana, says she had to flee that night. Her husband, a Marine, had been temporarily paralyzed after contracting meningitis while on active duty. He became depressed following his injury, which led to a downward spiral of alcohol abuse. Doris's father had been an alcoholic, and she vowed she would never subject her children to the difficult childhood that she had, living with a drinker. "His sickness was causing me to be sick. I didn't want that for my children," she says of her husband. She told her husband that she was taking Emily and leaving, and that he needed to decide if he was going to come clean. The next day, her husband agreed to check himself into a twenty-eight-day treatment program. He hasn't touched a drop of liquor since that day twenty-three years ago, and the two have had a happy marriage ever since. "I do admire her for all she did" that night, says Emily, now 28 and living in Wisconsin.

Emily can rattle off countless examples where her mother put her children's needs above her own. Since her family needed extra money, Doris worked for a lawyer, proofreading documents at home every morning from 4:00 A.M. to 8:00 A.M. "That was how committed my mom was to being home with me." Emily didn't even realize her mother was working in those wee hours of the morning.

Doris's commitment to family is something that Emily always planned to emulate. When she met her future husband, she told him on their first date that she had every intention of being a stay-at-home mom, "so I hope you can make enough money to support that," she says. She wanted to be a young mom like her mother. Now the mother of a 2-year-old boy and a 6-week-old girl, she's achieved that goal. Though she had been a schoolteacher, she quit her job once she gave birth to her son—just as she had told her husband on their first date.

Emily says her mother is there for her in the best way. Doris pitched in after Emily's daughter was born and Emily suffered post-partum depression, rocking the newborn so that Emily could have time with her son. She brought dinner, cleaned house, and did laundry so Emily wouldn't have to worry about housework. One night, she sat with the baby until after midnight so Emily could sleep. Doris says she listened to her daughter and told her that struggles in life only make you stronger. She says helping out wasn't a chore and she was only doing what comes naturally. Plus, she enjoys spending time with her grandchildren. "I love those kids. I just can't get enough of them."

Even though she lives an hour away, Emily sees her mother once a week. Her friends ask her why she wants to see her so often. "It's like seeing a friend," Emily says. The two have fun together. They attend country music concerts and talk on the phone every day. "I know a lot of people who don't have a mom like mine. I am very lucky," Emily says.

Doris agrees her daughter is one of her best friends and that she's fun to hang out with. But she never loses sight of the fact that "she's my daughter and I'm her mother" and doesn't want Emily to share every intimate detail with her. "We love each other deeply and, I think, have an appreciation of how precious life is." She says she can't understand how other people have power struggles. She never has such issues with her daughter because life is too short and you need to live in the moment, she says.

Emily looks to her mother as a model in raising her children. "I've got some pretty big shoes to fill," she says. She tells her parents all the time she wishes she had the "magic tools" they used to make her and her brother turn out so well. Doris's advice for mother-daughter harmony is to "love each other as if it's your last day together." Emily believes that Mother does know best. "You should know you can always go back to Mom and she'll always be there for you, because that's what moms are for."

The Heaven-Sent Mother-in-Law

While most of the daughters we interviewed talked about their mothers, we found that some women also had the benefit of a supportive mother-in-law who stood by their side during tough times. That was the case for Jodi Johnson, age 43, and her mother-in-law, Dorothy Davies, age 69. As Dorothy pushes her granddaughter on the swing set in a park in Jodi's neighborhood and watches her squeal with laughter, it's clear she relishes her grandmother role. With twinkling blue eyes, a warm smile, and thick, gray hair, Dorothy is the model grandma.

When Jodi was 31, she decided to switch careers and start medical school. She began her grueling medical residency when her oldest son was just a toddler, and her rigorous training program kept her away from home for days at a time. Her husband's parents retired early and were happy to routinely drive ten hours from their home in Ontario, Canada, to their son's house in the Midwest to pitch in, spending weeks at a time grocery shopping, mowing the lawn, doing laundry, and babysitting. "I feel very lucky that my kids have relatively young grandparents who are energetic and healthy and incredibly generous," says Jodi. Now that her residency is long over and Jodi has two children, ages 10 and 5, her in-laws still visit four times a year. They also take care of the children for a week each year while Jodi and John go on their annual scuba-diving vacation.

By contrast, Jodi's own mother is now 80 and doesn't have the energy or stamina to play with the children. Dorothy can play dolls with her granddaughter or military games with her grandson for hours, something Jodi never had the patience for. "We're different and that's a nice thing," she says. Dorothy says that these times with her grandchildren are "precious" and she's grateful for them. It helps, Jodi says, that Dorothy isn't judgmental. Jodi's far more defensive and sensitive to her own mother's remarks. Dorothy says she may not always agree with Jodi, but she'll say diplomatically, "Here's another option." The two enjoy being together and Jodi is grateful that her children have such a loving grandmother.

At face value, women like Jodi, a doctor, and Emily, a teacher turned stay-at-home mother, have little in common. But they and other mothers and daughters in this chapter share an important trait: they're able to rally and come together when times are tough. What lessons can the rest of us learn from them?

Special Considerations for Mothers-in-Law and Daughters-in-Law

Mothers-in-law have long been demonized in American humor and culture, but most women have excellent relationships with them. Dr. Berman says that mothers-in-law can be a wonderful source of support for adult women. And, there's little truth to the old wives' tale that mothers-in-law are threatened by their sons' wives. Although some mothers-in-law may fear they will no longer be the most important woman in their son's life, once their son assures her she's still well loved, those worries subside, and the mother-in-law is delighted to have the extra family around. Many women embrace their daughters-in-law as much as they do their daughters. The daughter-in-law, by the same token, often finds a nonjudgmental ally in an older mother figure who doesn't carry the emotional baggage of the lifelong mother-daughter relationship.

Dr. Sanford points out that these are successful relationships because the mothers are there to support their children physically and emotionally in every way. They're generally an optimistic lot. They think positively. They're mature, adult women who are able to put their needs aside to be there for their daughters, says Dr. Sanford. They are making family their priority. These days, she says, people are too caught up in what they have and comparing themselves to others. Kids are in too many activities. Moms are overscheduled and families are falling apart. In the examples of successful relationships, the mothers are saying they're committed to having a family life. Gina and her husband could have moved to a warmer climate, but instead decided to stay close to her daughter, "to fully support her in the ways that she needed them," Dr. Sanford says. That's what strong families do. They also recognize the importance of give and take. Gina was there for her daughter and now her daughter is making time to help her mother cope with her husband's illness. "That's what it's all about," Dr. Sanford says.

ADVICE FOR MOTHERS

Let your daughter know you support her, but won't protect her. Erin's mother handled her daughter's unplanned pregnancy in the best possible way. She talked to her openly and helped Erin weigh her options. She offered Erin support, but didn't protect her from the consequences of her actions. That's Erin's job. She also didn't let her pride get in the way of helping her daughter make mature decisions. Despite her dismay at finding her teenage daughter pregnant, she did not stop offering the love and support Erin so desperately needed, Dr. Sanford says.

ADVICE FOR MOTHERS AND DAUGHTERS

Use open, direct communication. Each of these cases is a model of open, honest, and nondefensive communication. The mothers express their opinions, the daughters respond, and then they move on, even if they disagree. They're not screaming at each other, or breaking into tears, or getting angry, or giving each other the silent treatment. That's how it should be done.

Love each other unconditionally. Each of these vignettes also reveals a healthy dose of unconditional love. The mothers and daughters support each other and accept one another's differences. They approach each other in a loving, caring, respectful way. Even if the mother disagrees with her daughter's choices, she still sends the message "I love and support you." They don't let their pride get in the way of having strong relationships, which makes sense, because "in the end, we really only have each other," Dr. Sanford says.

Coming Full Circle: From Adversaries to Allies

Elise Buono, 61, and her stepdaughter, Mia Buono Farber, 36, agree that their relationship has been a rocky one, but now that Mia is a stepmother herself, she has a new appreciation for the struggles that Elise faced as the young stepmother to five children. And Elise, who divorced Mia's father at age 49, returned to college at 52, and found exciting work as a college development officer at 55, says her stepdaughter has been her biggest cheerleader as Elise carved out her "new life." It wasn't always that way, however.

When Mia, the youngest of five children, was 5 years old, her biological mother—an intelligent, adventurous free spirit—abandoned her children and husband for missionary work in the South Pacific. Mia and her brothers and sisters were devastated, and their father, Vincenzo, a pediatrician in a Washington, D.C., suburb, quickly remarried. He met his second wife, Elise, when she was a divorced mother who brought her young son into Dr. Buono's office for his annual checkup. At first, the two were friends, sharing stories of their divorces, but their relationship soon blossomed into romance. They married in 1976, and Elise's world was transformed. She had a 10-year-old son from her first marriage and, at age 30, she instantly became stepmother to Vincenzo's five children, then ages 6, 8, 10, 12, and 14. Elise and Vincenzo eventually had three children together, bringing the household count up to nine children. By both Elise's and Mia's accounts, they were not "one big happy family."

Elise tried not to "replace" her stepkids' mother, often keeping her distance from them and withholding her advice. Her children took this as a sign that she didn't love them and didn't want to become close. Elise recalls, "I never got 'You're not my mother,' but I also didn't get the enthusiasm, the hugs, the kisses." She admits this may be partly due to her own trepidation: "Being the stepmother, you always wonder if you're stepping over the line or if you're doing something that's interpreted as not your role. Kids want to hear advice from their mother, not from you." She also says she didn't have a rule book to follow; divorce and remarriage were still relatively rare at that time, and she had no one to turn to for guidance.

Mia agrees that she and Elise had a frosty relationship for much of the time she was growing up. "She didn't want to replace my mother and she had her own kids and these five crazy stepkids, so there was definitely a line there." Mia now says that she would have liked a more close-knit and sincere relationship: "That line shouldn't have been there. She should have been more of a mother to us. She rarely was critical of us [kids], so there was almost a falseness to the relationship."

Their strained relationship was worsened by the fact that Vincenzo was often mean-spirited and insulting to his wife and children. "He always had to be the smartest guy in the room," says Mia. She says she lost respect for her stepmother because she wouldn't leave Vincenzo. Elise admits this was a source of tension, but says leaving him wasn't an option at the time, even though her husband was difficult. "I didn't feel I had the economic power to make it on my own, with all those kids."

Mia and Elise had very little contact when Mia was in her teens and twenties. Mia attended a prestigious college and graduate school, and now works in the art department of a national magazine in New York. At age 35, she married Joshua Farber, the divorced father of 5-year-old Serena. Mia told us that the hardest part of her marriage is navigating her relationship with Serena's biological mother, who she describes as "selfish and mean-spirited."

As Mia was learning to navigate her new role as stepmother, Elise was undergoing her own transformation. She divorced Vincenzo after twenty-eight years of marriage, went back to college, started a job she loves, and—in her own words—"became a new person." Returning to school helped her realize she was smart and capable: "It's an amazing thing. I have this new freedom and income; I don't want to give it up."

As Mia and Elise each experienced their own personal transformations, they now have a new appreciation for each other's opinions— even though those opinions drove them apart two decades earlier. At age 61, Elise is now the self-assured, independent career woman that Mia wanted her to be. As a development officer for a small college, Elise says she works with a dynamic group of women ranging in age from 30 to 84. They recently organized a major event for their college's sixtieth anniversary. "Our pictures were in the newspaper. It was wonderful."

In the same year her college celebrated sixty years, Elise celebrated her sixtieth birthday. At a family get-together, Elise told her stepdaughters that she was beginning the "decade of Elise." She plans to make this decade a time to focus on her own feelings and goals, rather than catering to the needs of her nine children and ex-husband, with whom she remains friendly. The next day, Mia told her she wanted to give her stepmother "something special to begin the new decade." She presented her with a beautiful necklace. "It was a genuinely thoughtful gesture. It was touching for me that she heard the significance of what I was saying, and wanted to share in this important change," says Elise.

Elise has returned the gesture by tentatively and gingerly sharing her thoughts about stepparenting with Mia. Mia constantly grapples with challenges, like how to silence her negative thoughts about her husband's ex-wife and how to handle her frustration when she's not allowed to take her stepdaughter, Serena, for a haircut, "because it's not my jurisdiction." Elise experienced all those challenges. Her main piece of advice to Mia is to "take the high road. Don't put down the former wife. It will only end up hurting you." She also advises her not to take things personally if her stepdaughter acts out; she may still be smarting from the pain of her parents' divorce. "It's not always you they're fighting against. You have to develop a bit of a personal detachment from all the emotion that's swirling around," she tells Mia.

Their relationship still isn't perfect. Elise says she still walks on eggshells a bit when talking to Mia. "We go out of our way not to upset each other, so we often don't discuss the past." Elise wishes both felt safer discussing controversial topics. Still, she's hopeful that things will change. Mia's biological mother recently died, which Elise thinks will free her up to discuss painful issues of her past. And, as Mia's stepdaughter matures, Elise thinks that she can be a source of support: "She's only been a stepmother for a short while. I hope we'll be able to discuss things more in the future." By both accounts, this optimism is warranted. At a recent baby shower with her stepdaughters, Elise said she finally felt like she had been accepted by Mia and her siblings. "All the stepdaughters were there, and we sat around talking like old friends. We talked about sex and marriage and makeup and wrinkles and babies. It was an inclusive group of women. That's the direction that we're going. We're all women, we're all on the same page."

The ups and downs of Mia's and Elise's relationship reveal a key aspect of mother-daughter relationships: mothers and daughters are constantly changing and evolving. With maturity and new life experiences, one's values and attitudes change—and often the two generations of women become closer, more similar, and more empathetic with the passage of time.

Special Considerations for Stepmothers and Stepdaughters

Stepmothers have gotten a bad rap, dating back to the wicked stepmother in fairy tales like *Cinderella*. Nearly all of the advice that therapists offered for mothers and daughters can apply to stepmothers and daughters, as well, although stepmoms and daughters may need to tread lightly, says Dr. High.

Step relationships vary tremendously, depending on many factors—including when the two came into each other's life. Another important influence is the quality of the relationships between the stepdaughter and her biological mother, and the stepmother and her biological children. Being a stepmother can be difficult, especially if the biological mother is around, since the stepmother may have a hard, if not impossible, time trying to fill shoes already filled by her. And the older the daughter is when a stepmom arrives, the more difficult it can be for the stepmother to fill the role as mother figure.

Stepmother-daughter relationships also may be complicated by the feeling that the two are not really on the same team. Most daughters expect, and hopefully receive, unconditional love from their biological mothers. By contrast, stepdaughters may feel that their stepmothers may be taking something from them—namely, their father's attention. A stepmother, fearful of stepping on the biological mother's toes or of imposing herself on the stepdaughter, may have her guard up and keep her stepdaughter at arm's length.

Dr. High says a good approach for stepmothers is to wait until they're asked for advice before offering it to their stepdaughters. They should turn to their husband (the stepdaughter's biological father) for his thoughts about what the appropriate roles and rules are for the child's biological mother and herself.

CHAPTER 11

Peacetime and Parting Thoughts: Final Tips for Bridging the Generation Gap

W e've learned a tremendous amount while researching and writing this book. We are extremely grateful to the many women who so honestly and candidly shared their stories. We're heartened that even mothers and daughters with the most contentious relationships desperately want to move beyond their bickering toward a more harmonious future. We also believe we've found the answer to the age-old question: What do women want? Personal and professional accomplishment, fulfilling family and romantic relationships, and the unconditional support of their mothers. Many of the daughters we spoke with provided eloquent answers to our questions, "What do women want in their mother-daughter relationships?" and "How do we get there?" Here's what they told us . . .

> When I was growing up, my mother really made me feel like I was the most important part of her life. That's something I want my daughters to feel. Even though I want to have something else going on in my life besides my domestic life, I want my children to feel that they're number one, because that was something I felt when I was growing up.
>
> —REBECCA MARSHALL, 36

> Early in my childhood, my mom convinced me that I could do anything I desired. . . . She opened up the world. I grew up

knowing that I could do whatever I wanted to do. I never felt limited because of my gender.

—CARRIE SMITH, 42

My mother taught me to have hope and believe in better days, to be a positive-thinking individual. I think that helped me tremendously.

—RAQUEL ANDRADE, 41

Daughters also shared their honest assessments of their relationships with their mothers. Many believed their mothers didn't want them to be independent-minded individuals. Most mothers agreed that stifling a daughter's individuality was the worst thing they could do. For instance:

A happy mom makes for a happy child. Just keep yourself happy and your kid will be fine. I had an unhappy mom. My mom just felt like she didn't have control over her own destiny and that made her really unhappy. Her unhappiness with her lot made the whole house a difficult place to be.

—JANET INGERSOLL, 42

Don't have the "my happiness should be your happiness" issue. Let your children find their passion, whatever makes them happy in life and try not to pick that for them.

—STACY FINES, 44

Respect and listen to each other and try not to impose your choices on your daughter. With my own daughter, I try not to criticize whom she's dating or spending her time with. I trust her and respect the choices she makes and her passions.

—MARY KLEINSCHMIDT, 46

Talking is crucial. I sometimes make the mistake of not talking enough with both my mother and daughters and I always regret it. More time is spent undoing the damage than would have been spent talking in the first place.

—KIM RODRIGUEZ, 46

Vivian Kleinschmidt, 77, probably put it best, and most succinctly, when she shared her thoughts about the key to a healthy mother-daughter relationship: "Don't give advice unless somebody asks you what you think. Don't be judgmental or critical. Try to understand where your child is coming from."

Eight Important Lessons We've Learned

After speaking with roughly a hundred mothers and daughters and interviewing nearly two dozen counselors, therapists, and experts, we uncovered some important discoveries about mothers and daughters. Even though each mother-daughter pair had their own idiosyncratic disagreements on issues like breast-feeding, spending patterns, single parenthood, and childlessness, we identified eight common patterns across nearly all our pairs.

1. Moms Are Truth Tellers

Mothers like to tell it like it is. And that honesty can be a breath of fresh air. Most of our friends and coworkers are constrained by a desire to be tactful, so they're reluctant to tell us that we've put on weight or that our child behaves like a spoiled brat. That information—if delivered in the right way—can be an important catalyst for making proactive and productive changes.

Because our mothers have known us our entire lives, they often feel they have the exclusive right, or even obligation, to tell it like it is. This can hurt, especially if it's regarding an area where we're already insecure. Even when we know our mother is right, our instinct is to fight her, either because we don't want to admit she's correct, or because we don't want to acknowledge that an important part of our life has gone seriously awry. In the end, we'll benefit from recognizing that our mothers have important insights and wisdom, gleaned not only from years of life experience in general, but from years of experience in watching their daughters grow up. The truth may hurt, but if our mothers won't tell us, who will?

2. Your Mom Is No Longer Your Mommy (and Susan Is No Longer Susie)

None of us are the same person today as we were twenty-five years ago, fortunately. As women reach their fifties, sixties, and older, they become more open-minded, self-assured, and better able to roll with the emotional ups and downs of life. And as young women mature past their teens and twenties and into their thirties, they become less self-centered, more empathetic, and less judgmental.

It's not just women's psychology that changes; the cultural environment around us also has changed, and those shifts shape our opinions and actions. Women who once believed that "a woman's place is in the home" or "premarital sex is wrong" may rethink their views, as they see the world around them changing.

Yet many mothers and daughters have difficulty recognizing that the other has changed with time—often for the better. Though a mother may have chastised her daughter for public displays of affection with her boyfriend in high school, that doesn't mean that she can't help her daughter through a marital crisis years later. And though a teenage daughter may have once screamed, "Mom, I hate you" when forced to study for an algebra exam instead of attending a school dance, it doesn't mean the daughter will always shut her mother out when she's trying to be helpful. We all change. Mothers and daughters should recognize that the way one reacted to a family crisis twenty-five years ago may have reflected her age at that time or a unique historical moment. By accepting change in each another, mothers and daughters can forge more mature and understanding relationships today.

3. Mom's Approval Is a Daughter's Holy Grail

Even the most poised, polished, and self-assured professional woman we interviewed admitted she could be brought to tears or a temper tantrum by an off-handed criticism or disapproving glance from her mother. Why do mothers get under their daughters' skin so? And why does a daughter's curt answer to a well-intended question hurt her mother so much?

The answer is simple; the mother-daughter bond is one of the closest and most important relationships that any woman will have in her life. Mothers and daughters crave each other's love, respect, and support, even if they don't always admit to it. But, the mother-daughter relationship is so important and enduring that both women often take it for granted. Ask yourself, honestly, when was the last time you thanked your mother for helping you solve a problem? When did you last compliment your daughter for turning out well-behaved children? It's likely the answer is, "Not lately."

We take for granted the most constant and important elements in our lives because we can't imagine life without them. Mothers and daughters who take the time to acknowledge and praise one another when times are good also do the best job of supporting each other during life's hardships.

4. Imitation May Be the Sincerest Form of Flattery, but That Doesn't Mean That Difference Is the Highest Form of Insult

Many mothers we interviewed wish their daughters would be more like them. But even if a daughter chooses a different life path than her mother doesn't mean she's rejecting her or her choices. As we've mentioned before, women today have many work and family options their mothers didn't have. They can make choices that match their personalities, preferences, and situational constraints. And few choose a life path simply to defy their mothers.

Of course, there are instances when daughters intentionally choose the opposite path of their mothers. We interviewed several women who tried to avoid what they saw as misery in their mothers' lives. Daughters of depressed homemakers sought fulfilling professions, while daughters of trailblazing career women often chose a more child-focused path. That's not surprising. It's inevitable that a mother's happiness or unhappiness will shape her daughter's actions. But decisions motivated solely by reaction to a negative situation are rarely good. Daughters who were the most satisfied were those who chose a life path because it worked for them, rather than avoiding the choice that brought pain to their mothers.

And for their part, mothers need to encourage their daughter's individuality. As Janet Ingersoll so eloquently told us, "You have to accept your children for who they are. Don't try to make them into what you would have liked to be. As much as it is tempting to see your child correct your own mistakes, that's not what they're there for."

5. No One Person Can Meet All Your Needs

Very few women have just one friend. Most of us have a friend we turn to for emotional support, another whom we rely on for laughs and adventure, and another who gives us practical help and tough love when we need it. One-stop shopping is impossible when it comes to mother-daughter relationships, too, so it's helpful to cultivate a cadre of supporters to get you through life's tough times.

Lifetime Television movies and Hallmark card ads depict mothers and daughters who can do everything for one other. That's an unrealistic expectation that inevitably leads to disappointment. Instead of striving for the ideal relationship, our goal should be for one that's good enough, flaws and all. Recognize the limits of what you have. Though you can usually improve your relations, accept that you may never have one that meets all of your practical and emotional needs. And that's okay. Mothers and daughters need to accept each other for who they are and not berate or judge the other for what they lack.

6. Daughters Think "Choice" Is a Right, Not a Privilege

In just about every aspect of life—work, education, kid's activities, and so on—the daughters we interviewed had far more options than their mothers. At face value, this is great. Yet it also was the underlying source of tension for most of our mothers and daughters. Mothers often felt their daughters took their options for granted, and they didn't appreciate just how good they had it.

The daughters, however, found that choice can have a dark side. After making a decision, we can't help but ruminate about whether we did the right thing. Would option A have been better than option B? The daughters' emotional struggles were often made worse by their moms, who couldn't understand their daughters' choices. Some daughters weighed options that were alien to their mothers, like visiting a sperm bank for a baby's father or taking a two-week business trip and leaving the kids behind. Most of us fear the new and unfamiliar, and our mothers are no exception. Daughters who chose novel paths found that these decisions often created a wedge between them and their mothers.

The mothers and daughters who weathered these storms best were those who took the time to discuss the reasons behind the daughters' choices and the rejected options. A mother should support her daughter's decision once that decision is final—even if she doesn't agree with it. There are, of course, exceptions to this situation, where a mother should speak up, for example, if a daughter is involved with a man who is abusive, alcoholic, or addicted to drugs.

7. Don't Blame Everything on Psychological Problems

Most of us enjoy playing the role of armchair psychologist. People who watch enough *Dr. Phil* believe they know how to diagnose the psychological demons of others. That's certainly the case with mothers and daughters. When mothers and daughters have a problem with each other, their knee-jerk explanations are psychological—often attributing one's actions to an underlying pathology. We heard things like, "My daughter can't commit to a relationship because she has attachment issues," or "My mother tells me how to style my hair because she has control issues."

There may be a kernel of truth to these assessments. But there may be other nonpsychological factors, like stress or the social environment, that also influence what women do and say. Perhaps a daughter is single because she wants to pursue her career rather than marriage right now. Maybe a mom offers grooming tips because she was raised in an era when women seldom had a hair out of place. The problem with automatically viewing every action as indicative of a deep-seated psychological trait is that those conditions don't easily change. It's a static and pessimistic approach and stops us from really trying to understand the forces behind mothers' and daughters' actions.

8. One Person's Turning Point Is Another Person's Afterthought

Many mothers and daughters blame the emotional climate of their relationship on a single event that happened years ago. They say things like, "I haven't trusted my mother ever since she read my diary in seventh grade," or "My daughter never accepts my help, ever since that time she told me I couldn't help design her fourth-grade science project."

What's interesting about those life-altering turning points is that they often were important only to *one person* in the relationship. We were surprised to discover that an event defining one woman's life barely registered in the memories of the other. Mothers don't remember reading their daughters' diaries. Daughters can't recall the time when they rebuffed their mothers' efforts to help with a science fair diorama. Still, the memory is critically important, says therapist Julia Davies. These "screen memories," as Davies calls them, symbolize in one person's mind the very essence of their relationship. Rather than continuing to silently dwell on some perceived wrongdoing, mothers and daughters need to revisit the memory, talk about why it was important, and then focus on the future rather than the past.

Practical Steps for Improving Mother-Daughter Relationships

How can mothers and daughters transcend these eight patterns and move toward a healthier and more harmonious relationship? We recap here the best pieces of advice shared by our team of therapists. Not all women will be comfortable with each technique. But we encourage mothers and daughters to try one piece of advice and move on to another if that one doesn't work.

ADVICE FOR MOTHERS

Try not to mold your daughter in your own image. Many mother-daughter conflicts were rooted in the mother's attempt to make her daughter into something she had no desire to be. This is a recipe for disaster. If the daughter's choice is inconsistent with her mother's expectations, she feels compelled to justify and defend those choices. But if she follows her mother's desires instead of her own, she may end up unhappy. Mothers need to listen to their daughters rather than impose choices that may be completely wrong for them. It's not a mother's job to dictate her daughter's marital status or college major, so loosen the reins and let her go. Give your daughter the freedom to live her own life, even if it's not the life you'd like her to lead.

Don't judge or criticize. One of the most common complaints we heard from daughters was that their mothers were constantly criticizing them. Mothers responded they were only trying to be helpful, not judgmental. Be careful of the way you word your messages, so they don't come across as negative and hurtful. If you can't find a diplomatic way to broach the subject without sounding judgmental, stay mum.

Learn when to advise and when to butt out. If a mother has done her job, she should trust her daughter to learn from her mistakes and make good decisions. A mother may fret over her daughter's choices, but it's not her job to tell her she "shouldn't" do something. It will only infantilize and anger her daughter. There is one important exception, though: if your daughter is putting herself or her children in harm's way, then it's a mother's duty to speak up.

A good grandmother follows the mother's lead. Dr. Berman told us that a good grandmother offers advice gently and infrequently, loves her children, and follows the rules of her child's household. If parents say "No candy," then Grandma needs to follow the family rules. In cases where you disagree with your daughter, you can try saying, "It worries me," but after you've said it a couple of times, you need to let it go.

ADVICE FOR DAUGHTERS

Try to see your mother as a friend rather than a disciplinarian or parent. As we mentioned earlier, the mother who scolded you as a child isn't the same person today. She might just surprise you with her flexibility. It's important to come to terms with the fact that the woman who changed your diapers, cooked your dinner, and tucked you in bed at night can also be your equal. Stop thinking of yourselves as care-giver mom and care-recipient daughter and instead find activities or conversation topics that you both enjoy. Once the power imbalance is removed and mothers and daughters are on equal footing, they'll feel a greater sense of affiliation and friendship.

Explore who your mother was before she became your mom. Much of your mother's behavior is rooted in the way she was raised. To better understand where she is coming from, take time to get to know her as a person. We can guarantee you'll have more empathy for her and her choices once you learn about her past. Making a scrapbook about her life, featuring pictures from childhood, personal mementos, and written memories, or conducting an oral history will bring you two closer together. The final product will be a lasting record of your mom's life. (See page 283 for tips on starting an oral history with your family members.)

Stop seeking your mother's approval. Many women we interviewed are still trying to win their mother's approval for everything they do. Therapists say a more productive approach is to say, "Mom, I'm a grown-up" and accept that she might not be 100 percent on board with all your choices. That doesn't mean she doesn't love you. Remember that your choice of a job, the house you bought, or the way you feed your child is just one small part of who you are. It might be nice to get your mother's approval for every decision you make, but you can't live your life looking for it.

Make Mom feel genuinely needed in those instances when she can help you. Some daughters we interviewed shut their mother out from important moments of their life, fearing she would be critical or judgmental. Rebuffing a mother's help is hurtful to her and counterproductive for you. Take her up on that offer to babysit, even if it means your kids may occasionally end up wired from too much sugar and a late bedtime. Find areas where you can use her assistance so she feels useful and valued. If your mother says, "I want to bring food over," agree, even if you don't care for her cooking.

Moms often send their grown-up kids off in the car with leftover holiday turkey because they want to give them *something;* it's hard to give something meaningful to a grown daughter who has a career and a family of her own. The tinfoil-wrapped turkey, the holiday sweater, or the apple cobbler recipe that your mom offers is often a symbolic gesture, a way for her to continue giving to a daughter who may have a full life and very few needs. Daughters should also feel free to solicit Mom's help when needed. For instance, try asking her how to cook a favorite dish from her native country or her childhood. She will feel validated that you respect her enough to ask for her input.

ADVICE FOR MOTHERS AND DAUGHTERS

Focus on the positive. Like the old saying goes, you catch more flies with honey than vinegar. Everyone likes to hear what they're doing right, rather than what they're doing wrong. Why not tell each other what you appreciate? If your best friend were to ask you what you admire most about your mother or daughter, what would you say? The compliment can be simple: "She makes delicious meatloaf." Or profound: "She lives by her principles." An unsolicited, unexpected, *sincere* compliment can make someone's day.

Realize that no one is perfect. Mothers and daughters who put each other on a pedestal will always be disappointed. We all make mistakes, yet even the most problematic misstep seldom comes from a place of cruelty or ill will. Mothers and daughters need to recognize each other's imperfections, yet not dwell on them. Our team of therapists says mothers and daughters may spend vast amounts of time rehashing painful memories or burying old wounds without confronting the issues. A better approach is to forgive and forget and talk openly with each other about your disappointments. If you continue to dwell silently on issues that bother you, you can never move past it and have a healthy relationship.

Try to see the other's perspective. There are two sides to every story. The next time you have an argument, think about the issues from the other person's viewpoint. It will make you a more sensitive person, and you'll be more flexible in developing a solution to the problem. Listening is key. It's not possible to adopt another's perspective if you argue rather than listen when they speak.

Have a heart-to-heart conversation. Mothers and daughters should muster their courage to openly share what's on their minds. That's easier said than done. Women who have had an emotionally distant relationship may not be ready to reveal their private thoughts to each other. We suggest one way to spark conversation is to first talk about similar issues facing *other* women. Depersonalizing matters will make them easier to discuss. Another way to spark a conversation is by getting together to watch a movie or discuss a book. By focusing on the issues facing other women—even those who are fictitious—mothers and daughters can slowly begin to open the lines of communication. (See page 287 for "conversation starter" movies, novels, and plays.)

Think before you speak. Mothers and daughters can get under each other's skin like no one else. When provoked, we often snap—without carefully weighing our words. These impromptu outbursts can be harmful. Therapists suggest thinking out what you plan to say before uttering your words out loud. Another strategy is to make a mental or written note of all the things you've said in a given day. How many times do you roll your eyes, use an angry or sarcastic tone, or give unsolicited advice? By jotting down a log of your words, you may be shocked to find out how counterproductive many of your conversations are. You may also find that a relationship contract can be helpful.

Put It in Writing:
Making a Relationship Contract

Mothers and daughters with adversarial relationships may benefit from writing up a relationship contract, suggests Dr. Merrill. A contract can be helpful when "we are not being the people we want to be," he says. By drafting and trying to live up to the terms of a contract, mothers and daughters can become aware of their unhealthy patterns and devise concrete steps to stop these patterns. Here's how the contract works:

1. Both mother and daughter independently make a list of what they'd like in a relationship.

2. Mother and daughter share their lists with one another and together agree on qualities they would like to see in their relationship. Those qualities can be elements like being honest with each other, agreeing not to criticize each other, or complimenting each other regularly.

3. Have a conversation about how to best achieve your goals. The conversation should emphasize what's good about the relationship, as well as those things that need to change.

4. Both mother and daughter should think about what they need to do *as individuals* to fulfill the terms of the contract. Also think about what they need to do *together* to uphold those terms.

5. Remember that the contract is a living, breathing document. Come together every couple of months and ask each other, "How are we doing?" Are both of you doing everything you can to live up to the terms of the contract? If the answer is no, either ramp up your efforts to abide by the contract or recognize that the terms are unrealistic. If it's the latter, revise them to better reflect the reality of your relationship. Ideally, when goals are formally stated in the contract, mother and daughter may be more inclined to live up to them.

Send along "just thinking of you" notes. When life gets busy, mother-daughter communication often falls by the wayside. One way to maintain good feelings, even during busy times, is to send along a quick greeting card or e-mail that says, "I'm thinking of you." Most Americans tend to write or call their mother once a week, says Dr. Berman. E-mail or text-messaging are good ways to quickly say hi or I love you.

It prevents you from having to get into a twenty-minute conversation when neither mother nor daughter may want it. (See Chapter 6 for tips for sending effective e-mails.)

Celebrate your differences. Just because mothers and daughters share DNA doesn't mean they share everything else—values, tastes, and child-rearing practices. You don't need an identical personality to get along well. Try to appreciate the qualities that make each of you unique instead of focusing on differences as deficiencies. Though that may be challenging if mothers' and daughters' temperaments or personalities differ radically from each other, give it a try. You may find that when you try to appreciate each other's idiosyncrasies, you'll get along better.

If all else fails, find a stand-in. If your relationship is strained to the point that it brings nothing but misery, take a break from one another. Find other women who can be a source of affirmation or support during those difficult times. Once the tension diffuses, mothers and daughters may gradually be able to reconnect and try to resolve their differences.

Epilogue

Julie's Story

On the opening pages of this book, I admitted that my mother inspired me to explore mother-daughter conflicts. Her nagging questions, criticisms, and attempts to clean my house were a constant thorn in my side. Sometimes she makes me feel like I can do nothing right. In our closing pages, I want to acknowledge the many things my *mother* has done right. The best thing I can say about my mom is that she is always there for me and my family.

My mother lives an hour away and attends every family event, big and small. She was at the hospital for the birth of each of my children. She would have climbed into my hospital bed with me if I let her. Now that the kids are older, she attends every birthday party, dance recital, school concert, play, and tennis tournament. And there have been many. She was there when, just as I was getting ready to attend a business lunch with my *Newsweek* bureau chief, I got the call from school to pick up my 7-year-old daughter, who was found by the school nurse to have head lice. While I lunched, my mom deloused, without complaint. She was there to take care of my three children for a weekend when I surprised my husband with a getaway trip for his fortieth birthday. When I returned, the kids were happy and well-fed, and my kitchen cabinets and refrigerator were sparkling clean and reorganized.

Yes, my mother feels the need to give her advice incessantly. It can be irritating. But I know she does it because she's trying to help. I'm not perfect either, often snapping at her when she offers advice, creating conflicts I regret. But my children and I know she cares. My kids view Nana as a very big part of their lives. She knows them better than my grandmother knew me. My grandmother lived in California, thousands of miles from our Michigan home. Our main contact was through the homemade rhyming birthday card she sent me every year.

I've tried to use some of the advice gleaned from the therapists in this book: to be more empathetic, to deliver my messages with love instead of defensiveness, to tell my mother which topics are not up for discussion. This, I believe, has helped me to better communicate with her. I'm now better able to savor her good qualities, instead of dwelling on our arguments. I've also learned that there's no such thing as a single, ideal mother-daughter relationship. Some bicker loudly. Others don't raise their voices. Some sling insults. Others never utter an unkind word. Most mothers and daughters may never have a perfect relationship, but we hope that our book will bring them to a more honest and sincere level, where they're better able to enjoy and respect each other.

Getting to Know You . . .
Through Oral History

One of the best ways to understand your mother is to learn what she was like before she became your mom. More Americans today are conducting oral histories with their loved ones. That means either tape recording, writing down, or videotaping stories of Mom's life. Start by asking questions about her childhood. What did she want to be when she grew up? What was her favorite subject in school? What kind of music did she enjoy when she was young? What was her most embarrassing moment? Did she have a happy childhood? Then, move on to courtship. How did she meet her husband? How did she know he was "the one"? Was he a good father? Then, ask about childbearing. What went through her mind when she found out she was pregnant with her first child? What scared her most about becoming a mother? What did she love most about being a mom? How was her life as a mother different from that of mothers raising children today? Ask a general question: What is the one secret about her that she's never shared before? Allow her to talk freely, without interruption. We guarantee you will learn something surprising. And you may have more empathy for her and her choices once you learn about her past. If you can't think of questions to ask, have your children or siblings draw up a list of questions (or turn to the questions that we've drafted for you in this section).

Conducting an oral history with Mom doesn't just benefit daughters. Grandchildren will be intrigued to hear about what Grandma was like when she was their age. And reminiscing about the past is a wonderful activity for older adults. Gerontologists call it "calisthenics for the brain." Reviewing one's past experiences helps older people make sense of their earlier life decisions and may guide them in deciding how they want to spend the future. According to Mary Alice Wolf, a gerontology professor at Saint Joseph College in West Hartford, Connecticut, and a reminiscence specialist, these interviews are also cathartic: "When you really stop and listen to them, what they're doing is settling scores and making sense of their lives."

Overall Life Review

What is the most important thing someone should know about you and your life?

What do you think is the most significant experience from the past that helped make you the person you are now?

What are you proudest of?

If you could live your life over, what would you do differently?

Specific Life Events

Family

When were you born? Where? What jobs or activities did your parents have?

When you were a child, what values did your parents instill in you? Do you believe that similar values are instilled in children growing up today?

When did you move out of your parents' home for the first time? Where did you move to? Whom did you live with? Why did you decide to move?

Are your parents still alive today? If not, when and how did they die?

How did you meet your spouse? How did you decide this was the person you wanted to marry? How long did you know each other before you got married?

Work and Education

How far did you go in school? Where did you go to school? Was your school experience different from that of your children or grandchildren? How?

What was your first job? What was your favorite job, or the most important job you've ever had? How did you decide on your career? Did you have other jobs first? All things considered, have you enjoyed your work? If you didn't work, how did you feel about that? Were you happy at home raising your kids? Did you have any regrets about that? Do you wish you could have had a career? If so, what kind of career would you have wanted?

Hobbies and Civic Activities

I have you ever belonged to any groups or organizations? Could you tell me about the hobbies, activities or interests you have most enjoyed pursuing in life?

Attitudes and Personal Change

Think about the attitudes and views you've held in the course of your life. These attitudes can be toward politics, religion, people, etc. Have your attitudes changed much? How? Why?

Historical Background

What historical event, trend, or invention do you believe has been the most important in your lifetime?

When you look back at your life, do you think American society has changed for better or for worse? Why? What has changed?

Mother–Daughter Movie Night and Book Group

A great way to spark conversation is to watch a movie together or discuss a good book. Sharing your favorite book or movie is a simple way to show who you really are, and it can open up a meaningful conversation about a topic that's important to you. It can also mitigate mother-daughter tension by encouraging lively chats about an intellectually engaging topic, rather than focusing on and sniping at one another. Here are ten of our favorite picks for classic tales of mother-daughter relationships and stories of how women's lives have changed in the past century.

Books and Plays

- *The Joy Luck Club* by Amy Tan (G. P. Putnam's Sons, 1989)
  This novel opens with the tale of a Chinese woman who bought an unusual bird at a Shanghai market. It was born a duck but stretched its neck to resemble the more elegant swan. The woman vowed to give her daughter this swan, because it was "a creature that became more than what was hoped for." The book tells the story of four older Chinese women and how their heartaches, hopes, and triumphs shaped the choices of their twenty-something American-born daughters. By listening to each other's stories, the vast generation gap and cultural divide slowly slips away.

- *One True Thing* by Anna Quindlen (Random House, 1994)
  This novel describes how the relationship between a driven
  journalist daughter, Ellen, and her stay-at-home mother, Kate,
  is transformed when Ellen becomes caretaker to her cancer-
  stricken mother. Ellen had always identified with her father, a
  professor, and was never close to her mother. As Ellen starts to
  care for her mom, she gathers surprising insights into her
  mother's life. The plot takes several unexpected twists and
  turns, yet at the book's end, readers will feel inspired to learn
  much more about their mothers.

- *The Bluest Eye* by Toni Morrison (Plume, 1970)
  This classic is a heartbreaking portrayal of how racism affects
  the lives of women and their families. The story is told from
  five different perspectives and focuses on Pecola Breedlove and
  her mother, Pauline. Pauline is cruel to her family members because they are a constant reminder that her life can never mea-
  sure up to the ideal world of the white family for whom she
  works as a maid. Not only is Pecola's mother distant and aloof,
  but her father is unreliable and unsupportive. After a series of
  traumatic events, Pecola's life takes a final tragic turn. *The
  Bluest Eye* opens up conversation about injustices in the world,
  especially against women and those with the fewest advantages
  to fight back.

- *The Giving Tree* by Shel Silverstein (HarperCollins, 1964)
  This short, illustrated book is not just for kids. This simple
  story raises important questions about the limits of maternal
  love and sacrifice. An apple tree starts out as a leafy play-
  ground, shade provider, and apple bearer for a spirited little
  boy. Making the boy happy makes the tree happy, but with
  time it becomes more challenging for the generous tree to
  meet his needs. As the boy continues to demand more, the
  tree keeps giving, even when there is only a stump for the boy
  to sit upon. The tree is happy to give to the boy until the bitter
  end, although it's not clear whether the boy appreciates her
  devotion.

- *The Heidi Chronicles* by Wendy Wasserstein (Dramatists Play Service, 1988)
  This riveting play opens at a high school dance in the early 1960s, when young Heidi dreams of boys and marriage. Through the next two decades, she becomes swept up in the women's movement and ultimately becomes a feminist art historian and the single mother of an adopted daughter. The play traces the heartaches she and her friends face as they try to juggle romantic relationships and rewarding professions at a time when women's roles were being transformed. It raises important questions about ambition, love, and sacrifice. And it asks whether it really is possible for women to have it all. Playwright Wendy Wasserstein became a single mother herself at age 48 and, tragically, died of cancer at age 55.

- *We Are Our Mothers' Daughters* by Cokie Roberts (William Morrow, 1998)
  Renowned journalist Cokie Roberts shares her personal experiences as a pioneer with a demanding career. She focuses on her group of devoted women friends and relatives, including eccentric aunts, who have had such a positive influence on her life. She makes clear the importance of having strong women in your life. And she sends the message that women before us were the real pioneers and are a true source of inspiration. This is a wonderful book for women of two generations to discuss. It offers a fascinating glimpse into the hurdles that women crossed in earlier decades and will give daughters a newfound appreciation for what their mothers' generation faced.

- *The Glass Castle* by Jeanette Walls (Scribner, 2006)
  A *New York Times* bestseller, this memoir describes the author's life on the run, as part of a homeless family. Jeanette's father is an alcoholic who can't hold down a job and often uproots the family, while her mother, Rose Mary, a frustrated artist, is the quintessential laissez-faire mom. She leaves her children to roam on their own most of the time, rooting

through the garbage to find food. Despite this difficult childhood, the daughter doesn't malign or turn her back on her parents. Ultimately, she becomes a successful writer. The book explores how the now successful adult daughter comes to terms with and accepts her eccentric mother, who is still homeless today.

Movies

- *Terms of Endearment* starring Shirley MacLaine and Debra Winger (1983)
  The epitome of tearjerkers, this film traces the relationship between a quirky yet exceedingly close mother-daughter pair. Aurora is a strong-willed, independent, and exasperating woman, while her daughter is an aimless free spirit who's devoted her life to her philandering husband and three young children. Through their daily telephone conversations, they cajole, annoy, and support each other through failed marriages, affairs, and, ultimately, a diagnosis of terminal cancer.

- *A League of Their Own* starring Geena Davis and Tom Hanks (1992)
  This film traces the adventures of two sisters who leave their farm home in Oregon to join the All American Pro Girls League, an all-women's baseball team that played at a time when most male major leaguers were fighting overseas in World War II. The two sisters and their charismatic teammates achieve more than they could ever hope for, shining as athletes and providing entertainment and inspiration to a nation at war. As the war draws to a close, the women are quietly pushed back into their "old" lives as homemakers and mothers. The story shows how much joy accomplishment brings to women, even those who thought they were happy to spend their lives toiling away in their kitchens.

- *The Turning Point* starring Shirley MacLaine and Anne
  Bancroft (1977)
  Deedee and Emma were once talented ballerinas and arch-
  rivals. Deedee quits dancing when she finds herself pregnant
  and decides to marry the father, a fellow dancer. Emma makes
  dance her life. The two reunite many years later, when
  Deedee's daughter, Amelia, a promising ballerina, decides to
  join a New York ballet company. Emma immediately takes
  Amelia under her wing as a protégé. The film traces the relationship between two women who envy each other's lives; one
  longs for a daughter and marriage, while the other wonders
  what she could have achieved if she had continued as a professional dancer.

Notes

PROLOGUE

1. L. Belkin, "Anxious? Sleepless? In a Survey, Your Mom, Again, Tells You Why," Life's Work, *New York Times,* Dec. 5, 2001.

CHAPTER 1. MOTHERS AND DAUGHTERS

1. For more information on theories of mother-daughter relationships, see J. Bowlby, *Attachment and Loss* (New York: Basic Books, 1969); C. J. Boyd, "Mothers and Daughters: A Discussion of Theory and Research," *Journal of Marriage and Family* 51 (1989): 291–301; P. Caplan, *The New Don't Blame Mother: Mending the Mother-Daughter Relationship* (New York: Routledge, 2000); N. Chodorow, *The Reproduction of Mothering* (Berkeley: University of California Press, 1978); E. Erikson, *Childhood and Society* (New York: W. W. Norton, 1950); L. R. Fischer, "Transitions in the Mother-Daughter Relationship," *Journal of Marriage and Family* 43 (1981): 613–622; S. Freud, *New Introductory Lectures* (New York: W. W. Norton, 1933).

2. For more information on cognitive dissonance, see L. Festinger, *A Theory of Cognitive Dissonance* (Stanford, CA: Stanford University Press, 1957); L. Festinger and J. M. Carlsmith, "Cognitive Consequences of Forced Compliance," *Journal of Abnormal and Social Psychology* 58 (1959): 203–211.

3. For more information on age differences in emotional reactivity, see L. Cartensen and S. Turk-Charles, "The Salience of Emotion Across the Adult Life Span," *Psychology and Aging* 9 (1994): 259–264; M. Lawton, M. H. Kleban, D. Rajagopal, and J. Dean, "Dimensions of Affective Experience in Three Age Groups," *Psychology and Aging* 7 (1992): 171–184.

CHAPTER 2. FROM *GOOD HOUSEKEEPING* TO *WORKING WOMAN*

1. For more information on historical trends in women's work and family roles, see S. M. Bianchi and D Spain, *American Woman in Transition* (New York: Russell Sage Foundation, 1986); S. M. Bianchi and D. Spain, "Women, Work, and Family in America," *Population Bulletin* 51, no. 3 (1996).

2. J. Lawler Dye, "Fertility of American Women: June 2004," *Current Population Reports* (2005), U.S. Department of Commerce, Economics and Statistics Administration, U.S. Census Bureau (www.census.gov).

3. For more information on the ways that childbearing affect women's earnings, see M. Budig and P. England, "The Wage Penalty for Motherhood," *American Sociological Review* 66 (2001): 204–225; General Accounting Office, "Women's Earnings: Work Patterns Partially Explain Difference Between Men's and Women's Earnings," *Report to Congressional Requesters* (Washington, D.C., GAO, 2003); C. Goldin, *Understanding the Gender Gap: An Economic History of American Women* (New York: Oxford University Press, 1990).

4. Adlai Stevenson, "A Purpose for Modern Woman," *Women's Home Companion* (September 1955): 30–31.

5. For more information on consumption and advertising, see American Academy of Pediatrics, Committee on Communications, "Children, Adolescents, and Advertising," *Pediatrics* 118 (2006): 2563–2569; G. Comstock and E. Scharrer, *Television: What's on, Who's Watching, and What It Means* (San Diego, CA: Academic Press, 1999); J. Schor, *The Overspent American: Why We Want What We Don't Need* (New York: Basic Books, 1999).

6. For more information on husbands' and wives' earnings, see Bureau of the Census, "Married-Couple Families with Wives' Earnings Greater than Husband's Earnings: 1981 to 2001," *Historical Income Tables—Families* (Washington, D.C., Author, 2003); M. Conlin, "Look Who's Bringing Home More Bacon," *BusinessWeek*, January 28, 2003; S. Winslow-Bowe, "The Persistence of Wives' Income Advantage," *Journal of Marriage and Family* 68 (2006): 824–842.

7. For more information on the hours that married couples spend on housework and child care, see S. M. Bianchi, "Maternal Employment and Time with Children: Dramatic Change or Surprising Continuity?" *Demography* 37 (2000): 401–414; S. M. Bianchi, J. P. Robinson, and M. A. Milkie, *Changing Rhythms of American Family Life* (New York: Russell Sage Foundation Press, 2006); S. M. Bianchi, M. Milkie, L. Sayer, and J. P. Robinson, "Is Anyone Doing the Housework? Trends in the Gender Division of Household Labor," *Social Forces* 79 (2000): 191–228.

8. A. Hochschild, *The Second Shift* (New York: Viking Adult, 1989).

9. M. Bolton, *The Third Shift: Managing Hard Choices in Our Careers, Homes, and Lives as Women* (New York: Jossey-Bass, 2001).

10. A. Pearson, *I Don't Know How She Does It* (New York: Random House, 2002).

CHAPTER 3. COURTSHIP, COHABITATION, AND CHINA PATTERNS

1. Recent U.S. Census statistics on women's marital status can be found at the Bureau of the Census, *Statistical Abstract of the United States,* Tables 54 to 56 (Washington, D.C.: Bureau of the Census, 2007).

2. For more information on the delayed transition to adulthood, see F. F. Furstenberg Jr., S. Kennedy, V. C. Mcloyd, R. G. Rumbaut, and R. A. Settersten Jr., "Growing Up Is Harder to Do," *Contexts* 3, no. 13 (2004): 33–41.

3. Ibid.

4. Ibid.

5. B. DePaulo, author of *Singled Out: How Singles Are Stereotypes, Stigmatized, and Ignored, and Still Live Happily Ever After* (New York: St. Martin's Press, 2006).

6. J. Spindel, author of *Get Serious About Marriage: 365 Proven Ways to Find Love in Less Than a Year* (New York: Regan Books, 2006).

7. T. Merrill and B. Sandoz-Merrill, *Settle for More: You Can Have the Relationship You Always Wanted . . . Guaranteed!* (New York: Select Books, 2005); B. Sandoz-Merrill, *Parachutes for Parents: 12 New Keys to Raising Children for a Better World* (New York: Contemporary Books, 1995).

8. For more information on cohabitation patterns, see S. L. Brown, "How Cohabitation Is Reshaping American Families," *Contexts* 4 (2005): 33–37; T. Simmons and M. O'Connell, "Married-Couple and Unmarried-Partner Households: 2000," *Census 2000 Special Reports* (Washington, D.C.: U.S. Bureau of the Census, 2003).

9. P. J. Smock and S. Gupta, "Cohabitation in Contemporary North America," in *Just Living Together: Implications of Cohabitation on Families, Children, and Social Policy* (Mahwah, NJ: Erlbaum, 2002) pp. 53–84; P. J. Smock, P. Huang, W. Manning, and C. Bergstrom-Lynch, "Heterosexual Cohabitation in the United States: Motives for Living Together Among Young Men and Women," *Population Studies Center Research Report 06–606.* Population Studies Center, Institute for Social Research, University of Michigan, 2006.

10. For more information on what young women today seek in a spouse, see P. Schwartz, *Love Between Equals: How Peer Marriage Really Works* (New York: Touchstone, 1995); D. Siegel, "The New Trophy Wife," *Psychology Today* (January/February 2004); B. D. Whitehead and D. Popenoe, *The State of Our Unions: The Social Health of Marriage in America* (New Brunswick, NJ: National Marriage Project, 2004).

11. B. D. Whitehead and D. Popenoe, "Marriage and Children: Coming Together Again," *The State of Our Unions: The Social Health of Marriage in America* annual report (New Brunswick, NJ: National Marriage Project, 2003), p. 12.

12. B. D. Whitehead and D. Popenoe, "Who Wants to Marry a Soul Mate?" *The State of Our Unions* annual report (2001).

13. For more information on divorce patterns in the United States, see P. Amato, "The Consequences of Divorce for Adults and Children," *Journal of Marriage and the Family* 62 (2000): 1269–1287; M. D. Bramlett and W. D. Mosher, *Cohabitation, Marriage, Divorce and Remarriage in the United States*, Vital and Health Statistics, Series 23, no. 22 (Hyattville, MD: National Center for Health Statistics, 2002); J. Goldstein, "The Leveling of Divorce in the United States," *Demography* 36 (1999): 409–414; R. M. Kreider, *Number, Timing, and Duration of Marriages and Divorces: 2001* (Washington, D.C.: U.S. Census Bureau, 2005); S. Ruggles, "The Rise of Divorce and Separation in the United States, 1880–1990," *Demography* 34 (1997): 455–466; J. Teachman, "Stability Across Cohorts in Divorce Risk Factors," *Demography* 39 (2002): 331–351.

CHAPTER 4. HAVING A BABY

1. For further information on trends in contraceptive use, see C. Goldscheider and W. D. Mosher, "Religions Affiliation and Contraceptive Usage: Changing American Patterns, 1955–1982," *Studies in Family Planning* 19, no. 1 (1988): 48–57; J. M. Riddle, *Eve's Herbs: A History of Contraception and Abortion in the West* (Cambridge, MA: Harvard University Press, 1997).

2. For further information on chidlessness, see J. C. Abma and G. M. Martinez, "Childlessness Among Older Women in the United States: Trends and Profiles," *Journal of Marriage and Family* 68, no. 4 (2006): 1045–1056; E. T. May, *Barren in the Promised Land: Childless Americans and the Pursuit of Happiness* (Cambridge, MA: Harvard University Press, 1997).

3. For further information on patterns of adoptions in the United States, see D. Carr, "Baby Blues," *Contexts* 6, no. 2 (2007): 62; K. S. Stolley, "Statistics on Adoption in the United States," *The Future of Children: Adoption* 3, no. 1 (1993): 26–42.

CHAPTER 5. THE STRUGGLE OVER WORK

1. S. A. Hewlett, *Creating a Life: Professional Women and the Quest for Children* (New York: Miramax Books, 2002).

2. M. Eberstadt, *Home-Alone America: The Hidden Toll of Day Care, Behavioral Drugs, and Other Parent Substitutes* (New York: Sentinel Trade, 2004).

3. L. Hirshman, *Get to Work: A Manifesto for Women of the World* (New York: Viking Basic, 2006).

4. L. Bennetts, *The Feminine Mistake: Are We Giving Up Too Much?* (New York: Voice, 2007).

5. D. Carr, " 'My Daughter Has a Career—I Just Raised Babies': Women's Intergenerational Social Comparisons," *Social Psychology Quarterly* 67, no. 2 (2004): 132–154.

6. For more information on women's attainment of advanced and professional degrees, see C. E. Freeman, *Trends in Educational Equity of Girls and Women: 2004* (Washington, D. C.: National Center for Education Statistics, 2004).

7. J. Warner, *Perfect Madness: Motherhood in the Age of Anxiety* (New York: Riverhead, 2005).

CHAPTER 6. BREAST-FEED OR BOTTLE?
TIME-OUTS OR SPANKINGS?

1. V. Iovine, *The Girlfriends' Guide to Pregnancy: Or, Everything Your Doctor Won't Tell You* (New York: Pocket Books, 1995); H. Murkoff, A. Eisenberg, and S. Hathaway, *What to Expect When You're Expecting,* 3rd ed. (New York: Workman, 2002).

2. For further information the history and prevalence of breast-feeding, see B. Hausman, *Mother's Milk: Breastfeeding Controversies in American Culture* (New York: Routledge, 2003); M. L. Hediger, M. D. Overpeck, W. J. Ruan, and J. F. Troendle, "Early Infant Feeding and Growth Status of U. S.-Born Infants and Children Aged 4–71 Months: Analyses from the Third National Health and Nutrition Examination Survey, 1988–1994," *American Journal of Clinical Nutrition* 72 (2000): 159–167; A. S. Ryan, Z. Wenjun, and A. Acosta, "Breastfeeding Continues to Increase into the New Millennium," *Pediatrics* 110, no. 6 (2002): 1103–1109; A. S. Ryan, W. F. Pratt, J. L. Wysong, G. Lewandowski, J. W. McNally, and F. W. Krieger, "A Comparison of Breastfeeding Data from the National Surveys of Family Growth and the Ross Laboratories Mothers Surveys," *American Journal of Public Health* 81 (1991): 1049–1052; P. Stuart-Macadam and K. Dettwyler, *Breastfeeding: Biocultural Perspectives (Foundations of Human Behavior)* (New York: Aldine de Gruyter, 1995).

3. R. Cohen-Sandler, author of *Stressed-Out Girls: Helping Them Thrive in the Age of Pressure* (New York: Viking, 2005) and coauthor, with M. Silver, of *I'm Not Mad, I Just Hate You! A New Understanding of Mother-Daughter Conflict* (New York: Penguin, 2000).

4. B. Spock, *The Common Sense Book of Baby and Child Care* (New York: Duell, Sloan, & Pearce, 1946).

5. A. Hulbert, *Raising America: Experts, Parents, and a Century of Advice About Children* (New York: Vintage, 2004).

6. W. Sears and M. Sears, *The Attachment Parenting Book: A Commonsense Guide to Understanding and Nurturing Your Baby* (New York: Little, Brown, 2001).

7. For more information on the history of child-rearing advice, see R. D. Apple, *Perfect Motherhood: Science and Childrearing in America* (New Brunswick, NJ: Rutgers University Press, 2006); A. R. Simpson, "The Role of the Mass Media in Parenting Education," Center for Health Communication, 1997, at parenthood.library.wisc.edu, accessed June 20, 2007.

8. C. Pickhardt, *The Connected Father: Understanding Your Unique Role and Responsibilities During Your Child's Adolescence* (New York: Palgrave MacMillan, 2007).

9. J. Belsky, D. L. Vandell, M. Burchinal, K. A. Clarke-Stewart, K. McCartney, M. T. Owen, and NICHD Early Child Care Research Network, "Are There Long-Term Effects of Early Child Care?" *Child Development* 78, no. 2 (2007): 681–701.

10. For further information on child-care practices and attitudes, see Federal Interagency Forum on Child and Family Statistics, *America's Children in Brief: Key National Indicators of Well-Being,* 2006 (Washington, D.C.: Federal Interagency Forum on Child and Family Statistics, 2006); J. Robison, "Should Mothers Work?" Princeton, NJ: Gallup Poll, August 27, 2002.

11. Federal Interagency Forum on Child and Family Statistics, *America's Children in Brief.*

CHAPTER 7. FROM PLAYING OUTSIDE TO PLAYDATES AND PLAYSTATIONS

1. S. M. Bianchi, J. P. Robinson, and M. A. Milkie, *Changing Rhythms of American Family Life* (New York: Russell Sage Foundation Press, 2006).

2. E. Berger, *Raising Kids with Character: Developing Trust and Personal Integrity in Children* (Lanham, MD: Rowman & Littlefield, 2006).

3. Gallup Poll, June 8, 2007, at www.galluppoll.com, accessed June 20, 2007.

CHAPTER 8. HIS, HERS, AND THEIRS

1. For more information on men's and women's housework hours, see S. M. Bianchi et al., "Is Anyone Doing the Housework?"

2. A. N. Schwartz, "Message of the Month," at www.allanschwartz.com, accessed June 20, 2007.

3. Divorce Financial Solutions, "Women and Finances," posted at www.divorcenet
.com on November 2, 2006.

4. A. G. Berg, *How to Stop Fighting About Money and Make Some: A Couple's Guide
to Personal Harmony and Financial Success* (New York: Avon Books, 1989).

CHAPTER 9. PERSONAL TIME

1. National Sleep Foundation, *2007 Sleep in America Poll: Summary of Findings*
(Washington, D.C.: National Sleep Foundation, 2007), at www.sleepfoundation.org,
accessed June 20, 2007.

2. Ibid.

3. Ibid.

4. Reuters, "Yawn! Most Mothers Don't Get Enough Sleep," posted at www.msnbc
.msn.com on October 20, 2006.

5. J. M. Jones, "Parents of Young Children Are Most Stressed Americans, Working
Moms Least Likely to Have Adequate Relaxation Time," Gallup Poll, November 8,
2002.

6. P. Orenstein, *Flux: Women on Sex, Work, Love, Kids, and Life in a Half-Changed
World* (New York: Anchor Books, 2001), p. 16.

7. B. Friedan, *The Feminine Mystique* (New York: Dell, 1963), p. 15.

CHAPTER 10. MANAGING CRISES

1. For further information on residential transitions and the well-being of older
adults, see R. C. Atchley, "A Continuity Theory of Normal Aging," *Gerontologist* 29,
no. 2 (1989): 183–190; C. C. Cook, P. Martin, M. Yearns, and M. L. Damhorst, "Attachment to 'Place' and Coping with Loss in Changed Communities: A Paradox for
Aging Adults," *Family and Consumer Sciences Research Journal* 35, no. 3 (2007):
201–214; H. L. Menne, J. M. Kinney, and D. J. Morhardt, " 'Trying to Continue to Do
as Much as They Can Do': Theoretical Insights Regarding Continuity and Meaning
Making in the Face of Dementia," *Dementia* 1, no. 3 (2002): 367–382.

Acknowledgments

We are indebted to the nearly one hundred mothers and daughters who took time out of their busy lives to share with us their stories of joy and frustration. We were continually amazed at their honesty, frankness, and desire to make things right with one another, even if they were in the midst of a rough emotional patch. We could not have written this book without them. We would like to thank Edie Broida, who helped us find women of the mothers' generation to interview, and who enthusiastically supported this book from its inception.

We also thank our team of experts. They were incredibly generous in sharing their time, expertise, and wisdom with us. We hope they are gratified to know that their words of wisdom may make the lives of American mothers and daughters better. We are particularly grateful to Elizabeth Berger, Ellen Berman, Margaret Buttenheim, Renée A. Cohen, Roni Cohen-Sandler, Julia Davies, Pamela High, Barbara Howard, Donna Mayerson, Bobbie Sandoz-Merrill, Tom Merrill, John Northman, Carl Pickhardt, Diane Sanford, Tom Sullivan, and Howard Weinblatt, who carefully read through our vignettes and shared their wise insights with us.

Thanks are also due to our creative advisers, who helped us transform our ideas into a proposal, and ultimately this book. Our book never would have happened if it weren't for the persistence, enthusiasm, and good humor of our agent, Daniel Lazar, of Writers House. We are indebted to Erin Brown, our editor at Thomas Dunne/St. Martin's Press. Thanks also to Eileen Pollack, who helped us navigate the book publishing world, and who brought us to our wonderful agent,

Dan. We hope that our book fulfills the promise that they saw in our proposal.

We would each like to thank our own teams of friends, family, and colleagues who shared their insights and support as we struggled in the long, tedious writing process.

First and foremost, I thank my family for believing in me—not only in writing this book, but in every project I've undertaken. My mother, Naomi Bojar Carr, is the most creative and supportive mother I know. She not only marches to the beat of her own drum, she provides the piano accompaniment to liven things up a bit, and she expects nothing less in her children. My late father, Raymond Carr, like my mother, encouraged us to follow our passions and talents, regardless of whether these pursuits paid the bills. My brothers and sisters (and their significant others), Tracy Carr, Mark DalPorto, David Carr, Shellie Carr, François Minaux, Dan Carr, and Yumi Kagamihara, and my aunt Fanny Bojar, are always a source of laughter and an endless supply of memories of our raucous and happy childhood.

I have a terrific group of friends who have long shared their stories of mother-daughter woes and joys, even years before this book was a gleam in my eye. Their insights into women's issues, their humor, and their support have been inspiring. There are too many to name, but I'm particularly grateful to Mary Ann Gallo (and her mother, Nancy Gallo), Hiromi Ono, Kathy Passero (and her mother, Ginny Passero), Amy Pienta, Marci Resnicoff, Jenn Sheridan, Debbie Siegel, and Pam Smock.

Finally, Rutgers University and the University of Wisconsin have provided me the institutional support to do precisely the kind of research I want. I've been fortunate to work with kind and brilliant people who have given me intellectual inspiration and warm collegiality— and encouraged me to tear myself away from the computer to join them for music, good conversation, and the occasional beer. I have too many colleagues to name them all, but a special thanks to Ira and Reggie Cohen, Laurie Cohen, Bob and Tess Hauser, Ellen Idler, Allan Horwitz, David Mechanic, Jane Miller, Fernando Riosmena, Sal Rivas,

Carol Ryff, Kristen Springer, Hal and Shirley Winsborough, and Eviatar and Yael Zerubavel. —D.C.

I wish to thank my parents. My mother, Joanna Edelson, was a role model for me in navigating the balance between work and family life. My father, Alvin Edelson, was a "Mr. Mom" of his generation, cheerfully taking on domestic tasks, regularly providing much appreciated emotional support to his children, and never losing his characteristic good humor. My sister, and best friend, Karin Edelson, was a constant source of encouragement during this project and always makes me laugh, even when times are tough. My brother, Andrew Edelson, provided perspective, teaching me to never sweat the small stuff.

My husband, Scott, took on a second job as editor and proofreader of this project. He was my biggest cheerleader and supported my writing even when this book was only a germ of an idea. He is incredible and I never take him for granted. My amazing children, Alyson, Garrett, and Madeline, deserve major thanks and appreciation. They were sorely neglected during the final phases of this book, but they haven't held it against me.

I wish to thank my women friends, who were often the sounding board for my ideas, and who supported this project from its inception. This includes my monthly coffee club group, especially Jean Rorke, Mary Salley, Sarah Nicoli, and Becky Targett, and my dear friends Stephanie Kosarin, Wendy Uhlmann, Lynn Heumann, Laurie Blume, Julie Yolles, Stefany Freeman, and Amy Weiner. Thanks to Catherine McCurrach, Ellen Janke, and Cindy and Anthony Brooks, who graciously provided many hours of child care during the book-writing process. I can't forget the many parents of my children's friends, too numerous to mention, who patiently endured my endless discussions of mother-daughter issues on the sidelines of kids' soccer games.

I'm grateful to my relatives across the country who eagerly found me subjects to interview, including my cousin Karen Grossman, who met an untimely death just a month before this book was finished and was so looking forward to reading it. For all of these sources of support, I am truly grateful. —J.H.